The Economic and Legal Foundations of Managing Innovative Development
in Modern Economic Systems

Interdisciplinary Thought of the 21st Century

——

Management, Economics and Law

Series Editors
Elena G. Popkova and Artem I. Krivtsov

Volume 2

The Economic and Legal Foundations of Managing Innovative Development in Modern Economic Systems

Edited by
Elena G. Popkova, Aleksei V. Bogoviz
and Artem I. Krivtsov

DE GRUYTER

ISBN 978-3-11-063975-9
e-ISBN (PDF) 978-3-11-064370-1
e-ISBN (EPUB) 978-3-11-063990-2
ISSN 2626-7063

Library of Congress Control Number: 2020946055

Bibliographic information published by the Deutsche Nationalbibliothek
The Deutsche Nationalbibliothek lists this publication in the Deutsche Nationalbibliografie;
detailed bibliographic data are available on the Internet at http://dnb.dnb.de.

MIX
Papier aus verantwor-
tungsvollen Quellen
FSC
www.fsc.org   FSC® C083411

Introduction: Managing the Innovative Development of Economic Systems as a Challenge for the Modern Economics and Law

Innovative development is one of the most important manifestations of the modern economic systems, which gives them a range of advantages. Firstly, innovations have a counter-cyclical influence on economic systems, allowing preventing and overcoming economic crises. Innovations accelerate economic growth and create new jobs, ensuring employment and growth of population's incomes. At the same time, innovations could be the causes of crises – e.g., technological changes in the stock market became a reason of the 2008 crisis, and technological changes cause unemployment due to expansion of automatizaton – which was observed during each industrial revolution.

Secondly, technological progress stimulates the increase of quality of life. New benefits become accessible, ensuring the improved satisfaction of society's needs. Innovations could raise the level of social justice, level social disproportions, and stimulate social integration. Digitization, for example, erases geographical borders and ensures global communication of people. However, new inventions could pose a threat for human health and environment, causing a delayed effect. For example, the fuel & energy achievements of the 20th century in the sphere of car building and nuclear energy became a reason of ecological crises in the 21st century – mass pollution of air from wide use of cars, disasters at nuclear power plants, etc.

Thirdly, innovations move competition, increasing the effectiveness of economic systems. Innovations allow achieving competitive advantages and increasing the economic systems' competitiveness. At the same time, competition could be destructive – when investments in innovations are not returned, do not bring profit, and are aimed only at undermining the rivals' positions in the target market. Competition could also be false – when economic systems copy and adapt each other's technologies instead of creating new ones. The risks of innovative activities could be manifested in negative results of R&D, due to which investments in them will not be returned.

Fourthly, innovations allow realizing human potential, which is accumulated by economic systems. Progress conforms to the logic of society's development, and its absence causes social tension. High level of education, which has been achieved – though, to a different extent – in all modern economic systems, requires the application of population's intellectual capabilities. However, in case of the network form of organization of entrepreneurship, innovative development could take place only in the economic system with the intellectual & managerial center; in other economic systems, where production is located, skilled workers are not required, for cheap labor resources or automatization means are used.

https://doi.org/10.1515/9783110643701-202

Thus, advantages of innovative development are contradictory, and its regulation is a "market gap", which could be overcome by state regulation. Innovations management allows balancing private commercial advantages from the innovative activities and the public interests of innovative development, as well as preventing the negative consequences and increasing the probability of obtaining profit from the innovative activities. This complex task on managing the innovative development of economic systems is a challenge for the modern economics and law and is an important scientific and practical problem.

This book aimed at developing a scientific basis of economic & legal management of innovative development of modern economic systems. The book contains seven parts, which dwell on the essence and perspectives of solving the set problem. Part I considers the theoretical foundations and the methodology of managing the innovative development of economic systems, as well as conceptual approach to studying innovations and their paradigm modern treatment. Innovations are studied as opposed to traditions. The economic and legal mechanism of managing the innovative development of a modern economic system is determined.

Part II is devoted to evaluation of effectiveness of economic systems' innovative development. Effectiveness is treated as the key criterion of successfulness of managing the innovative development of modern economic systems. The indicators of effectiveness of economic systems' innovative development are given, and the methodological approach to evaluating the effectiveness of economic systems' innovative development is offered.

Part III forms the legal foundations of managing the innovative development of economic systems. The modern institutions of managing the innovative development of economic systems and the standards and norms of managing the innovative development of modern of economic systems are described. The role of international organizations in managing the innovative development of modern economic systems is formulated.

Part IV is contains the overview of the modern practical experience of economic & legal management of economic systems' innovative development. The authors determine specific features of economic & legal management of innovative development of modern economic systems in developed countries and outline the economic & legal specifics of managing the innovative development of modern economic systems in developing countries. The specifics of economic & legal management of innovative development of the modern Russia's economic system are also considered.

Part V sets the current economic & legal problems of managing the innovative development of economic systems. The authors dwell on the economic & legal gaps in managing the innovative development of modern economic systems, substantiate inconsistency and imbalance of managing the innovative development of modern economic systems, and analyze the global disproportions in managing the innovative development of developed and developing countries.

Part VI contains recommendations for economic & legal management of economic systems' innovative development. A concept of consistent and well-balanced economic & legal management of innovative development of modern economic systems is offered; a perspective algorithm of economic & legal management of innovative development of modern economic systems is compiled; and a model of leveling the global disproportions in managing the innovative development of modern economic systems is created. Future scenarios of innovative development of the global economic system depending on the economic & legal specifics of this process management are determined.

Elena G. Popkova, Aleksei V. Bogoviz and Artem I. Krivtsov

Contents

Leonid V. Stolyarov, Dina N. Savinskaya, Camila I. Weisman,
Tatiana P. Saraldaeva and Ekaterina S. Safronova

18 A Perspective Algorithm of Economic and Legal Management
of the Modern Economic Systems' Innovative Development —— 161

Ekaterina S. Vasiutina, Olga G. Kryukova, Oksana E. Ivanova, Elena V. Popova
and Olga A. Ageeva

19 The Model of Leveling the Global Disproportions in Modern Economic
Systems' Innovative Development Management —— 169

Aleksandr E. Suglobov, Ekaterina A. Orlova, Oleg G. Karpovich,
Evgeny V. Vologdin and Irina P. Drachena

20 Future Scenarios of Innovative Development of the Global Economic
System Depending on the Economic and Legal Features of Managing
this Process —— 177

Lee Jae Sung and Elena Zavyalova

21 Public-Private Prartnerships as an Efficient Boost for the Economic
Development. The Case of the Republic of Korea —— 187

Elena G. Popkova, Aleksei V. Bogoviz and Artem I. Krivtsov

Conclusions: Economic and Legal Management of Modern Economic
Systems' Innovative Development: A View into the Future —— 203

List of Figures —— 205

List of Tables —— 209

Part I: **Theoretical Foundations and Evaluation of Effectiveness of Economic Systems' Innovative Development**

Aleksei V. Bogoviz, Erastus Mwanaumo, Lubinda Haabazoka
and Astra T. Surambaeva

1 The Economic and Legal Mechanism of Managing the Innovative Development of a Modern Economic System

Introduction

Management of innovative development is one of the main components of the national economic policy of a modern economic system, but, despite the strategic significance, there is a large gap in science and practice regarding this component. The scientific basis of management of innovative development is based on the provisions of the Theory of economic cycled, formulated in the 20th century.

According to this, the economic theory treats management of innovative development as a factor and a tool of managing the economic system's cyclicity. The essence of innovative development management is conceptually connected to restraint of risky innovations for preventing the decline and support for innovative activity during a crisis, in the interests of quick overcoming of economic depression.

Economic practice – under the influence of globalization and pressure of the technological progress – is based on the idea of innovations as a universal mechanism of intensification of economic growth and development. The empirical essence of innovative development management is brought down to selecting the most perspective innovative projects, which, in the conditions of the digital economy, are concentrated in the sphere of Industry 4.0, and forming the attitude to globalization of the innovative activities in the aspect of international technological cooperation, export, import, and import substitution of innovations and innovative and hi-tech products.

However, new experience shows that adoption of the national strategies of innovative development is not enough for obtaining the expected results, due to which the sphere of this process management should be expanded. Economics should not only provide estimate qualitative treatment of innovations at different stages of the economic cycle but also offer the methodological recommendations for achieving the strategic goals of economic systems' innovative development.

Aleksei V. Bogoviz, Independent Researcher, Moscow, Russia
Erastus Mwanaumo, Department of Civil and Environmental Engineering, School of Engineering, University of Zambia, Lusaka, Zambia
Lubinda Haabazoka, Director of the University of Zambia Graduate School of Business, Zambia
Astra T. Surambaeva, M. Ryskulbekov University of Economics, Kyrgyzstan

https://doi.org/10.1515/9783110643701-001

Thus, it is necessary to study the logic of innovative development, its economic and legal factors, their change in dynamics, and the differences between developed and developing countries. That's why the purpose of this chapter is to determine the economic and legal mechanism of managing the innovative development of a modern economic system.

Materials and Method

General issues of innovative development management are studied in the works Atkinsonk and Ezell (2012), García-Quevedo et al. (2018), Gumba and Vlasenko (2017), Haabazoka (2019), Harfst et al. (2017), Kuznetsova et al. (2017), Li et al. (2018), Ramanathan et al. (2018), and Yao et al. (2018).

The modern specifics of innovative development management of a modern economic system are shown in the works Andronova et al. (2019), Petrenko and Shevyakova (2019), Popkova (2019), Popkova and Sergi (2020), Popkova et al. (2019), Popkova and Gulzat (2020), Popkova and Parakhina (2019), Popkova et al. (2017), Popkova and Zmiyak (2019), Popkova and Sergi (2018), Popkova and Sergi (2019), Ragulina (2019), Ragulina et al. (2019), Sergi (2003), Sergi (2019), Sergi et al. (2019a), Sergi et al. (2019b), Shulus et al. (2020), Stolyarov et al. (2020), and Zavyalova et al. (2018).

In this chapter, the research is performed by the example of top 5 developed countries and top 5 developing countries, which have the highest values of the Global Innovation Index in 2020. Trend analysis is used for determining the growth rate of the resulting indicators of innovative development – technological innovations (new knowledge and technologies) and organizational & managerial and marketing innovations in 2020, as compared to 2013.

Correlation analysis is used for determining the contribution of each economic and legal factor – institutional basis (institutions), human capital and research, infrastructure, market sophistication, and business sophistication – into achievement of the results of innovative development, and for determining the change of this influence in 2020, as compared to 2013. The selection of statistical data for the research is shown in Tables 1.1 and 1.2.

Table 1.1: Statistics of innovations and their hypothetical consequences in developed and developing countries in 2020 (as a result of 2019), points 1–100.

Category of countries	Country (by decease of the Global Innovation Index)	Institutions	Human capital and research	Infrastructure	Market sophistication	Business sophistication	Knowledge and technology outputs	Creative outputs
		x_1	x_2	x_3	x_4	x_5	y_1	y_2
Top 5 countries of the OECD by the Global Innovation Index (developed)	Switzerland	89.1	61.9	68.2	68.4	67.5	70.3	56.6
	Sweden	90.1	62.1	69.1	62.1	68.8	61.8	51.9
	USA	89.7	55.7	59.2	87.0	62.7	59.7	45.5
	Netherlands	90.9	52.4	61.8	58.2	63.7	61.8	53.2
	UK	87.1	59.3	64.4	76.0	54.3	56.6	52.2
Countries of BRICS (progressive developing)	Brazil	58.9	36.0	46.8	44.2	37.6	23.0	22.8
	South Africa	65.9	30.4	41.1	58.6	32.7	23.9	20.8
	India	59.5	33.5	43.0	56.3	31.0	33.5	23.5
	Russia	60.9	48.3	47.1	49.4	40.0	27.1	25.1
	China	64.1	47.6	58.7	58.6	55.4	57.2	48.3

Source: compiled by the authors based on Cornell, INSEAD, WIPO (2020).

Table 1.2: Statistics of innovations and their hypothetical consequences in developed and developing countries in 2013, points 1–100.

Category of countries	Country (by decease of the Global Innovation Index)	Institutions	Human capital and research	Infrastructure	Market sophistication	Business sophistication	Knowledge and technology outputs	Creative outputs
		x_1	x_2	x_3	x_4	x_5	y_1	y_2
Top 5 countries of the OECD by the Global Innovation Index (developed)	Switzerland	87.3	55.4	57.0	77.5	55.3	61.5	71.8
	Sweden	89.9	62.5	63.1	71.8	52.0	54.1	55.6
	USA	86.0	61.1	52.5	87.1	59.2	53.6	49.2
	Netherlands	92.8	50.6	55.5	69.2	52.9	53.9	62.3
	UK	88.4	56.2	59.4	84.6	52.3	51.1	57.5
Countries of BRICS (progressive developing)	Brazil	53.8	30.3	37.2	44.9	38.0	26.5	37.2
	South Africa	70.1	23.7	28.5	66.0	31.5	24.7	37.8
	India	51.9	21.7	27.5	49.5	28.3	34.5	38.6
	Russia	56.0	44.1	37.2	45.4	36.1	30.4	30.8
	China	48.3	40.6	39.8	54.2	42.9	56.4	31.9

Source: compiled by the authors based on Cornell, INSEAD, WIPO (2020).

Results

Dynamics of average results of innovative development management in developed and developing countries in 2013 and 2020 are shown in Figure 1.1.

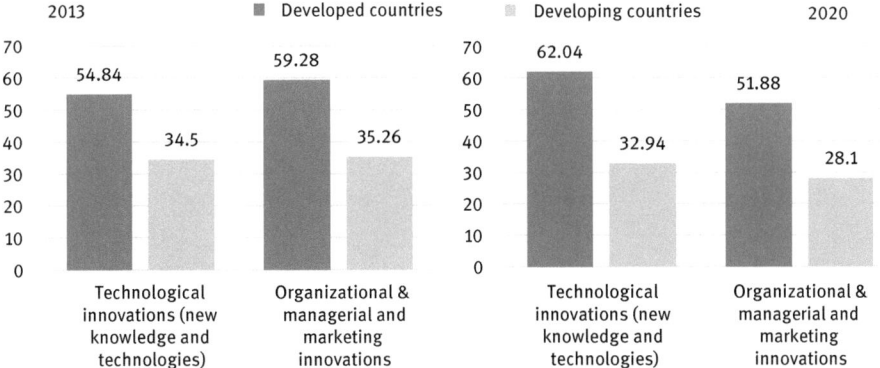

Figure 1.1: Dynamics of average results of innovative development management in developed and developing countries in 2013 and 2020, points.
Source: calculated and compiled by the authors.

As shown in Figure 1.1, technological innovations in developed countries grew by 13.13% in 2020 (62.04 points), as compared to 2013 (54.84 points), and organizational & managerial innovations reduced by 12.43% in 2020 (51.88 points), as compared to 2013 (59.28 points). In developing countries, technological innovations reduced by 4.73% in 2020 (34.5 points), as compared to 2013 (32.94 points), and organizational & managerial innovations reduced by 20.31% in 2020 (28.1 points) as compared to 2013 (35.26 points). Correlation of factors and results of innovative development management is shown in Figures 1.2–1.5.

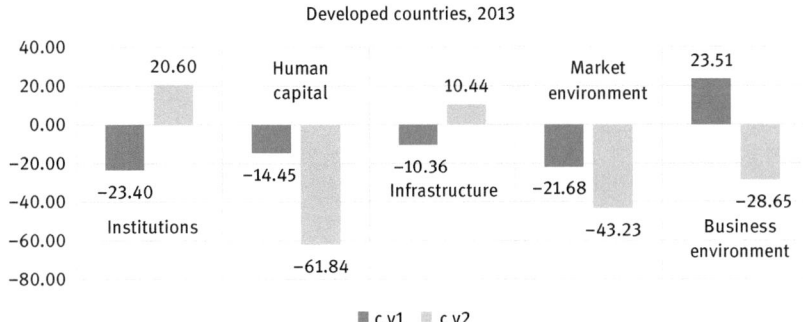

Figure 1.2: Correlation of the factors and results of innovative development management in developed countries in 2013.
Source: calculated and compiled by the authors.

As shown in Figure 1.2, influence of all factors is contradictory and inconsistent in developed countries in 2013.

As shown in Figure 1.3, developing countries have the same situation – influence of all factors is contradictory and inconsistent in 2013.

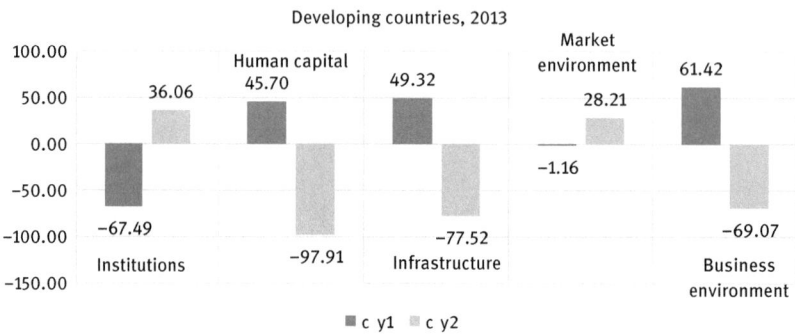

Figure 1.3: Correlation of the factors and results of innovative development management in developing countries in 2013.
Source: calculated and compiled by the authors.

As shown in Figure 1.4, three key factors of innovative development management formed in developed countries in 2020 – they show positive correlation with the both results: human capital, infrastructure, and business environment.

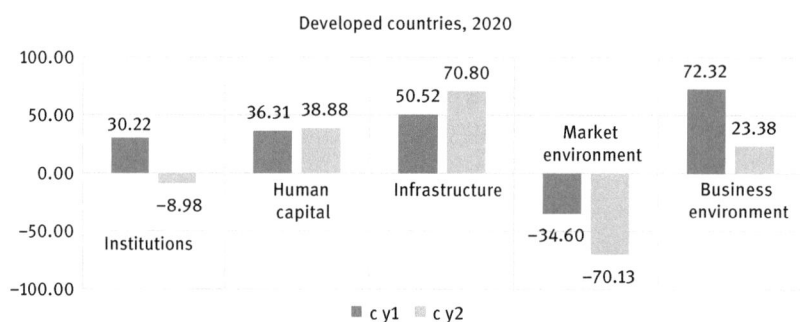

Figure 1.4: Correlation of the factors and results of innovative development management in developed countries in 2020.
Source: calculated and compiled by the authors.

As shown in Figure 1.5, all factors in developing countries in 2020 have strong and positive influence on the results of innovative development management.

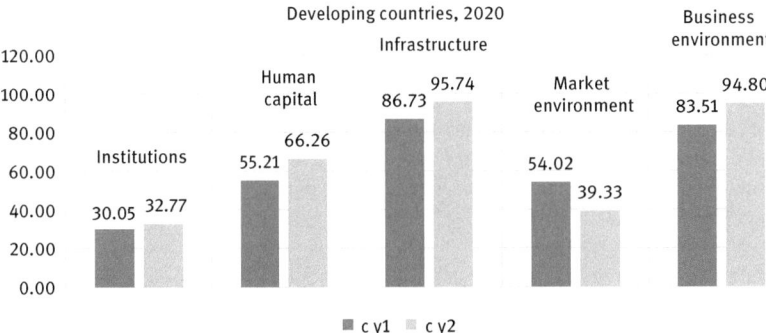

Figure 1.5: Correlation of the factors and results of innovative development management in developing countries in 2020.
Source: calculated and compiled by the authors.

Conclusion

It is possible to conclude that the economic and legal mechanism of innovative development management of a modern economic system should be flexible and subject to modernization in the course of evolution of the innovative economy, which does not necessarily mean progress (regress is also possible). In the period of its formation in 2013, innovative development in developed and developing countries was not subject to management. At present (2020), there are clear factors of innovative development – human capital, infrastructure, and business environment in developed countries, and also institutional basis and market environment (in addition to the above) in developing countries.

References

Andronova, I.V., Chernova, V.Y., Starostin, V.S., Degtereva (2019). Study of sector-specific innovation efforts: The case from Russian economy. Entrepreneurship and Sustainability Issues, Vsl Entrepreneurship and Sustainability Center, 7 (1), p. 540–552.

Atkinsonk, R.D., Ezell, S.J. (2012). Innovation Economics: the Race for Global Advantage, New Haven, CT: Yale University Press.

Cornell, INSEAD, WIPO (2020). Global innovation index. URL: https://www.globalinnovationindex.org/analysis-economy (data accessed: 18.03.2020).

García-Quevedo, J., Segarra-Blasco, A., Teruel, M. (2018). Financial constraints and the failure of innovation projects. Technological Forecasting and Social Change, 127, p. 127–140.

Gumba, H.M., Vlasenko, V.A. (2017). Strategy of development of innovative activity in industry and construction: The rationale of the regional dimension. Izvestiya Vysshikh Uchebnykh Zavedenii, Seriya Teknologiya Tekstil'noi Promyshlennosti, 2017-January(2), p. 14–18.

Haabazoka, L. (2019). A Study of the Effects of Technological Innovations on the Performance of Commercial Banks in Developing Countries – A Case of the Zambian Banking Industry. In:

Popkova E. (eds) The Future of the Global Financial System: Downfall or Harmony. ISC 2018. Lecture Notes in Networks and Systems, vol 57. Springer, Cham, Online ISBN 978-3-030-00102-5, https://doi.org/10.1007/978-3-030-00102-5_132

Harfst, J., Pichler, P., Fischer, W. (2017). Regional Ambassadors-An Innovative Element for the Development of Rural Areas? European Countryside, 9(2), p. 359–374.

Kuznetsova, O., Kuznetsova, S., Yumaev, E., Kuznetsov, V., Galtseva, O. (2017). Formation and Development of the Training System for Innovative Development of Regional Industry. E3S Web of Conferences, 15,04019.

Li, X., Subrahmanyam, A., Yang, X. (2018). Can financial innovation succeed by catering to behavioral preferences? Evidence from a callable options market. Journal of Financial Economics, 2(1), p. 34–42.

Petrenko, E.S., Shevyakova, A.L. (2019). Features and perspectives of digitization in Kazakhstan. Studies in Computational Intelligence, 826, p. 889–899.

Popkova, E.G. (2019). Preconditions of formation and development of industry 4.0 in the conditions of knowledge economy. Studies in Systems, Decision and Control, 169(1), 65–72.

Popkova, E.G., Sergi, B.S. (2020). Human Capital and AI in Industry 4.0. Convergence and Divergence in Social Entrepreneurship in Russia. Journal of Intellectual Capital, In press, 2020. https://doi.org/10.1108/JIC-09-2019-0224

Popkova, E.G., Egorova, E.N., Popova, E., Pozdnyakova, U.A. (2019). The model of state management of economy on the basis of the internet of things. Studies in Computational Intelligence, 826, pp. 1137–1144.

Popkova, E.G., Gulzat, K. (2020). Technological Revolution in the 21st Century: Digital Society vs. Artificial Intelligence. Lecture Notes in Networks and Systems, 91, p. 339–345.

Popkova, E.G., Parakhina, V.N. (2019). Managing the global financial system on the basis of artificial intelligence: possibilities and limitations. Lecture Notes in Networks and Systems, 57, pp. 939–946.

Popkova, E.G., Poluyufta, L., Beshanova, Y., Popova, L.V., Kolesnikova, E. (2017). Innovations as a basis for marketing strategies of Russian oil companies in the conditions of oil prices reduction. Contributions to Economics, (9783319606958), p. 449–455.

Popkova, E.G., Zmiyak, K.V. (2019). Priorities of training of digital personnel for industry 4.0: social competencies vs technical competencies. On the Horizon, 27 (3–4), p. 138–144.

Popkova, E.G., Sergi, B.S. (2018). Will Industry 4.0 and Other Innovations Impact Russia's Development? In Bruno S. Sergi (Ed.) Exploring the Future of Russia's Economy and Markets: Towards Sustainable Economic Development (pp. 51–68). Bingley, UK: Emerald Publishing Limited.

Popkova, E.G., Sergi, B.S. (Eds.) (2019). Digital Economy: Complexity and Variety vs. Rationality. Berlin: Springer International Publishing.

Ragulina, Y.V. (2019). Priorities of development of industry 4.0 in modern economic systems with different progress in formation of knowledge economy. Studies in Systems, Decision and Control, 169, p. 167–174.

Ragulina, Y.V., Alekseev, A.N., Strizhkina, I.V., Tumanov, A.I. (2019). Methodology of criterial evaluation of consequences of the industrial revolution of the 21st century. Studies in Systems, Decision and Control, 169, p. 235–244.

Ramanathan, R., Ramanathan, U., Bentley, Y. (2018). The debate on flexibility of environmental regulations, innovation capabilities and financial performance – A novel use of DEA. Omega (United Kingdom), 75, p. 131–138.

Sergi, B.S. (2003). Economic Dynamics in Transitional Economies: The Four-P Governments, the EU Enlargement, and the Bruxelles Consensus. New York: Routledge.

Sergi, B.S. (Ed.) (2019). Tech, Smart Cities, and Regional Development in Contemporary Russia. Bingley, UK: Emerald Publishing Limited.

Sergi, B.S., Popkova, E.G. Bogoviz, A.V., Ragulina J.V. (2019a). Costs and Profits of Technological Growth in Russia. In Bruno S. Sergi (Ed.) Tech, Smart Cities, and Regional Development in Contemporary Russia. Bingley, UK: Emerald Publishing Limited.

Sergi, B.S., Popkova, E.G. Bogoviz, A.V., Ragulina J.V. (2019b). Entrepreneurship and Economic Growth: The Experience of Developed and Developing Countries. In Bruno S. Sergi and Cole C. Scanlon (Eds.) Entrepreneurship and Development in the 21st Century (pp. 3–32). Bingley, UK: Emerald Publishing Limited.

Shulus, A.A., Akopova, E.S., Przhedetskaya, N.V., Borzenko, K.V. (2020). Intellectual Production and Consumption: A New Reality of the 21st Century. Lecture Notes in Networks and Systems, 92, pp. 353–359.

Stolyarov, N.O., Petrenko, E.S., Serova, O.A., Umuralieva, A.S. (2020). The Digital Reality of the Modern Economy: New Actors and New Decision-Making Logic. Lecture Notes in Networks and Systems, 87, p. 882–888.

Yao, M., Di, H., Zheng, X., Xu, X. (2018). Impact of payment technology innovations on the traditional financial industry: A focus on China. Technological Forecasting and Social Change, 2(1), p. 22–29.

Zavyalova, E.B. Studenikin, N.V. Starikova, E.A. (2018). Business participation in implementation of socially oriented Sustainable Development Goals in countries of Central Asia and the Caucasus region. Central Asia and the Caucasus, 19(2), p. 56–63.

Aleksei V. Bogoviz, Erastus Mwanaumo, Lubinda Haabazoka
and Bermet M. Kadyrova

2 Effectiveness as the Key Criterion of Successfulness of Managing the Innovative Development of a Modern Economic System

Introduction

Successfulness of managing the innovative development of a modern economic system, like any other regulatory practice, should be evaluated from the positions of effectiveness. This envisages determination of positive effects that are generated by innovations. Here we speak of the innovations' positive consequences for an economic system. Also, it is necessary to establish the level of completeness of these effects. In view of the fact that, like any changes, innovations are connected to risks and changes, the positive effects that are created by them should be vivid and significant for economic systems.

Also, it is necessary to determine the sources of emergence of positive effects – i.e., determining the key directions and measures of state management of innovations. Despite the high level of elaboration of the theory of innovations as one of the basic spheres of research in economics, these aspects are not studied sufficiently. This is due to the fact that studies of these aspects are very narrow: they are performed either according to certain technologies (e.g., digital technologies), or according to innovations – but not their regulation.

Thus, an important problem of economic theory and practice is uncertainty regarding the necessity for state management of innovative development of a modern economic system and the logic of its implementation. Absence of the scientific basis of this management undermines the foundations of its implementation, which negatively influences the general economic policy. The purpose of the chapter is to solve the set problem through determining the positive effects from innovative development in modern economic systems, the level of their completeness, and the sources of creation of the effects, which are connected to state management.

Aleksei V. Bogoviz, Independent researcher, Moscow, Russia
Erastus Mwanaumo, Department of Civil and Environmental Engineering, School of Engineering, University of Zambia, Lusaka, Zambia
Lubinda Haabazoka, Director of The University of Zambia Graduate School of Business, Zambia
Bermet M. Kadyrova, Academy of State Mnagement under the President of Kyrgyzstan, Kyrgyzstan

https://doi.org/10.1515/9783110643701-002

Materials and Method

The theoretical basis of the research includes scientific works that consider the general issues of innovative development of a modern economic system and state management of this process: Atkinsonk and Ezell (2012), García-Quevedo et al. (2018), Gumba and Vlasenko (2017), Haabazoka (2019), Harfst et al. (2017), Kuznetsova et al. (2017), Li et al. (2018), Ramanathan et al. (2018), and Yao et al. (2018).

Also, the materials of the works on the topic of evaluation of effectiveness of digitization as the most popular direction of modern economic systems' innovative development are used: Andronova et al. (2019), Petrenko and Shevyakova (2019), Popkova (2019), Popkova and Sergi (2020), Popkova et al. (2019), Popkova and Gulzat (2020), Popkova and Parakhina (2019), Popkova et al. (2017), Popkova and Zmiyak (2019), Popkova and Sergi (2018), Popkova and Sergi (2019), Ragulina (2019), Ragulina et al. (2019), Sergi (2003), Sergi (2019), Sergi et al. (2019a), Sergi et al. (2019b), Shulus et al. (2020), Stolyarov et al. (2020), and Zavyalova et al. (2018).

It is possible to see that effectiveness – as the key criterion of successfulness of managing the innovative development of a modern economic system – is poorly studied and requires further research. Based on the advantages, which are noted in the existing studies by the example of digital technologies and innovations, we select the following positive effects, which could appear due to state management of innovations: development of the "green" economy, human development, improvement of business environment, and increase of The Global Competitiveness Index 4.0.

The potential sources of the above effects could be investments in innovations (managing the expenditure side of the state budget, investment policy), export of hi-tech products (foreign trade regulation, globalization management), and level of education (managing the development of human capital, formation of the "knowledge economy"). The data for the selected indicators in 2020 (as a result of 2019) by the example of the most innovative developed and developing countries are shown in Table 2.1.

The methodology of this research includes creation of regression curves, which reflect regression (value of coefficient b in the model $y = a + b * x$) and correlation (value R^2) of influence of the sources on creation of effects from state management of innovations. The logic of the performed research is that regression reflects the effect, and correlation – the level of its completeness. In the course of the research, the most vivid effects and the most effective/reliable sources of their creation are selected.

Results

Regression curves are built based on the data from Table 2.1 (Figures 2.1–2.4).

Based on the results of the performed regression analysis (Figure 2.1–2.4), we have compiled Table 2.2, which shows the effects of managing the innovative

Table 2.1: Statistics of innovations and their hypothetical consequences in developed and developing countries in 2020.

Category of countries	Country (by decease of the Global Innovation Index)	Effects from innovations				Sources of effects		
		Green economy index, points 1–100	Human development index, points 1–100	Doing business index, points 1–100	Global competitiveness Index 4.0, points 1–100	Investments in innovations, % of GDP	Export of hi-tech products, % of commodity export	Level of education, points 1–100
Top 5 countries of the OECD by the Global Innovation Index (developed)	Switzerland	0.7594	0.946	88.4	82.3	3.37	13.0	86.7
	Sweden	0.7608	0.937	93.1	81.2	3.31	14.0	83.7
	USA	0.5471	0.920	91.6	83.7	2.80	19.0	82.5
	Netherlands	0.5937	0.933	94.3	82.4	2.00	23.0	84.6
	UK	0.6230	0.920	94.6	81.2	1.67	22.0	81.9
Countries of BRICS (progressive developing)	Brazil	0.5417	0.761	81.3	60.9	1.27	13.0	56.4
	South Africa	0.4376	0.705	81.2	62.4	0.82	5.0	58.1
	India	0.5398	0.647	81.6	61.4	0.62	9.0	50.5
	Russia	0.4115	0.824	78.2	66.7	1.11	11.0	68.3
	China	0.55231	0.758	94.1	73.9	2.13	31.0	64.1

Source: compiled by the authors based on Dual Citizen (2020), Institute of Scientific Communications (2020), UNDP (2020), World Bank (2020a), World Bank (2020b), World Economic Forum (2020).

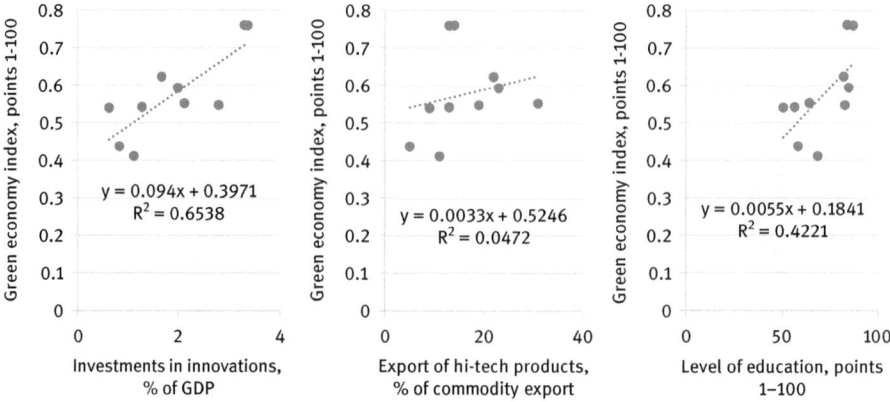

Figure 2.1: Regression curve of contribution of potential sources into effect of innovations management, connected to development of the "green" economy.
Source: developed and compiled by the authors.

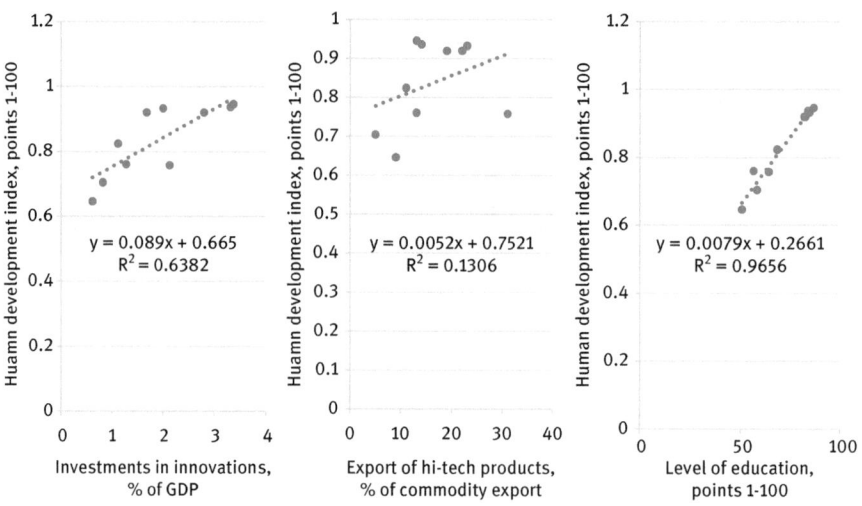

Figure 2.2: Regression curve of contribution of potential sources into effect of innovations management, connected to human development.
Source: developed and compiled by the authors.

development of the most progressive developed and developing countries, and their completeness and sources in 2020.

As shown in Figure 2.2, the most vivid effect of managing the economic systems' innovative development in 2020 is increase of their The Global Competitiveness Index 4.0 (6.59). Improvement of business environment (2.54) is ranked 2nd among

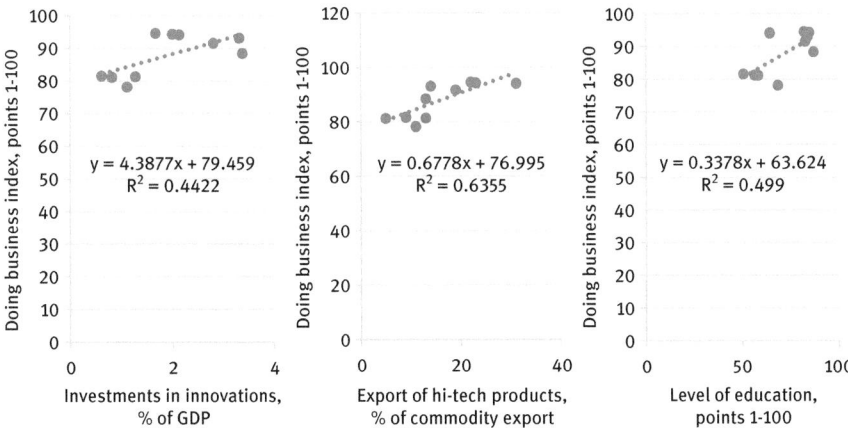

Figure 2.3: Regression curve of contribution of potential sources into effect of innovations management, connected to improvement of business environment.
Source: developed and compiled by the authors.

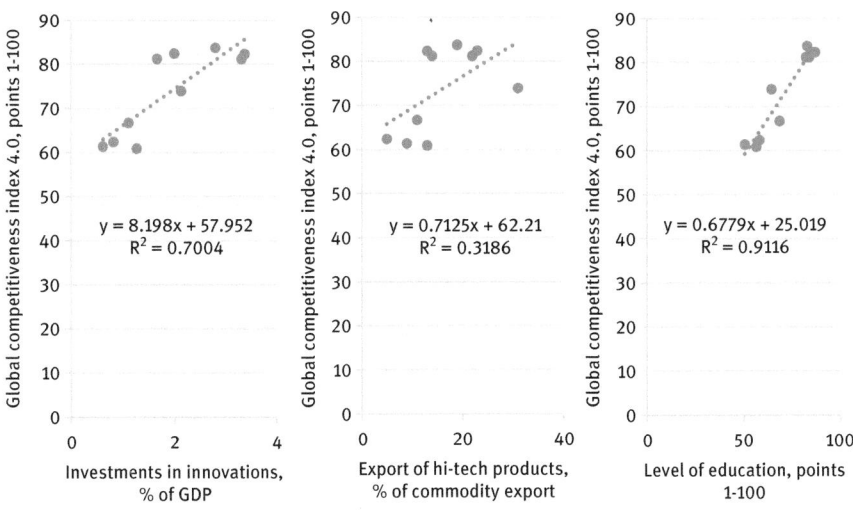

Figure 2.4: Regression curve of contribution of potential sources into effect of innovations management, connected to increase of competitiveness.
Source: developed and compiled by the authors.

the effects. Such effects as development of the "green" economy (0.06) and human development (0.07) are poorly expressed. The most reliable and the only significant source of creation of the studied effects is investments in innovations (5.74). Other sources are insignificant: export of hi-tech products (0.23) and level of education (0.62).

Table 2.2: Effects of managing the economic systems' innovative development, their completeness, and sources in 2020.

Source of the effect	Indicator	Green economy index, points 1–100	Human development index, points 1–100	Doing business index, points 1–100	The Global Competitiveness Index 4.0, points 1–100
Investments in innovations, % of GDP	Regression	0.094	0.089	4.3877	8.198
	Correlation	0.6538	0.6382	0.4422	0.7005
	Effect (regression *correlation)	0.06	0.06	1.94	5.74
	Integral effect: 0.06+0.06+1.94+5.74=7.80				
Export of hi-tech products, % of commodity export	Regression	0.0033	0.0052	0.6778	0.7125
	Correlation	0.0472	0.1306	0.6355	0.3186
	Effect (regression *correlation)	0.00	0.00	0.43	0.23
	Integral effect: 0.00+0.00+0.43+0.23=0.66				
Level of education, points 1–100	Regression	0.0055	0.0079	0.3378	0.6779
	Correlation	0.4225	0.9656	0.499	0.9116
	Effect (regression *correlation)	0.00	0.01	0.17	0.62
	Integral effect: 0.00+0.01+0.17+0.62=0.80				
Aggregate contribution of the source into integral effect		0.06+0.00+ +0.00=0.06	0.06+0.00+ +0.01=0.07	1.94+0.43 +0.17=2.54	5.74+0.23+ +0.62=6.59

Source: calculated and compiled by the authors.

Conclusion

Thus, the performed analysis of effectiveness shows that when managing the innovative development of a modern economic system it is necessary to focus efforts on financing of innovations. Increase of the level of population's education should not seek the goal of formation of the innovative economy, and export of hi-tech products should be limited – as it generates insignificant positive effects, but, at the same time, leads to a loss of competitive advantages – it is better to seek production of hi-tech products for internal needs.

The main effects that should be used for evaluating the successfulness of state management of innovative development in the modern economic systems should be the Global Competitiveness Index and doing business. These effects are vivid and are the basis for targeted state management of modern economic systems' innovative development.

References

Andronova, I.V., Chernova, V.Y., Starostin, V.S., Degtereva (2019). Study of sector-specific innovation efforts: The case from Russian economy. Entrepreneurship and Sustainability Issues, Vsl Entrepreneurship and Sustainability Center, 7 (1), p. 540–552.

Atkinsonk, R.D., Ezell, S.J. (2012). Innovation Economics: the Race for Global Advantage, New Haven, CT: Yale University Press.

Dual Citizen (2020). The Global Green Economy Index. URL: https://dualcitizeninc.com/global-green-economy-index/index.php#interior_section_link (data accessed: 18.03.2020).

García-Quevedo, J., Segarra-Blasco, A., Teruel, M. (2018). Financial constraints and the failure of innovation projects. Technological Forecasting and Social Change, 127, p. 127–140.

Gumba, H.M., Vlasenko, V.A. (2017). Strategy of development of innovative activity in industry and construction: The rationale of the regional dimension. Izvestiya Vysshikh Uchebnykh Zavedenii, Seriya Teknologiya Tekstil'noi Promyshlennosti, 2017-January(2), p. 14–18.

Haabazoka, L. (2019). A Study of the Effects of Technological Innovations on the Performance of Commercial Banks in Developing Countries – A Case of the Zambian Banking Industry. In: Popkova E. (eds) The Future of the Global Financial System: Downfall or Harmony. ISC 2018. Lecture Notes in Networks and Systems, vol 57. Springer, Cham, Online ISBN 978-3-030-00102-5, https://doi.org/10.1007/978-3-030-00102-5_132

Harfst, J., Pichler, P., Fischer, W. (2017). Regional Ambassadors-An Innovative Element for the Development of Rural Areas? European Countryside, 9(2), p. 359–374.

Institute of Scientific Communications (2020). Data set "Big data of the modern world economy: digital platform for intelligent analytics – 2020". URL: https://www.archilab.online/en/data/sounting-data-set (data accessed: 18.03.2020).

Kuznetsova, O., Kuznetsova, S., Yumaev, E., Kuznetsov, V., Galtseva, O. (2017). Formation and Development of the Training System for Innovative Development of Regional Industry. E3S Web of Conferences, 15,04019.

Li, X., Subrahmanyam, A., Yang, X. (2018). Can financial innovation succeed by catering to behavioral preferences? Evidence from a callable options market. Journal of Financial Economics, 2(1), p. 34–42.

Petrenko, E.S., Shevyakova, A.L. (2019). Features and perspectives of digitization in Kazakhstan. Studies in Computational Intelligence, 826, p. 889–899.

Popkova, E.G. (2019). Preconditions of formation and development of industry 4.0 in the conditions of knowledge economy. Studies in Systems, Decision and Control, 169(1),65–72.

Popkova, E.G., Sergi, B.S. (2020). Human Capital and AI in Industry 4.0. Convergence and Divergence in Social Entrepreneurship in Russia. Journal of Intellectual Capital, In press, 2020. https://doi.org/10.1108/JIC-09-2019-0224

Popkova, E.G., Egorova, E.N., Popova, E., Pozdnyakova, U.A. (2019). The model of state management of economy on the basis of the internet of things. Studies in Computational Intelligence, 826, pp. 1137–1144.

Popkova, E.G., Gulzat, K. (2020). Technological Revolution in the 21st Century: Digital Society vs. Artificial Intelligence. Lecture Notes in Networks and Systems, 91, p. 339–345.

Popkova, E.G., Parakhina, V.N. (2019). Managing the global financial system on the basis of artificial intelligence: possibilities and limitations. Lecture Notes in Networks and Systems, 57, pp. 939–946.

Popkova, E.G., Poluyufta, L., Beshanova, Y., Popova, L.V., Kolesnikova, E. (2017). Innovations as a basis for marketing strategies of Russian oil companies in the conditions of oil prices reduction. Contributions to Economics, (9783319606958), p. 449–455.

Popkova, E.G., Zmiyak, K.V. (2019). Priorities of training of digital personnel for industry 4.0: social competencies vs technical competencies. On the Horizon, 27 (3–4), p. 138–144.

Popkova, E.G., Sergi, B.S. (2018). Will Industry 4.0 and Other Innovations Impact Russia's Development? In Bruno S. Sergi (Ed.) Exploring the Future of Russia's Economy and Markets: Towards Sustainable Economic Development (pp. 51–68). Bingley, UK: Emerald Publishing Limited.

Popkova, E.G., Sergi, B.S. (Eds.) (2019). Digital Economy: Complexity and Variety vs. Rationality. Springer International Publishing.

Ragulina, Y.V. (2019). Priorities of development of industry 4.0 in modern economic systems with different progress in formation of knowledge economy. Studies in Systems, Decision and Control, 169, p. 167–174.

Ragulina, Y.V., Alekseev, A.N., Strizhkina, I.V., Tumanov, A.I. (2019). Methodology of criterial evaluation of consequences of the industrial revolution of the 21st century. Studies in Systems, Decision and Control, 169, p. 235–244.

Ramanathan, R., Ramanathan, U., Bentley, Y. (2018). The debate on flexibility of environmental regulations, innovation capabilities and financial performance – A novel use of DEA. Omega (United Kingdom), 75, p. 131–138.

Sergi, B.S. (2003). Economic Dynamics in Transitional Economies: The Four-P Governments, the EU Enlargement, and the Bruxelles Consensus. New York: Routledge.

Sergi, B.S. (Ed.) (2019). Tech, Smart Cities, and Regional Development in Contemporary Russia. Bingley, UK: Emerald Publishing Limited.

Sergi, B.S., Popkova, E.G. Bogoviz, A.V., Ragulina J.V. (2019a). Costs and Profits of Technological Growth in Russia. In Bruno S. Sergi (Ed.) Tech, Smart Cities, and Regional Development in Contemporary Russia (pp. 41–54). Bingley, UK: Emerald Publishing Limited. https://doi.org/10.1108/978-1-78973-881-020191005

Sergi, B.S., Popkova, E.G. Bogoviz, A.V., Ragulina J.V. (2019b). Entrepreneurship and Economic Growth: The Experience of Developed and Developing Countries. In Bruno S. Sergi and Cole C. Scanlon (Eds.) Entrepreneurship and Development in the 21st Century (pp. 3–32). Bingley, UK: Emerald Publishing Limited.

Shulus, A.A., Akopova, E.S., Przhedetskaya, N.V., Borzenko, K.V. (2020). Intellectual Production and Consumption: A New Reality of the 21st Century. Lecture Notes in Networks and Systems, 92, pp. 353–359.

Stolyarov, N.O., Petrenko, E.S., Serova, O.A., Umuralieva, A.S. (2020). The Digital Reality of the Modern Economy: New Actors and New Decision-Making Logic. Lecture Notes in Networks and Systems, 87, p. 882–888.

UNDP (2020). Human Development Report 2019. URL: http://www.hdr.undp.org/ (data accessed: 18.03.2020).

World Bank (2020a). Doing business 2020. URL: https://russian.doingbusiness.org/ru/data/doing-business-score?topic=starting-a-business (data accessed: 18.03.2020).

World Bank (2020b). Indicators. URL: https://data.worldbank.org/indicator (data accessed: 18.03.2020).

World Economic Forum (2020). The Global Competitiveness Report 2019. URL: https://www.
  weforum.org/reports/how-to-end-a-decade-of-lost-productivity-growth (data accessed:
  18.03.2020).
Yao, M., Di, H., Zheng, X., Xu, X. (2018). Impact of payment technology innovations on the
  traditional financial industry: A focus on China. Technological Forecasting and Social Change,
  2(1), p. 22–29.
Zavyalova, E.B. Studenikin, N.V. Starikova, E.A. (2018). Business participation in implementation of
  socially oriented Sustainable Development Goals in countries of Central Asia and the
  Caucasus region. Central Asia and the Caucasus, 19(2), p. 56–63.

Svetlana V. Lobova

3 Indicators of Effectiveness of Economic Systems' Innovative Development

Introduction

In the modern conditions, when struggle for hi-tech markets is observed around the world and scientific inventions define the potential of economic systems' development, as well as their economic independence and security, economic systems' innovative development is treated as a positive practice, stimulated by the state and supported by society. Effectiveness of the economy's innovative system is considered from the positions of its contribution into increase of competitiveness of entrepreneurship and increase of population's quality of life by solving socially important tasks.

The existing externally-oriented treatment of effectiveness of the economy's innovative system reflects only the results of this system's functioning, which does not help a scientific idea of effectiveness as a generated useful result (effect) by the unit of resources. Large attention to results actually justifies any expenditures for innovative activities. The existing treatment is convenient for international comparisons, as it allows comparing the level of economic systems' innovative activity and advantages that are ensured by this activity.

At the same time, the existing treatment of effectiveness of this process cannot be used for the purposes of state management of economic systems' innovative development. This is due to the fact that it is uncertainty by what means the results in an innovative system are achieved and how its efficiency could be raised. It is necessary to use a scientific paradigm for determining not only the results but also the resources spent for their achievement, and it is necessary to take into account all types of resources.

The purpose of this chapter is to offer a scientific concept of a new – internally-oriented treatment of effectiveness of economy's innovative system and to offer indicators for evaluating the effectiveness of economic systems' innovative development according to the new treatment.

Materials and Method

The issues of effectiveness of economic systems' innovative development are studied in the works Andronova et al. (2019), Bogoviz and Ragulina (2020), Petrenko

Svetlana V. Lobova, Altai State University, Barnaul, Russia and Ural State University of Economics, Yekaterinburg, Russia

https://doi.org/10.1515/9783110643701-003

and Shevyakova (2019), Popkova (2019), Popkova and Sergi (2020), Popkova et al. (2019), Popkova and Gulzat (2020), Popkova and Parakhina (2019), Popkova et al. (2017), Popkova and Zmiyak (2019), Popkova and Sergi (2018), Popkova and Sergi (2019), Ragulina (2019), Ragulina et al. (2019), Sergi (2003), Sergi (2019), Sergi et al. (2019a), Sergi et al. (2019b), Shulus et al. (2020), Stolyarov et al. (2020), and Zavyalova et al. (2018).

The sets of indicators that are used for evaluating and analyzing the effectiveness of economic systems' innovative development are given in the works Atkinsonk and Ezell (2012), García-Quevedo et al. (2018), Gumba and Vlasenko (2017), Haabazoka (2019), Harfst et al. (2017), Kuznetsova et al. (2017), Li et al. (2018), Ramanathan et al. (2018), and Yao et al. (2018). Though this topic is considered in a lot of works, they present a unilateral view of effectiveness of economic systems' innovative development, which reflect the results of this approach. For changing the results, the following indicators are offered: increase of the level of social justice and expansion of presence of domestic business in the world markets, and innovations are treated as their source.

Here we offer a new – internally-oriented – treatment of effectiveness of economy's innovative system, which conforms to the scientific idea of effectiveness to a larger extent. In the new treatment, expenditures are financial resources (state budget's expenses for innovations) and human resources (number of researchers per one million people). The result is that which is formed at the output of the innovative system – applications for trademarks and patents.

As the above indicators have different measuring units, they are not comparable in the absolute expression – which does not allow for evaluation of effectiveness with the help of these indicators. For solving this problem, indicators are converted into shares of 1 by calculating their ratio to direct average for all countries of the selection. The selection includes nine countries of different categories of innovative activity by the criterion of the volume of hi-tech export (three countries in each category). The systematized selection of data as of early 2020 is shown in Table 3.1.

For evaluation of effectiveness of economic systems' innovative development in view of the recommended indicators, we offer a proprietary scientific & methodological approach, which is based on the following formula:

$$EID = \frac{TA + PA}{BE + RS} \qquad (1)$$

where EID – effectiveness of economic system's innovative development;

TA – relative expenditures of state budget for innovations, shares of 1;

PA – relative number of researchers per one million people, shares of 1;

BE – relative number of trademark applications, shares of 1;

RS – relative number of patent applications, shares of 1;

Table 3.1: Statistics of economic systems' innovative development from different categories of hi-tech export in 2020.

Category of hi-tech export		Country	Research and development expenditure (% of GDP)	Researchers in R&D (per million people)	Trademark applications, direct resident	Patent applications, residents
Intensive export (31% of GDP and more)	61%	Philippines	0.16	106	21,625	529
	53%	Malaysia	1.44	2,397	19,863	1,116
	31%	China	2.15	1,225	1,997,058	1,393,815
Moderate export (20–30% of GDP)	26%	France	2.19	4,450	90,581	14,303
	21%	Mexico	0.49	252	109,353	1,555
	11%	Russia	1.11	2,822	49,132	29,426
Restrained export (below 20% of GDP)	9%	India	0.60	253	197,750	16,289
	8%	Indonesia	0.27	216	56,583	1,407
	8%	Italy	1.35	2,245	37,320	8,921
On average for the selection			1.084	1,551.778	286,585.000	163,040.111

Source: compiled by the author based on World Bank (2020).

If EID is below 1, economic system's innovative development is considered to be ineffective and unprofitable and could be conducted only for public benefit and with state financing. The higher the value of EID (if it exceeds 1), the more effective (profitable) the innovative development of the economic system and the wider the opportunities for attraction of private investments in innovations.

Results

Evaluation of the effectiveness of economic systems' innovative development from different categories of hi-tech export in 2020, according to the offered proprietary scientific & methodological approach, is performed in Table 3.2.

For better clarity, the results of evaluation of the effectiveness of economic systems' innovative development from different categories of hi-tech export in 2020 are shown in Figure 3.1.

As shown in Figure 3.1, large effectiveness of innovative development in 2020 is observed in China – 12.30. The second position belongs to India (2.39), the third position belongs to Mexico (1.39), and the fourth position belongs to Indonesia (1.19). For more precise determination of causal connections and explanation of the successful experience of the above developing countries from the scientific point of

Table 3.2: Evaluation of the effectiveness of economic systems' innovative development from different categories of hi-tech export in 2020.

Ratio to average: expenditures, shares of 1		Ratio to average: results, shares of 1		Calculation of effectiveness based on the proprietary methodology, shares of 1
BE	RS	TA	PA	
0.15	0.07	0.08	0.00	(0.08+0.00)/(0.15+0.07)=0.36
0.65	0.57	0.07	0.01	(0.07+0.01)/(0.65+0.57)=0.06
0.97	0.29	6.97	8.55	(6.97+8.55)/(0.97+0.29)=12.30
0.99	1.07	0.32	0.09	(0.32+0.09)/(0.99+1.07)=0.20
0.22	0.06	0.38	0.01	(0.38+0.01)/(0.22+0.06)=1.39
0.50	0.68	0.17	0.18	(0.17+0.18)/(0.50+0.68)=0.30
0.27	0.06	0.69	0.10	(0.69+0.10)/(0.27+0.06)=2.39
0.12	0.05	0.20	0.01	(0.20+0.01)/(0.12+0.05)=1.19
0.61	0.54	0.13	0.05	(0.13+0.05)/(0.61+0.54)=0.16

Source: calculated and compiled by the authors.

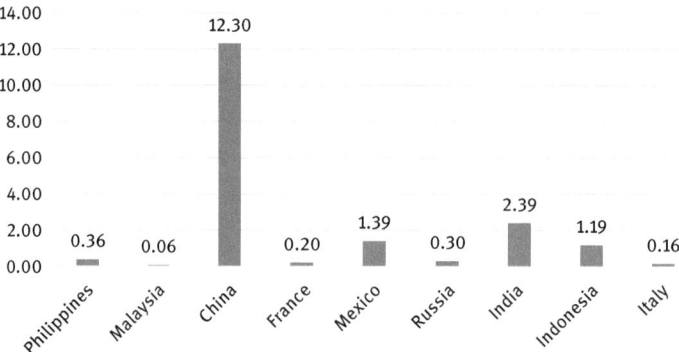

Figure 3.1: Effectiveness of economic systems' innovative development from different categories of hi-tech export in 2020.
Source: calculated and compiled by the authors.

view, the indicators of the cost of economic systems' innovative development in 2020 are shown in Figure 3.2, and the indicators of efficiency are shown in Figure 3.3.

As shown in Figure 3.2, the world's lowest expenditures for R&D are observed in India, Indonesia, and Mexico; China's expenditures are medium.

As shown in Figure 3.3, China has very high indicators of efficiency of innovative development in 2020. High values of these indicators are also observed in India,

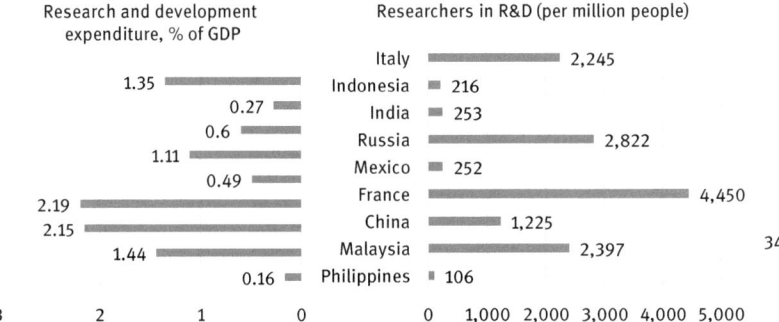

Figure 3.2: Indicators of cost of economic systems' innovative development in 2020.
Source: calculated and compiled by the authors.

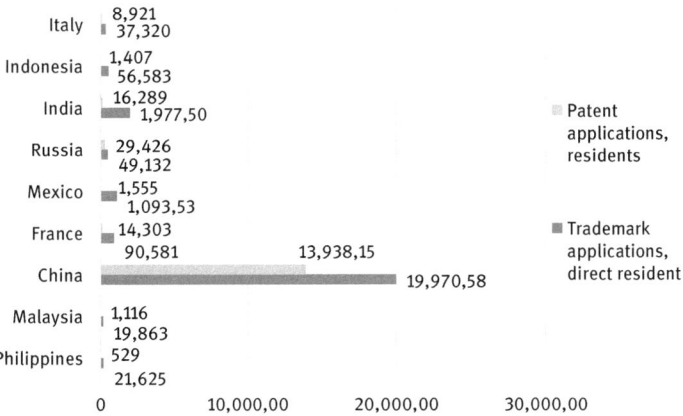

Figure 3.3: The indicators of efficiency of economic systems' innovative development in 2020.
Source: calculated and compiled by the authors.

Indonesia, and Mexico. Therefore, high efficiency is the source of large effectiveness of innovative development in these countries.

Conclusion

Thus, the performed research allows offering a scientific concept of internally-oriented treatment of effectiveness of economy's innovative system. According to the new treatment, a proprietary scientific & methodological approach to evaluation of effectiveness has been developed – it distinguishes internal indicators of expenditures and internal indicators of results. Due to this, effectiveness reflects not macro-economic (external) advantages of innovations but return from investments and commercial attractiveness. The authors' conclusions and recommendations supplement the Theory of innovations by creation of a scientific & methodological provision of the process of state monitoring and attraction of private investments in innovative activities in the economic system.

References

Andronova, I.V., Chernova, V.Y., Starostin, V.S., Degtereva (2019). Study of sector-specific innovation efforts: The case from Russian economy. Entrepreneurship and Sustainability Issues, Vsl Entrepreneurship and Sustainability Center, 7 (1), p. 540–552.

Atkinsonk, R.D., Ezell, S.J. (2012). Innovation Economics: the Race for Global Advantage, New Haven, CT: Yale University Press.

Bogoviz, A.V., Ragulina, Y.V. (2020). Industry competitiveness in the new economy. Lecture Notes in Networks and Systems, 115, p. v–vi.

García-Quevedo, J., Segarra-Blasco, A., Teruel, M. (2018). Financial constraints and the failure of innovation projects. Technological Forecasting and Social Change, 127, p. 127–140.

Gumba, H.M., Vlasenko, V.A. (2017). Strategy of development of innovative activity in industry and construction: The rationale of the regional dimension. Izvestiya Vysshikh Uchebnykh Zavedenii, Seriya Teknologiya Tekstil'noi Promyshlennosti, 2017-January(2), 2(1), p. 14–18.

Haabazoka, L. (2019). A Study of the Effects of Technological Innovations on the Performance of Commercial Banks in Developing Countries – A Case of the Zambian Banking Industry. In: Popkova E. (eds) The Future of the Global Financial System: Downfall or Harmony. ISC 2018. Lecture Notes in Networks and Systems, vol 57. Springer, Cham, https://doi.org/10.1007/978-3-030-00102-5_132

Harfst, J., Pichler, P., Fischer, W. (2017). Regional Ambassadors-An Innovative Element for the Development of Rural Areas? European Countryside, 9(2), p. 359–374.

Kuznetsova, O., Kuznetsova, S., Yumaev, E., Kuznetsov, V., Galtseva, O. (2017). Formation and Development of the Training System for Innovative Development of Regional Industry. E3S Web of Conferences, 15,04019.

Li, X., Subrahmanyam, A., Yang, X. (2018). Can financial innovation succeed by catering to behavioral preferences? Evidence from a callable options market. Journal of Financial Economics, 2(1), p. 34–42.

Petrenko, E.S., Shevyakova, A.L. (2019). Features and perspectives of digitization in Kazakhstan. Studies in Computational Intelligence, 826, p. 889–899.

Popkova, E.G. (2019). Preconditions of formation and development of industry 4.0 in the conditions of knowledge economy. Studies in Systems, Decision and Control, 169(1),65–72.

Popkova, E.G., Sergi, B.S. (2020). Human Capital and AI in Industry 4.0. Convergence and Divergence in Social Entrepreneurship in Russia. Journal of Intellectual Capital, In press, 2020. https://doi.org/10.1108/JIC-09-2019-0224

Popkova, E.G., Egorova, E.N., Popova, E., Pozdnyakova, U.A. (2019). The model of state management of economy on the basis of the internet of things. Studies in Computational Intelligence, 826, pp. 1137–1144.

Popkova, E.G., Gulzat, K. (2020). Technological Revolution in the 21st Century: Digital Society vs. Artificial Intelligence. Lecture Notes in Networks and Systems, 91, p. 339–345.

Popkova, E.G., Parakhina, V.N. (2019). Managing the global financial system on the basis of artificial intelligence: possibilities and limitations. Lecture Notes in Networks and Systems, 57, pp. 939–946.

Popkova, E.G., Poluyufta, L., Beshanova, Y., Popova, L.V., Kolesnikova, E. (2017). Innovations as a basis for marketing strategies of Russian oil companies in the conditions of oil prices reduction. Contributions to Economics, (9783319606958), p. 449–455.

Popkova, E.G., Zmiyak, K.V. (2019). Priorities of training of digital personnel for industry 4.0: social competencies vs technical competencies. On the Horizon, 27 (3–4), p. 138–144.

Popkova, E.G., Sergi, B.S. (2018). Will Industry 4.0 and Other Innovations Impact Russia's Development? In Bruno S. Sergi (Ed.) Exploring the Future of Russia's Economy and Markets: Towards Sustainable Economic Development (pp. 51–68). Bingley, UK: Emerald Publishing Limited.

Popkova, E.G., Sergi, B.S. (Eds.) (2019). Digital Economy: Complexity and Variety vs. Rationality. Berlin: Springer International Publishing.

Ragulina, Y.V. (2019). Priorities of development of industry 4.0 in modern economic systems with different progress in formation of knowledge economy. Studies in Systems, Decision and Control, 169, p. 167–174.

Ragulina, Y.V., Alekseev, A.N., Strizhkina, I.V., Tumanov, A.I. (2019). Methodology of criterial evaluation of consequences of the industrial revolution of the 21st century. Studies in Systems, Decision and Control, 169, p. 235–244.

Ramanathan, R., Ramanathan, U., Bentley, Y. (2018). The debate on flexibility of environmental regulations, innovation capabilities and financial performance – A novel use of DEA. Omega (United Kingdom), 75, p. 131–138.

Sergi, B.S. (2003). Economic Dynamics in Transitional Economies: The Four-P Governments, the EU Enlargement, and the Bruxelles Consensus. New York: Routledge.

Sergi, B.S. (Ed.) (2019). Tech, Smart Cities, and Regional Development in Contemporary Russia. Bingley, UK: Emerald Publishing Limited.

Sergi, B.S., Popkova, E.G. Bogoviz, A.V., Ragulina J.V. (2019a). Costs and Profits of Technological Growth in Russia. In Bruno S. Sergi (Ed.) Tech, Smart Cities, and Regional Development in Contemporary Russia. pp. 41–54. Bingley, UK: Emerald Publishing Limited. https://doi.org/10.1108/978-1-78973-881-020191005

Sergi, B.S., Popkova, E.G. Bogoviz, A.V., Ragulina J.V. (2019b). Entrepreneurship and Economic Growth: The Experience of Developed and Developing Countries. In Bruno S. Sergi and Cole C. Scanlon (Eds.) Entrepreneurship and Development in the 21st Century (pp. 3–32). Bingley, UK: Emerald Publishing Limited.

Shulus, A.A., Akopova, E.S., Przhedetskaya, N.V., Borzenko, K.V. (2020). Intellectual Production and Consumption: A New Reality of the 21st Century. Lecture Notes in Networks and Systems, 92, pp. 353–359.

Stolyarov, N.O., Petrenko, E.S., Serova, O.A., Umuralieva, A.S. (2020). The Digital Reality of the Modern Economy: New Actors and New Decision-Making Logic. Lecture Notes in Networks and Systems, 87, p. 882–888.

World Bank (2020). Indicators. URL: https://data.worldbank.org/indicator (data accessed: 17.03.2020).

Yao, M., Di, H., Zheng, X., Xu, X. (2018). Impact of payment technology innovations on the traditional financial industry: A focus on China. Technological Forecasting and Social Change, 2(1), p. 22–29.

Zavyalova, E.B. Studenikin, N.V. Starikova, E.A. (2018). Business participation in implementation of socially oriented Sustainable Development Goals in countries of Central Asia and the Caucasus region. Central Asia and the Caucasus, 19(2), p. 56–63.

Elena L. Emelyanenkova, Aleksandr N. Abramov,
Valentina Y. Dianova, Marina V. Karp and Tatiana N. Morgun

4 Methodological Approach to Evaluation of Effectiveness of Economic Systems' Innovative Development

Introduction

Effectiveness is the most important criterion of any economic activities. Though the general logic of measuring of effectiveness is always brought down to comparison of expenditures and profits, the approaches to its determination are different. Each of the existing methodological approaches to evaluating the effectiveness of economic systems' innovative development has certain advantages and drawbacks.

The most popular globally-oriented approach describes in detail the macroeconomic advantages of innovative development of economy and also allows for precise determination of the contribution of innovations into achievement of each (separately) strategic priority of economic systems' development. However, innovations are generalized here. The financial & investment approach allows for a well-balanced view of the results and expenditures and for assessment of investment attractiveness and commercial effectiveness of the innovative activities in economy.

However, both existing approaches allow only for limited conclusions regarding the economic effectiveness of innovative activities, which are insufficient for justified managerial decisions of state regulators. The problem is that expenditures and profits are differentiated in both approaches. Thus, in the first approach profits belong to the sphere of international trade, and expenditures to the sphere of innovations. In the second approach, expenditures belong to the resource sphere, and profits to the sphere of intellectual property protection.

These drawbacks do not allow describing the causal connections of innovative activities – in particular, their social and ecological manifestations. That's why it is necessary to develop a new methodological approach that would allow analyzing not aggregated indicators from different spheres of economy but detailed indicators that are unified by a common sphere.

Elena L. Emelyanenkova, Research and Design Institute For Information Technology, Signalling and Telecommunications in Railway Transportation, Moscow, Russia
Aleksandr N. Abramov, Moscow Region State University, Mytishchi, Russia
Valentina Y. Dianova, Plekhanov Russian University of Economics, Moscow, Russia
Marina V. Karp, State University of Management, Moscow, Russia
Tatiana N. Morgun, Russian Presidential Academy of National Economy and Public Administration, Smolensk Branch, Smolensk, Russia

https://doi.org/10.1515/9783110643701-004

Materials and Method

General issues of economic systems' innovative development are studied in the works Andronova et al. (2019), Bogoviz and Ragulina (2020), Petrenko and Shevyakova (2019), Popkova (2019), Popkova and Sergi (2020), Popkova et al. (2019), Popkova and Gulzat (2020), Popkova and Parakhina (2019), Popkova et al. (2017), Popkova and Zmiyak (2019), Popkova and Sergi (2018), Popkova and Sergi (2019), Ragulina (2019), Ragulina et al. (2019), Sergi (2003), Sergi (2019), Sergi et al. (2019a), Sergi et al. (2019b), Shulus et al. (2020), Stolyarov et al. (2020), and Zavyalova et al. (2018).

The methodological foundations of evaluation of effectiveness of economic systems' innovative development are set in the works Atkinsonk and Ezell (2012), García-Quevedo et al. (2018), Gumba and Vlasenko (2017), Haabazoka (2019), Harfst et al. (2017), Kuznetsova et al. (2017), Li et al. (2018), Ramanathan et al. (2018), and Yao et al. (2018).

This chapter presents a proprietary methodological approach to evaluation of effectiveness of economic systems' innovative development, which envisages consecutive comparison of expenditures and profits separately in each sphere where the consequences of innovations are manifested:

- entrepreneurship – determination of ratio of economic growth (according to the World Bank) to entrepreneurial risk ("entrepreneurial culture" reflects the risks of business's innovative activities) (according to the World Economic Forum);
- labor – determination of ratio of quality of life (Numbeo) to unemployment (as a result of the changes) (IMF);
- ecology – determination of ratio of the sustainable development index (UNDP) to Energy Trilemma index (World Energy Council);
- social sphere – determination of ratio of competitiveness 4.0 (World Economic forum) to the happiness index (World Happiness Report)

Though the above indicators are unified by a common sphere, their measuring units are different. That's why, in order to compare the data it is offered to evaluate the consequences of innovative activities for one calendar year. It is offered to use not the values of the indicators in the current year but ratio of their values in the current year to their values in the previous year. Evaluation of effectiveness should be performed with the help of the following formula:

$$\int EI = \frac{BE + LE + EE + SE}{4} \qquad (1)$$

where $\int EI$ – integral effectiveness of innovative development, shares of 1;

BE – effectiveness in the sphere of entrepreneurship, shares of 1;

LE – effectiveness in the sphere of labor, shares of 1;

EE – effectiveness in the ecological sphere, shares of 1;

SE – effectiveness in the social sphere, shares of 1.

According to the traditional idea of effectiveness, the value of each indicator in formula (1) is treated in the following way:

- if the value is below 1, effectiveness is negative, and innovations are inexpedient;
- if the value exceeds 1, effectiveness is positive – the higher the better.

The statistical basis for approbation of the developed methodological approach is shown in Table 4.1. Two countries from each distinguished category of countries by the value of the Global Innovation Index (WIPO, 2020) in 2020 are selected.

Table 4.1: Data for evaluation of effectiveness of economic systems' innovative development in 2019–2020.

Indicator	Year	Category of countries by the Global Innovation Index (GEI) in 2020					
		Innovative leaders (GEI>50)		Innovative periphery (50≤GEI≤25)		Innovative outsiders (GEI<25)	
		Switzerland	Sweden	India	Russia	Zambia	Nepal
Economic block, %	2019	1.600	2.181	7.791	1.500	4.050	3.821
	2020	1.700	1.697	7.921	1.500	4.546	3.972
Business risk, points 1–100	2019	66.6	71.6	61.1	49.5	47.9	41.0
	2020	64.4	70.8	55.5	49.5	47.8	44.7
Quality of Life Index, points 1–100	2019	195.93	178.67	117.51	104.94	n/a	n/a
	2020	192.01	175.95	108.63	102.31	n/a	n/a
Unemployment, %	2019	2.914	6.600	n/a	5.500	n/a	n/a
	2020	2.880	2.880	n/a	5.500	n/a	n/a
Sustainable development index, shares of 1	2019	85.0	80.1	59.1	68.9	53.1	62.8
	2020	87.3	86.7	61.7	73.4	46.7	53.0
Energy Trilemma index, position	2019	2	3	88	59	112	118
	2020	1	2	109	42	112	117
The Global Competitiveness Index 4.0, points 1–100	2019	82.6	81.7	62.0	65.6	46.1	50.8
	2020	82.3	81.2	61.4	66.7	46.5	51.6
Happiness index, points 1–100	2019	7.487	7.314	4.190	5.810	5.286	4.740
	2020	7.480	7.343	4.015	5.648	4.107	4.913

Source: compiled by the authors based on Helliwell et al. (2020), Institute of Scientific Communications (2020), International Monetary Fund (2020), Numbeo (2020), UNDP (2020), World Economic Forum (2020), World Energy Council (2020).

Results

Evaluation of the effectiveness of economic systems' innovative development in 2020 (as a result of 2019), according to the developed methodological approach, is shown in Table 4.2.

Table 4.2: Evaluation of the effectiveness of economic systems' innovative development in 2020, according to the developed methodological approach.

	Category of countries by the Global Innovation Index (GEI) in 2020					
	Innovative leaders (GEI>50)		Innovative periphery (50≤GEI≤25)		Innovative outsiders (GEI<25)	
	Switzerland	Sweden	India	Russia	Zambia	Nepal
Economic growth, %	1.06	0.78	1.02	1.00	1.12	1.04
Business risk	0.97	0.99	0.91	1.00	1.00	1.09
Effectiveness in the sphere of entrepreneurship	1.10	0.79	1.12	1.00	1.12	0.95
Quality of Life Index,	0.98	0.98	0.92	0.97	n/a	n/a
Unemployment, %	0.99	0.44	n/a	1.00	n/a	n/a
Effectiveness in the sphere of labor	0.99	2.26	n/a	0.97	n/a	n/a
Sustainable development index, shares of 1	1.03	1.08	1.04	1.07	0.88	0.84
Energy Trilemma index, position in the world	0.50	0.67	1.24	0.71	1.00	0.99
Effectiveness in the ecological sphere	2.05	1.62	0.84	1.50	0.88	0.85
The Global Competitiveness Index 4.0	1.00	0.99	0.99	1.02	1.01	1.02
Happiness index	1.00	1.00	0.96	0.97	0.78	1.04
Effectiveness in the social sphere	1.00	0.99	1.03	1.05	1.30	0.98
Integral effectiveness of innovative development	1.29	1.41	1.00	1.13	1.10	0.93

Source: calculated and compiled by the authors.

The obtained results are shown in Figures 4.1–4.4.

As shown in Figure 4.1, among the innovative leaders, the highest values are observed with effectiveness in the sphere of labor (2.26 in Sweden) and effectiveness in

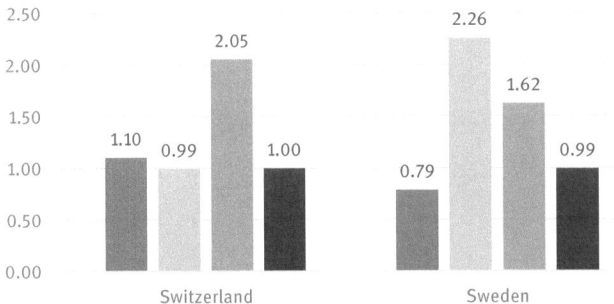

Figure 4.1: Effectiveness in different spheres with the innovative leaders in 2020, shares of 1. Source: calculated and compiled by the authors.

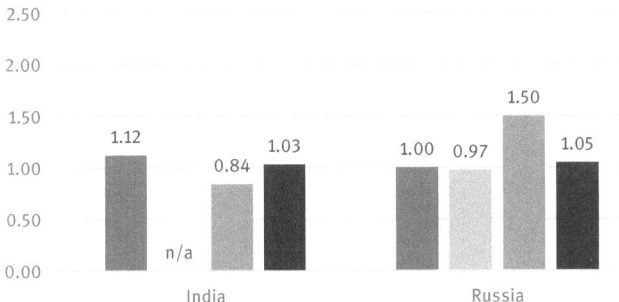

Figure 4.2: Effectiveness in different spheres for the innovative periphery in 2020, shares of 1. Source: calculated and compiled by the authors

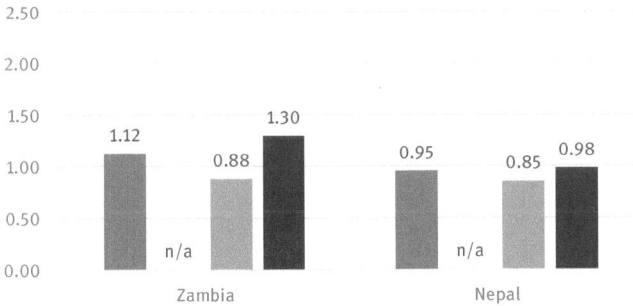

Figure 4.3: The innovative outsiders' effectiveness in different spheres in 2020, shares of 1. Source: calculated and compiled by the authors.

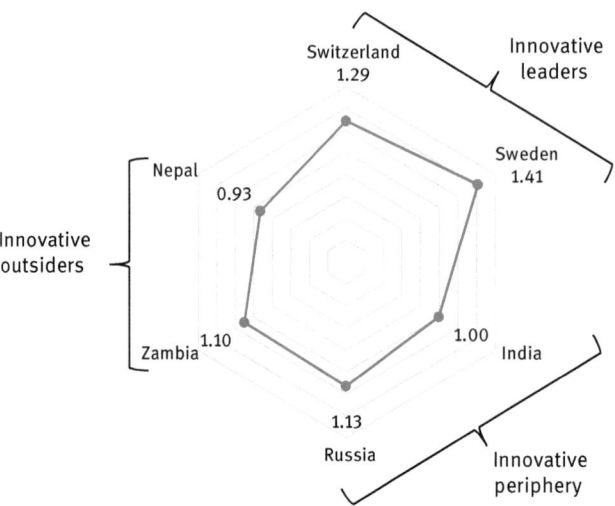

Figure 4.4: Integral effectiveness of innovative development in economic systems in 2020, shares of 1.
Source: calculated and compiled by the authors.

the ecological sphere (2.055 in Switzerland and 2.26 in Sweden). On the whole, innovations are justified in all spheres.

As shown in Figure 4.2, the innovative periphery's effectiveness in the ecological sphere is contradictory: 0.84 in India and 1.50 in Russia. Innovations are positive but not justified in all spheres.

As shown in Figure 4.3, the innovative outsiders' effectiveness in the ecological sphere is negative: 0.88 in Zambia and 0.85 in Nepal. Innovations are justified not in all spheres and require limitation or significant correction.

As shown in Figure 4.4, the only country in which integral effectiveness is negative is Nepal (0.93). It should be noted that integral effectiveness is the highest with the innovative leaders (1.29 in Switzerland and 1.41 in Sweden); low with the innovative periphery (1.13 in Russia and 1.00 in India), and very low with the innovative outsiders (1.10 in Zambia and 0.93 in Nepal). Therefore, effectiveness of the innovative activities grows with increase of their scale.

Conclusion

The developed methodological approach to evaluation of effectiveness of economic systems' innovative development allowed determining large differences in integral effectiveness and in effectiveness in different spheres for countries with different innovative activity. Thus, successful and problem spheres in each category of countries have been determined and it has been substantiated that it is necessary to increase the scale of innovative activities for raising the integral effectiveness.

References

Andronova, I.V., Chernova, V.Y., Starostin, V.S., Degtereva (2019). Study of sector-specific innovation efforts: The case from Russian economy. Entrepreneurship and Sustainability Issues, Vsl Entrepreneurship and Sustainability Center, 7(1), p. 540–552.

Atkinsonk, R.D., Ezell, S.J. (2012). Innovation Economics: The Race for Global Advantage, New Haven, CT: Yale University Press.

Bogoviz, A.V., Ragulina, Y.V. (2020). Industry competitiveness in the new economy. Lecture Notes in Networks and Systems, 115, p. v–vi.

Formation and Development of the Training System for Innovative Development of Regional Industry / O. Kuznetsova, S. Kuznetsova, E. Yumaev, V. Kuznetsov, O. Galtseva // International Innovative Mining Symposium (in memory of Prof. Vladimir Pronoza) : The 1st Scientific Practical Conference. – Kemerovo, 2017. Vol. – 15. – P. 04019. – DOI: 10.1051/e3sconf/20171504019.

García-Quevedo, J., Segarra-Blasco, A., Teruel, M. (2018). Financial constraints and the failure of innovation projects. Technological Forecasting and Social Change, 127, p. 127–140.

Gumba, H.M., Vlasenko, V.A. (2017). Strategy of development of innovative activity in industry and construction: The rationale of the regional dimension. Izvestiya Vysshikh Uchebnykh Zavedenii, Seriya Teknologiya Tekstil'noi Promyshlennosti, 2017-January(2), 2(1), p. 14–18.

Haabazoka, L. (2019). A Study of the Effects of Technological Innovations on the Performance of Commercial Banks in Developing Countries – A Case of the Zambian Banking Industry. In: Popkova E. (eds) The Future of the Global Financial System: Downfall or Harmony. ISC 2018. Lecture Notes in Networks and Systems, vol 57. Springer, Cham, https://doi.org/10.1007/978-3-030-00102-5-132.

Harfst, J., Pichler, P., Fischer, W. (2017). Regional Ambassadors-An Innovative Element for the Development of Rural Areas? European Countryside, 9(2), p. 359–374.

Helliwell, J.F., Layard, R., Sachs, J.D. (2020). World Happiness Report. URL: https://worldhappiness.report/ed/2019/ (data accessed: 27. 03.2020).

Institute of Scientific Communications (2020). Data set "Big data of the modern world economy: digital platform for intelligent analytics – 2020". URL: https://www.archilab.online/en/data/sounting-data-set (data accessed: 22.02.2020).

International Monetary Fund (2020). World Economic Outlook Database. URL: https://www.imf.org/external/pubs/ft/weo/2017/01/weodata/weoselgr.aspx (data accessed: 20. 02.2020).

Kuznetsova, O., Kuznetsova, S., Yumaev, E., Kuznetsov, V., Galtseva, O. (2017). Formation and Development of the Training System for Innovative Development of Regional Industry. E3S Web of Conferences, 15,04019.

Li, X., Subrahmanyam, A., Yang, X. (2018). Can financial innovation succeed by catering to behavioral preferences? Evidence from a callable options market. Journal of Financial Economics, 2(1), p. 34–42.

Numbeo (2020). Quality of Life Index for Country 2019 Mid-Year. URL: https://www.numbeo.com/quality-of-life/rankings_by_country.jsp (data accessed: 06.01.2020).

Petrenko, E.S., Shevyakova, A.L. (2019). Features and perspectives of digitization in Kazakhstan. Studies in Computational Intelligence, 826, p. 889–899.

Popkova, E.G. (2019). Preconditions of formation and development of industry 4.0 in the conditions of knowledge economy. Studies in Systems, Decision and Control, 169(1),65–72.

Popkova, E.G., Sergi, B.S. (2020). Human Capital and AI in Industry 4.0. Convergence and Divergence in Social Entrepreneurship in Russia. Journal of Intellectual Capital, In press, 2020. https://doi.org/10.1108/JIC-09-2019-0224

Popkova, E.G., Egorova, E.N., Popova, E., Pozdnyakova, U.A. (2019). The model of state management of economy on the basis of the internet of things. Studies in Computational Intelligence, 826, pp. 1137–1144.

Popkova, E.G., Gulzat, K. (2020). Technological Revolution in the 21st Century: Digital Society vs. Artificial Intelligence. Lecture Notes in Networks and Systems, 91, p. 339–345.

Popkova, E.G., Parakhina, V.N. (2019). Managing the global financial system on the basis of artificial intelligence: possibilities and limitations. Lecture Notes in Networks and Systems, 57, pp. 939–946.

Popkova, E.G., Poluyufta, L., Beshanova, Y., Popova, L.V., Kolesnikova, E. (2017). Innovations as a basis for marketing strategies of Russian oil companies in the conditions of oil prices reduction. Contributions to Economics, (9783319606958), p. 449–455.

Popkova, E.G., Zmiyak, K.V. (2019). Priorities of training of digital personnel for industry 4.0: social competencies vs technical competencies. On the Horizon, 27(3–4), p. 138–144.

Popkova, E.G., Sergi, B.S. (2018). Will Industry 4.0 and Other Innovations Impact Russia's Development? In Bruno S. Sergi (Ed.) Exploring the Future of Russia's Economy and Markets: Towards Sustainable Economic Development, pp. 51–68. Bingley, UK: Emerald Publishing Limited.

Popkova, E.G., Sergi, B.S. (Eds.) (2019). Digital Economy: Complexity and Variety vs. Rationality. Berlin: Springer International Publishing.

Ragulina, Y.V. (2019). Priorities of development of industry 4.0 in modern economic systems with different progress in formation of knowledge economy. Studies in Systems, Decision and Control, 169, p. 167–174.

Ragulina, Y.V., Alekseev, A.N., Strizhkina, I.V., Tumanov, A.I. (2019). Methodology of criterial evaluation of consequences of the industrial revolution of the 21st century. Studies in Systems, Decision and Control, 169, p. 235–244.

Ramanathan, R., Ramanathan, U., Bentley, Y. (2018). The debate on flexibility of environmental regulations, innovation capabilities and financial performance – A novel use of DEA. Omega (United Kingdom), 75, p. 131–138.

Sergi, B.S. (2003). Economic Dynamics in Transitional Economies: The Four-P Governments, the EU Enlargement, and the Bruxelles Consensus. New York: Routledge.

Sergi, B.S. (Ed.) (2019). Tech, Smart Cities, and Regional Development in Contemporary Russia. Bingley, UK: Emerald Publishing Limited.

Sergi, B.S., Popkova, E.G. Bogoviz, A.V., Ragulina J.V. (2019a). Costs and Profits of Technological Growth in Russia. In Bruno S. Sergi (Ed.) Tech, Smart Cities, and Regional Development in Contemporary Russia, pp. 41–54. Bingley, UK: Emerald Publishing Limited. https://doi.org/10.1108/978-1-78973-881-020191005.

Sergi, B.S., Popkova, E.G. Bogoviz, A.V., Ragulina J.V. (2019b). Entrepreneurship and Economic Growth: The Experience of Developed and Developing Countries. In Bruno S. Sergi and Cole C. Scanlon (Eds.) Entrepreneurship and Development in the 21st Century (pp. 3–32). Bingley, UK: Emerald Publishing Limited.

Shulus, A.A., Akopova, E.S., Przhedetskaya, N.V., Borzenko, K.V. (2020). Intellectual Production and Consumption: A New Reality of the 21st Century. Lecture Notes in Networks and Systems, 92, pp. 353–359.

Stolyarov, N.O., Petrenko, E.S., Serova, O.A., Umuralieva, A.S. (2020). The Digital Reality of the Modern Economy: New Actors and New Decision-Making Logic. Lecture Notes in Networks and Systems, 87, p. 882–888.

UNDP (2020). Sustainable Development Report 2019. URL: м https://sdgindex.org/reports/sustainable-development-report-2019/ (data accessed: 24.02.2019).

WIPO (2020). The Global Innovation Index – 2019. URL: https://www.globalinnovationindex.org/
    Home (data accessed: 20.02.2020).
World Economic Forum (2020). The Global Competitiveness Report 2019. URL: https://www.wefo
    rum.org/reports/how-to-end-a-decade-of-lost-productivity-growth (data accessed:
    07.01.2020).
World Energy Council (2020). Energy Trilemma Index. URL: https://trilemma.worldenergy.org/#!/en
    ergy-index (data accessed: 27.03.2020).
Yao, M., Di, H., Zheng, X., Xu, X. (2018). Impact of payment technology innovations on the
    traditional financial industry: A focus on China. Technological Forecasting and Social Change,
    2(1), p. 22–29.
Zavyalova, E.B. Studenikin, N.V. Starikova, E.A. (2018). Business participation in implementation of
    socially oriented Sustainable Development Goals in countries of Central Asia and the
    Caucasus region. Central Asia and the Caucasus, 19(2), p. 56–63.

Part II: **The Economic Foundations of Managing Economic Systems' Innovative Development**

Alexey V. Rodionov, Sergey V. Muzalev, Alsu R. Nabiyeva,
Dmitry M. Manyshin and Margarita V. Melnik

5 Economic Mechanisms of Innovative Development Management: Public-Private Partnership, Innovative Networks and Technological Parks

Introduction

The strategic role of innovative development for supporting effectiveness and competitiveness of the modern economic systems actualizes the problem of search for managerial mechanisms that allow for acceleration of this development. As the experience of developed countries shows, a large potential in this is observed with integration mechanisms, which are connected to interaction and cooperation of economic subjects. The principle of action of integration mechanisms consists in unifying the efforts and resources and joint implementation of innovative activities by economic subjects by the terms of division of labor, incomes, and risks.

The advantage of the integration mechanisms, as compared to state financing of innovations, is transfer of costs and risks to private investors. As compared to introduction of norms and standards of innovative activities for companies, their integration expends freedom of business, creating natural market stimuli for manifestation of innovative activity. This allows avoiding false innovations, which are announced by a company but are not implemented or are not new.

Developed countries actively use a wide diversity of the integration mechanisms, which include public-private partnership, clustering of business, innovative networks, and technological parks. However, contribution of these mechanisms into innovations is an additional positive effect, while they are initially created for increasing business activity and accelerating economic growth.

Based on this, we offer a hypothesis that the contribution of economic integration of entrepreneurship into economic system's innovative developments is not

Alexey V. Rodionov, Academy of the Federal Penitentiary Service of Russia, Ryazan, Russian Federation
Sergey V. Muzalev, Margarita V. Melnik, Financial University under the Government of the Russian Federation, Moscow, Russia
Alsu R. Nabiyeva, Russian University of Cooperation, Moscow, Russia
Dmitry M. Manyshin, State Educational Institution of Higher Education Moscow Region "University of Technology", Korolev, Russia

https://doi.org/10.1515/9783110643701-005

always ensured – it is predetermined by high inclination for innovative activities of business in developed countries, and it might not be achieved in developing countries, or might be achieved only in case of use of certain mechanisms of integration. The purpose of this chapter is to determine the most perspective and universal economic integration mechanisms of innovative development management, which are accessible not only for developed countries but also for developing countries.

Materials and Method

Various issues of innovative development management, as well as the use of the mechanisms of public-private partnership, clusters, innovative networks, and technological parks, are studied in the works Andronova et al. (2019), Bogoviz and Ragulina (2020), Petrenko and Shevyakova (2019), Popkova (2019), Popkova and Sergi (2020), Popkova et al. (2019), Popkova and Gulzat (2020), Popkova and Parakhina (2019), Popkova et al. (2017), Popkova and Zmiyak (2019), Popkova and Sergi (2018), Popkova and Sergi (2019), Ragulina (2019), Ragulina et al. (2019), Sergi (2003), Sergi (2019), Sergi et al. (2019a), Sergi et al. (2019b), Shulus et al. (2020), Stolyarov et al. (2020), and Zavyalova et al. (2018).

Specifics of innovative development management in developing countries are outlined in the works Atkinsonk and Ezell (2012), García-Quevedo et al. (2018), Gumba and Vlasenko (2017), Haabazoka (2019), Harfst et al. (2017), Kuznetsova et al. (2017), Li et al. (2018), Ramanathan et al. (2018), and Yao et al. (2018). However, experience and perspectives of application of the economic integration mechanisms in developing countries directly for acceleration of innovative development are not studied sufficiently and require further elaboration.

In this chapter, regression analysis is used for determining the dependence of the Global Innovation Index (calculated by WIPO (y)) on activity of application of the mechanisms of economic integration in entrepreneurship:
- public-private partnership (x_1) in the aspect of investments in information and communication technologies, water supply and sanitation, transport, and energy sphere, calculated by the World Bank – aggregate share in GDP according to the IMF;
- clustering (x_2) – indicator "12.02. State of cluster development", calculated by the World Economic Forum as the main element of the Global Competitiveness Index;
- innovative networks and technological parks – indicator of interaction and cooperation of companies (12.04b Collaboration between companies, x_3) and indicator of interaction and cooperation between universities and companies in R&D (12.04c University-industry collaboration in R&D, x_4), calculated by the World Economic Forum as an element of the Global Competitiveness Index;

The selection of countries for which the statistics for 2020 are accessible is shown in Tables 5.1 and 5.2.

Table 5.1: Statistics of public-private partnership and GDP in developing countries in 2020.

Country	Public private partnerships investment in ICT*	Public private partnerships investment in water and sanitation	Public private partnerships investment in transport	Public private partnerships investment in energy	Gross domestic product, USD million
Bangladesh	70.000	327.000	0.179	0.271	324,861
Brazil	n/a	0.140	1.041	4.929	2,447,245
China	n/a	1.617	25.965	0.449	15,066,667
Ghana	42.000	0.126	0.550	1.705	53,476
India	n/a	0.583	9.486	1.639	3,252,721
Indonesia	385.260	0.315	2.903	3.715	1,320,139
Mexico	946.000	0.537	0.589	3.486	1,153,302
Peru	273.700	0.121	0.215	0.311	245,766
Russia	n/a	1.200	1.762	0.189	1,712,024
South Africa	229.820	0.313	0.970	4.313	353,409
Tanzania	28.000	0.850	0.134	0.134	65,837

*ICT – information and communication technologies.
Source: compiled by the authors based on International Monetary Fund (2020), World Bank (2020).

Table 5.2: Statistics of public-private partnership, clusters, technological parks, and innovative networks in developing countries in 2020.

Country	PPP* aggregate investments, % of GDP	State of cluster development, points 1–7	Collaboration between companies, points 1–7	University-industry collaboration in R&D, points 1–7	Global Innovation Index, points 1–100
Bangladesh	0.001223	3.6	2.8	2.6	23.31
Brazil	0.000002	3.9	3.4	3.4	33.82
China	0.000002	4.6	4.4	4.4	54.82
Ghana	0.000830	4.0	3.9	3.9	25.27
India	0.000004	4.3	4.2	3.9	36.58

Table 5.2 (continued)

Country	PPP* aggregate investments, % of GDP	State of cluster development, points 1–7	Collaboration between companies, points 1–7	University-industry collaboration in R&D, points 1–7	Global Innovation Index, points 1–100
Indonesia	0.000297	4.6	4.7	4.2	29.72
Mexico	0.000824	4.3	3.5	3.5	36.06
Peru	0.001116	3.4	2.9	2.9	32.93
Russia	0.000002	3.4	3.6	3.8	37.62
South Africa	0.000666	4.3	3.7	4.3	34.04
Tanzania	0.000442	4.0	3.7	3.9	26.63

*PPP – public-private partnership.
Source: calculated and compiled by the authors based on Institute of Scientific communications (2020), World Economic Forum (2020).

Results

The activity of application of the mechanisms of public-private partnership, clustering, and creation of technological parks and innovative networks in developing countries in 2020 is shown in Figure 5.1.

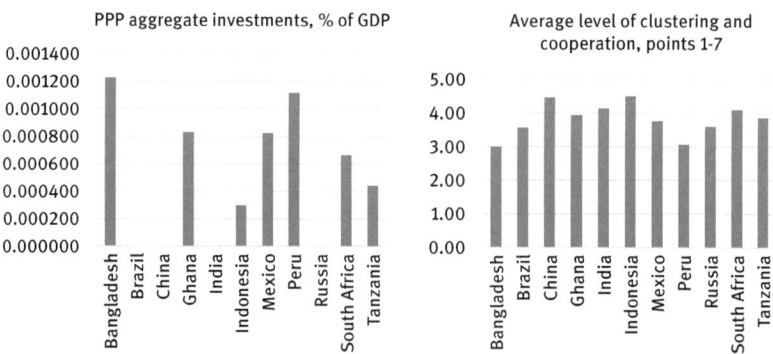

Figure 5.1: The level of application of the mechanisms of public-private partnership, clustering, and creation of technological parks and innovative networks in developing countries in 2020.
    *PPP – public-private partnership.
Source: developed and compiled by the authors.

As shown in Figure 5.1, the share of PPP aggregate investments in economy is different in developing countries – but in all cases it is below 0.5% (very small). The highest activity in the sphere of public-private partnership is observed in Bangladesh, Peru, Ghana, and Mexico; the lowest – in Brazil, China, India, and Russia. The average level of clustering and cooperation based on technological parks and innovative networks in all studied developing countries does not reach 5% and is more unified. The highest activity in the sphere of clustering and cooperation based on technological parks and innovative networks is observed in China and Indonesia; the lowest – in Bangladesh and Peru.

Regression analysis is used for creation of a multiple linear regression equation based on the data from Table 5.2: $y = 21.01 - 11,623.74^*x1 + 9.30^*x2 - 9.64^*x3 + 4.48^*x4$. According to the obtained equation, increase of the share of public-private partnership in GDP by 1% leads to decrease of the Global Innovation Index by 11,623.74; increase of the clustering index by 1 point leads to increase of the Global Innovation Index by 9.30 points; increase of collaboration between companies by 1 leads to decrease of the Global Innovation Index by 9.64 points; increase of university-industry collaboration by 1 point leads to increase of the Global Innovation Index by 4.48 points. The multiple correlation coefficient is assessed at 65.27% (moderate correlation).

Based on the established dependence, we determine the optimal combination of use of the integration mechanisms in entrepreneurship for the values of the Global Innovation Index up to 45 points – i.e., by 33.49% as compared to its average value in the selection of countries in 2020 (33.71 points). The condition is refusal from decrease of the indicators' values as compared to 2020. The results of optimization with the simplex methods are presented in Table 5.3.

Table 5.3: The optimal combination of using the integration mechanisms in entrepreneurship for increasing the values of the Global Innovation Index in developing countries up to 45 points.

Variable	Regression coefficient	Target value	Initial value in 2020	Growth of target value as compared to the initial value in 2020, %
PPP aggregate investments, % of GDP	−11623.74	0.000492	0.000492	0
Level of cluster development, points 1–7	9.30	5.19	4.04	28.54
Collaboration between companies, points 1–7	−9.64	3.71	3.71	0

Table 5.3 (continued)

Variable	Regression coefficient	Target value	Initial value in 2020	Growth of target value as compared to the initial value in 2020, %
University-industry collaboration in R&D, points 1–7	4.48	3.84	3.71	3.46
Global Innovation Index, points 1–100	Constant: 21.01	Goal: 45.00	33.71	33.49

Source: calculated and compiled by the authors.

As shown in Table 5.3, it is necessary to increase the level of cluster development by 28.54%, as compared to 2020 – up to 9.30 points, and to increase university-industry collaboration in R&D by 3.46%, as compared to 2020 – up to 4.48 points. Based on the obtained results, the comparative characteristics of the economic mechanisms of innovative development management are compiled (Table 5.4).

Table 5.4: Comparative characteristics of the economic mechanisms of innovative development management.

Characteristics for comparison	Public-private partnership	Clustering of business	Innovative networks and technological parks	
			Collaboration between companies	University-industry collaboration in R&D
Goal of the mechanism (connection to innovations)	Attraction of private investments in infrastructure (not connected)	Increase of business's effectiveness in the sphere (connected)	Growth of competitiveness (connected)	commercialization of university innovations (connected)
Mechanism's influence on competition	limits	stimulated	stimulates	stimulates
Creation and strengthening of competitive advantages from innovations	ensured	ensured	not ensured	ensured

Table 5.4 (continued)

Characteristics for comparison	Public-private partnership	Clustering of business	Innovative networks and technological parks	
			Collaboration between companies	University-industry collaboration in R&D
Mechanism's influence on accessibility of innovations	no influence	accessibility is increased	accessibility is increased	accessibility is increased
Recommendation to use the mechanism for the purpose of innovative development	application is not expedient or has to be limited	application of the mechanism is recommended	application is not expedient	application of the mechanism is recommended

Source: developed and compiled by the authors.

As shown in Table 5.4, only clustering of business and university-industry collaboration in R&D based on innovative networks and technological parks are initially aimed at increase of innovative activity of entrepreneurial subjects and integration unions, increase competition, create and strengthen of competitive advantages from innovations, and increase the accessibility of innovations for the subjects of innovative activities. That's why these two integration mechanisms are recommended for application in the interests of innovative development in developing countries.

Conclusion

Thus, it has been proved that natural stimuli for implementation of innovations are less vivid in developing countries than in developed countries. That's why not all integration mechanisms that are used in entrepreneurship allow increasing its innovative activity. Two universal mechanisms, which stimulate economy's innovative development, regardless of the market stimuli, are recommended for application in developed and developing countries – clustering and university-industry collaboration in R&D based on innovative networks and technological parks.

References

Andronova, I.V., Chernova, V.Y., Starostin, V.S., Degtereva (2019). Study of sector-specific innovation efforts: The case from Russian economy. Entrepreneurship and Sustainability Issues, Vsl Entrepreneurship and Sustainability Center, 7(1), p. 540–552.

Atkinsonk, R.D., Ezell, S.J. (2012). Innovation Economics: the Race for Global Advantage, New Haven, CT: Yale University Press.

Bogoviz, A.V., Ragulina, Y.V. (2020). Industry competitiveness in the new economy. Lecture Notes in Networks and Systems, 115, p. v–vi.

García-Quevedo, J., Segarra-Blasco, A., Teruel, M. (2018). Financial constraints and the failure of innovation projects. Technological Forecasting and Social Change, 127, p. 127–140.

Gumba, H.M., Vlasenko, V.A. (2017). Strategy of development of innovative activity in industry and construction: The rationale of the regional dimension. Izvestiya Vysshikh Uchebnykh Zavedenii, Seriya Teknologiya Tekstil'noi Promyshlennosti, 2017-January(2), 2(1), p. 14–18.

Haabazoka, L. (2019). A Study of the Effects of Technological Innovations on the Performance of Commercial Banks in Developing Countries – A Case of the Zambian Banking Industry. In: Popkova E. (eds) The Future of the Global Financial System: Downfall or Harmony. ISC 2018. Lecture Notes in Networks and Systems, vol 57. Springer, Cham, https://doi.org/10.1007/978-3-030-00102-5_132

Harfst, J., Pichler, P., Fischer, W. (2017). Regional Ambassadors-An Innovative Element for the Development of Rural Areas? European Countryside, 9(2), p. 359–374.

Institute of Scientific Communications (2020). Data set "Big data of the modern world economy: digital platform for intelligent analytics – 2020". URL: https://www.archilab.online/en/data/sounting-data-set (data accessed: 17.03.2020).

International Monetary Fund (2020). World Economic Outlook Database. URL: https://www.imf.org/external/pubs/ft/weo/2017/01/weodata/weoselgr.aspx (data accessed: 28. 03.2020).

Kuznetsova, O., Kuznetsova, S., Yumaev, E., Kuznetsov, V., Galtseva, O. (2017). Formation and Development of the Training System for Innovative Development of Regional Industry. E3S Web of Conferences, 15,04019. DOI: 10.1051/e3sconf/20171504019

Li, X., Subrahmanyam, A., Yang, X. (2018). Can financial innovation succeed by catering to behavioral preferences? Evidence from a callable options market. Journal of Financial Economics, 2(1), p. 34–42.

Petrenko, E.S., Shevyakova, A.L. (2019). Features and perspectives of digitization in Kazakhstan. Studies in Computational Intelligence, 826, p. 889–899.

Popkova, E.G. (2019). Preconditions of formation and development of industry 4.0 in the conditions of knowledge economy. Studies in Systems, Decision and Control, 169(1), 65–72.

Popkova, E.G., Sergi, B.S. (2020). Human Capital and AI in Industry 4.0. Convergence and Divergence in Social Entrepreneurship in Russia. Journal of Intellectual Capital, In press, 2020. https://doi.org/10.1108/JIC-09-2019-0224

Popkova, E.G., Egorova, E.N., Popova, E., Pozdnyakova, U.A. (2019). The model of state management of economy on the basis of the internet of things. Studies in Computational Intelligence, 826, pp. 1137–1144.

Popkova, E.G., Gulzat, K. (2020). Technological Revolution in the 21st Century: Digital Society vs. Artificial Intelligence. Lecture Notes in Networks and Systems, 91, p. 339–345.

Popkova, E.G., Parakhina, V.N. (2019). Managing the global financial system on the basis of artificial intelligence: possibilities and limitations. Lecture Notes in Networks and Systems, 57, pp. 939–946.

Popkova, E.G., Poluyufta, L., Beshanova, Y., Popova, L.V., Kolesnikova, E. (2017). Innovations as a basis for marketing strategies of Russian oil companies in the conditions of oil prices reduction. Contributions to Economics, (9783319606958), p. 449–455.

Popkova, E.G., Zmiyak, K.V. (2019). Priorities of training of digital personnel for industry 4.0: social competencies vs technical competencies. On the Horizon, 27(3–4), p. 138–144.

Popkova, E.G., Sergi, B.S. (2018). Will Industry 4.0 and Other Innovations Impact Russia's Development? In Bruno S. Sergi (Ed.) Exploring the Future of Russia's Economy and Markets: Towards Sustainable Economic Development, pp. 51–68. Bingley, UK: Emerald Publishing Limited.

Popkova, E.G., Sergi, B.S. (Eds.) (2019). Digital Economy: Complexity and Variety vs. Rationality. Berlin: Springer International Publishing.

Ragulina, Y.V. (2019). Priorities of development of industry 4.0 in modern economic systems with different progress in formation of knowledge economy. Studies in Systems, Decision and Control, 169, p. 167–174.

Ragulina, Y.V., Alekseev, A.N., Strizhkina, I.V., Tumanov, A.I. (2019). Methodology of criterial evaluation of consequences of the industrial revolution of the 21st century. Studies in Systems, Decision and Control, 169, p. 235–244.

Ramanathan, R., Ramanathan, U., Bentley, Y. (2018). The debate on flexibility of environmental regulations, innovation capabilities and financial performance – A novel use of DEA. Omega (United Kingdom), 75, p. 131–138.

Sergi, B.S. (2003). Economic Dynamics in Transitional Economies: The Four-P Governments, the EU Enlargement, and the Bruxelles Consensus. New York: Routledge.

Sergi, B.S. (Ed.) (2019). Tech, Smart Cities, and Regional Development in Contemporary Russia. Bingley, UK: Emerald Publishing Limited.

Sergi, B.S., Popkova, E.G. Bogoviz, A.V., Ragulina J.V. (2019a). Costs and Profits of Technological Growth in Russia. In Bruno S. Sergi (Ed.) Tech, Smart Cities, and Regional Development in Contemporary Russia, pp. 41–54. Bingley, UK: Emerald Publishing Limited. https://doi.org/10.1108/978-1-78973-881-020191005

Sergi, B.S., Popkova, E.G. Bogoviz, A.V., Ragulina J.V. (2019b). Entrepreneurship and Economic Growth: The Experience of Developed and Developing Countries. In Bruno S. Sergi and Cole C. Scanlon (Eds.) Entrepreneurship and Development in the 21st Century (pp. 3–32). Bingley, UK: Emerald Publishing Limited.

Shulus, A.A., Akopova, E.S., Przhedetskaya, N.V., Borzenko, K.V. (2020). Intellectual Production and Consumption: A New Reality of the 21st Century. Lecture Notes in Networks and Systems, 92, pp. 353–359.

Stolyarov, N.O., Petrenko, E.S., Serova, O.A., Umuralieva, A.S. (2020). The Digital Reality of the Modern Economy: New Actors and New Decision-Making Logic. Lecture Notes in Networks and Systems, 87, p. 882–888.

World Bank (2020). Indicators. URL: https://data.worldbank.org/indicator (data accessed: 28.03.2020).

Yao, M., Di, H., Zheng, X., Xu, X. (2018). Impact of payment technology innovations on the traditional financial industry: A focus on China. Technological Forecasting and Social Change, 2(1), p. 22–29.

Zavyalova, E.B. Studenikin, N.V. Starikova, E.A. (2018). Business participation in implementation of socially oriented Sustainable Development Goals in countries of Central Asia and the Caucasus region. Central Asia and the Caucasus, 19(2), p. 56–63.

Sergei V. Shkodinsky, Aleksandr E. Suglobov, Murat A. Bulgarov,
Elena N. Belkina and Anatoly V. Solodilov

6 The Role of Government in Managing the Innovative Development in the Market Economy

Introduction

Innovative activities are implemented based on a long algorithm, starting from offering ideas and developing innovative solutions and technologies to commercializing innovations – implementing the created solutions and technologies into the economic practice, manufacturing innovative products, and providing services in the innovative form. The direct participation of government in the innovative process – as the owner of research organizations that conduct R&D and/or companies that implement innovative solutions and technologies – is ineffective due to two reasons.

Firstly, full government financing of the innovative activities in economy causes a large burden on the state budget and should be provided only in rare cases – as a rule, during an intensive economic rise, by means of additional tax revenues from prospering business or in during a period of deep crisis, for overcoming it by means of the reserve fund's assets. Quick innovative development with the dominating deficit of financing will not allow achieving stable results of the innovative activities, and production capacities of the involved economic subjects will be at their minimum use. Thus, innovations will be unprofitable.

Secondly, innovative activities are not subject to planning, due to a vivid creative component and uncertainty of the results. For executing a government plan, the subjects of innovative activities will be implementing false innovations – copying the existing technologies for obtaining the guaranteed results. High risks of true innovations will be restraining their development, and commercialization will be difficult, as a government plan could be fulfilled differently by research institutes and companies, and created innovations will not be in demand in practice.

Thus, the role of government in managing the innovative development of the market economy should be more flexible, and financing of the innovative should be an exception, not a rule. Out of a large diversity of available tools of regulation it is

Sergei V. Shkodinsky, Research Institute of Finance of the Ministry of Finance of the Russian Federation Moscow, Russia, Moscow Region State University, Mytishchi, Russia
Aleksandr E. Suglobov, Financial University under the Government of the Russian Federation, Moscow, Russian Federation
Murat A. Bulgarov, Elena N. Belkina, "Kuban State Agrarian University named after I.T. Trubilin", Krasnodar, Russia
Anatoly V. Solodilov, Moscow Region State University,Mytishchi, Russia

https://doi.org/10.1515/9783110643701-006

necessary to choose the most effective ones, to become the basis for a universal approach to state management of economy's innovative development. The purpose of this research is to determine a perspective role of government in managing the innovative development of the market economy for maximizing the effectiveness of this management.

Materials and Method

The necessity for state management of innovative development of the market economy is noted in Atkinsonk and Ezell (2012), García-Quevedo et al. (2018), Gumba and Vlasenko (2017), Haabazoka (2019), Harfst et al. (2017), Kuznetsova et al. (2017), Li et al. (2018), Ramanathan et al. (2018), and Yao et al. (2018).

The traditional role of government in managing the innovative development of the market economy, which is brought down to financing of this development, is studied by Andronova et al. (2019), Bogoviz and Ragulina (2020), Petrenko and Shevyakova (2019), Popkova (2019), Popkova and Sergi (2020), Popkova et al. (2019), Popkova and Gulzat (2020), Popkova and Parakhina (2019), Popkova et al. (2017), Popkova and Zmiyak (2019), Popkova and Sergi (2018), Popkova and Sergi (2019), Ragulina (2019), Ragulina et al. (2019), Sergi (2003), Sergi (2019), Sergi et al. (2019a), Sergi et al. (2019b), Shulus et al. (2020), Stolyarov et al. (2020), and Zavyalova et al. (2018).

Despite a large number of publications on the topic of state management of innovative development of the market economy, the successful international experience of this management has not been studied sufficiently – which requires further scientific elaboration. In order to show this experience, we selected five countries which companies are in the list Forbes (2020) of the World's Most Innovative Companies:

- USA – in the ranking ServiceNow (innovation premium: 89.22%, 1st position);
- India – in the ranking Hindustan Unilever (innovation premium: 67.20%, 8th position);
- South Korea – in the ranking Naver (innovation premium: 64.62%, 9th position);
- Indonesia – in the ranking Unilever Indonesia (innovation premium: 63.91%, 12th position);
- Russia – in the ranking Norilsk Nickel (innovation premium: 34.92%, 100th position).

For obtaining the most correct results of, we use a complex of indicators that are calculated according to the same methodology and could be found in a general report by the World Economic Forum. Correlation analysis is used for determining the connection between various manifestations of state management and managerial

results: dynamics of business and innovative activity of business. The manifestations of state management are structured according to the following:
- Correction of state management on the whole, which manifestations are transparency of economy, orientation at the future, and supporting stability;
- Regulation of entrepreneurship, which manifestations are infrastructural provision, support for market competition, development of the labor market, and development of financial system;
- Non-financial stimulation of innovative activities, which manifestations are protection of property rights, provision of digitization, and development of education.

The values of the selected indicators as of early 2020 are shown in Table 6.1.

Table 6.1: Manifestations of state management of innovative development of the market economy
and its results in countries from the list of innovative business (Forbes) in 2020, points 1–100.

Indicator	Original title of the indicator	USA	India	South Korea	Indonesia	Russia
Transparency of economy	Transparency	71,0	41,0	57,0	38,0	28,0
Protection of property rights	Property rights	71.0	47.8	72.8	56.4	59.6
Orientation at the future	Future orientation of government	68.2	69.7	69.5	55.9	54.7
Infrastructural provision	2nd pillar: Infrastructure	87.9	68.7	92.1	67.7	73.8
Provision of digitization	3rd pillar: ICT adoption	74.3	32.1	92.8	55.4	77.0
Supporting stability	4th pillar: Macroeconomic stability	99.8	90.0	100.0	90.0	90.0
Development of education	6th pillar: Skills	82.5	50.5	74.0	64.0	68.3
Supporting market competition	7th pillar: Product market	68.6	50.4	56.1	58.2	52.9
Development of labor market	8th pillar: Labour market	78.0	53.9	62.9	57.7	61.0
Development of financial system	9th pillar: Financial system	91.0	69.5	84.4	64.0	55.7
Dynamics of business	11th pillar: Business dynamism	84.2	60.0	70.5	69.6	63.1
Innovative activity of business	12th pillar: Innovation capability	84.1	50.9	79.1	37.7	52.9

Source: compiled by the authors based on World Economic Forum (2020).

Results

Correlation analysis is performed based on Table 6.1 (Figure 6.1).

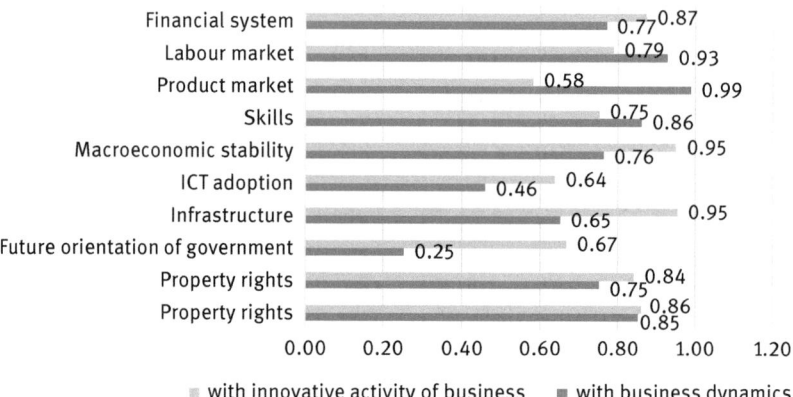

Figure 6.1: Correlation of the manifestations of state management of innovative development of the market economy with its results in countries from the list of innovative business by Forbes in 2020, shares of 1.
Source: calculated and compiled by the authors.

As shown in Figure 6.1, all the distinguished manifestations of state management of innovative development of the market economy are very important. This does not allow distinguishing or excluding any manifestation – all of them are necessary and should be achieved in practice. However, the obtained results do not allow ranking the distinguished manifestations by the level of their significance and effectiveness.

It has also been established that correlation of the studied manifestations of state management of innovative development of the market economy – on average – is with innovative activity of business (0.79) is higher than with dynamics of business (0.73). That's why during state management of innovative development of the market economy it is expedient to pay main attention to stimulation of not just changes but innovative activities of entrepreneurship. The pyramid of government's directions in managing the innovative development of the market economy is shown in Figure 6.2.

As shown in Figure 6.2, regulation of entrepreneurship is ranked 1st by significance and effectiveness: correlation – 0.82, variation – 3.86%, within which transparency of economy (0.86), macro-economic stability (0.86), and future orientation of government (0.46) are ensured.

The 2nd position belongs to correction of state management on the whole: correlation – 0.72, variation – 31.60%, within which development of the labor market (0.86), development of the financial system (0.82), infrastructural provision (0.80), and support for market competition (0.78) are conducted.

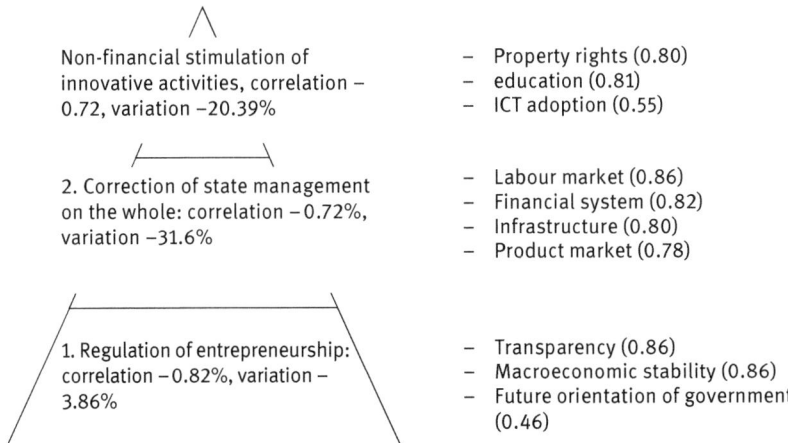

Figure 6.2: The pyramid of government's directions in managing the innovative development of the market economy.
Source: developed and compiled by the authors.

The 3rd position belongs to non-financial stimulation of innovative activities (correlation – 0.72, variation – 20.39%), within which property rights are protected (0.80), education is developed (0.81), and digitization is ensured (0.55).

Conclusion

As a result of the research by the example of countries with the highest innovative activity of entrepreneurship in 2020 it is proved that opportunities of state management of innovative development of the market economy beyond financing of innovations are very wide. Therefore, the role of government in managing the innovative development of the market economy is connected to creation and support for a favorable environment for the innovative activities of entrepreneurship.

It has been substantiation that while performing this role government should not limit itself with a certain direction of regulation and has to implement the whole complex of regulatory measures in three directions, which include correction of state management on the whole, regulation of entrepreneurship, and non-financial stimulation of the innovative activities.

At the same time, the results of the research showed different significance of these directions. That's why the resources for their implementation should be distributed not equally but according to the priority. For this, a pyramid of government's directions in managing the innovative development of the market economy is offered.

References

Andronova, I.V., Chernova, V.Y., Starostin, V.S., Degtereva (2019). Study of sector-specific innovation efforts: The case from Russian economy. Entrepreneurship and Sustainability Issues, Vsl Entrepreneurship and Sustainability Center, 7(1), p. 540–552.

Atkinsonk, R.D., Ezell, S.J. (2012). Innovation Economics: the Race for Global Advantage, New Haven, CT: Yale University Press.

Bogoviz, A.V., Ragulina, Y.V. (2020). Industry competitiveness in the new economy. Lecture Notes in Networks and Systems, 115, p. v–vi.

Forbes (2020). The World's Most Innovative Companies. URL: https://www.forbes.com/innovative-companies/list/#tab:rank (data accessed: 29.03.2020).

García-Quevedo, J., Segarra-Blasco, A., Teruel, M. (2018). Financial constraints and the failure of innovation projects. Technological Forecasting and Social Change, 127, p. 127–140.

Gumba, H.M., Vlasenko, V.A. (2017). Strategy of development of innovative activity in industry and construction: The rationale of the regional dimension. Izvestiya Vysshikh Uchebnykh Zavedenii, Seriya Teknologiya Tekstil'noi Promyshlennosti, 2017-January(2), 2(1), p. 14–18.

Haabazoka, L. (2019). A Study of the Effects of Technological Innovations on the Performance of Commercial Banks in Developing Countries – A Case of the Zambian Banking Industry. In: Popkova E. (eds) The Future of the Global Financial System: Downfall or Harmony. ISC 2018. Lecture Notes in Networks and Systems, vol 57. Springer, Cham, Online ISBN 978-3-030-00102-5, https://doi.org/10.1007/978-3-030-00102-5_132

Harfst, J., Pichler, P., Fischer, W. (2017). Regional Ambassadors-An Innovative Element for the Development of Rural Areas? European Countryside, 9(2), p. 359–374.

Kuznetsova, O., Kuznetsova, S., Yumaev, E., Kuznetsov, V., Galtseva, O. (2017). Formation and Development of the Training System for Innovative Development of Regional Industry. E3S Web of Conferences, 15,04019.

Li, X., Subrahmanyam, A., Yang, X. (2018). Can financial innovation succeed by catering to behavioral preferences? Evidence from a callable options market. Journal of Financial Economics, 2(1), p. 34–42.

Petrenko, E.S., Shevyakova, A.L. (2019). Features and perspectives of digitization in Kazakhstan. Studies in Computational Intelligence, 826, p. 889–899.

Popkova, E.G. (2019). Preconditions of formation and development of industry 4.0 in the conditions of knowledge economy. Studies in Systems, Decision and Control, 169(1),65–72.

Popkova, E.G., Sergi, B.S. (2020). Human Capital and AI in Industry 4.0. Convergence and Divergence in Social Entrepreneurship in Russia. Journal of Intellectual Capital, In press, 2020. https://doi.org/10.1108/JIC-09-2019-0224

Popkova, E.G., Egorova, E.N., Popova, E., Pozdnyakova, U.A. (2019). The model of state management of economy on the basis of the internet of things. Studies in Computational Intelligence, 826, pp. 1137–1144.

Popkova, E.G., Gulzat, K. (2020). Technological Revolution in the 21st Century: Digital Society vs. Artificial Intelligence. Lecture Notes in Networks and Systems, 91, p. 339–345.

Popkova, E.G., Parakhina, V.N. (2019). Managing the global financial system on the basis of artificial intelligence: possibilities and limitations. Lecture Notes in Networks and Systems, 57, pp. 939–946.

Popkova, E.G., Poluyufta, L., Beshanova, Y., Popova, L.V., Kolesnikova, E. (2017). Innovations as a basis for marketing strategies of Russian oil companies in the conditions of oil prices reduction. Contributions to Economics, (9783319606958), p. 449–455.

Popkova, E.G., Zmiyak, K.V. (2019). Priorities of training of digital personnel for industry 4.0: social competencies vs technical competencies. On the Horizon, 27(3–4), p. 138–144.

Popkova, E.G., Sergi, B.S. (2018). Will Industry 4.0 and Other Innovations Impact Russia's Development? In Bruno S. Sergi (Ed.) Exploring the Future of Russia's Economy and Markets: Towards Sustainable Economic Development (pp. 51–68). Bingley, UK: Emerald Publishing Limited.

Popkova, E.G., Sergi, B.S. (Eds.) (2019). Digital Economy: Complexity and Variety vs. Rationality. Berlin: Springer International Publishing.

Ragulina, Y.V. (2019). Priorities of development of industry 4.0 in modern economic systems with different progress in formation of knowledge economy. Studies in Systems, Decision and Control, 169, p. 167–174.

Ragulina, Y.V., Alekseev, A.N., Strizhkina, I.V., Tumanov, A.I. (2019). Methodology of criterial evaluation of consequences of the industrial revolution of the 21st century. Studies in Systems, Decision and Control, 169, p. 235–244.

Ramanathan, R., Ramanathan, U., Bentley, Y. (2018). The debate on flexibility of environmental regulations, innovation capabilities and financial performance – A novel use of DEA. Omega (United Kingdom), 75, p. 131–138.

Sergi, B.S. (2003). Economic Dynamics in Transitional Economies: The Four-P Governments, the EU Enlargement, and the Bruxelles Consensus. New York: Routledge.

Sergi, B.S. (Ed.) (2019). Tech, Smart Cities, and Regional Development in Contemporary Russia. Bingley, UK: Emerald Publishing Limited.

Sergi, B.S., Popkova, E.G. Bogoviz, A.V., Ragulina J.V. (2019a). Costs and Profits of Technological Growth in Russia. In Bruno S. Sergi (Ed.) Tech, Smart Cities, and Regional Development in Contemporary Russia, pp. 41–54. Bingley, UK: Emerald Publishing Limited. https://doi.org/10.1108/978-1-78973-881-020191005

Sergi, B.S., Popkova, E.G. Bogoviz, A.V., Ragulina J.V. (2019b). Entrepreneurship and Economic Growth: The Experience of Developed and Developing Countries. In Bruno S. Sergi and Cole C. Scanlon (Eds.) Entrepreneurship and Development in the 21st Century (pp. 3–32). Bingley, UK: Emerald Publishing Limited.

Shulus, A.A., Akopova, E.S., Przhedetskaya, N.V., Borzenko, K.V. (2020). Intellectual Production and Consumption: A New Reality of the 21st Century. Lecture Notes in Networks and Systems, 92, pp. 353–359.

Stolyarov, N.O., Petrenko, E.S., Serova, O.A., Umuralieva, A.S. (2020). The Digital Reality of the Modern Economy: New Actors and New Decision-Making Logic. Lecture Notes in Networks and Systems, 87, p. 882–888.

World Economic Forum (2020). The Global Competitiveness Report 2019. URL: https://www.weforum.org/reports/how-to-end-a-decade-of-lost-productivity-growth (data accessed: 29.03.2020).

Yao, M., Di, H., Zheng, X., Xu, X. (2018). Impact of payment technology innovations on the traditional financial industry: A focus on China. Technological Forecasting and Social Change, 2(1), p. 22–29.

Zavyalova, E.B. Studenikin, N.V. Starikova, E.A. (2018). Business participation in implementation of socially oriented Sustainable Development Goals in countries of Central Asia and the Caucasus region. Central Asia and the Caucasus, 19(2), p. 56–63.

Yuliya A. Agunovich

7 The Economic Model of Innovative Development of an Economic System: Private Stimuli/Government Expenditures Ratio

Introduction

An important role in the process of economic system's innovative development belongs to investments in innovations. Their subject could be government, which allocated funds from the budget for top-priority national innovative projects. The subject of financing of innovations could also be venture investors, which support the most perspective and breakthrough projects. Universities that conduct R&D could also finance their innovative activities, similarly to entrepreneurial structures that implement innovative technologies in their activities and start production of innovative products (goods and services).

The classical idea of economic model of innovative development of an economic system envisages foundation on private investments – venture (external) and entrepreneurial (internal). The justification is saving of budget assets and the existing idea of government as an ineffective subject of commercial activities management. In particular, the classical model is implemented in one of the most innovative market economies of the world – the USA – which became a case study during formation of the classical model.

At the same time, it is necessary to note that in the conditions of outflow of investments from economy and in the period of a crisis the foundation on the classical model means termination of the innovative activities. In countries with permanent deficit of investments and underdeveloped venture investing – because of investors and entrepreneurs' low inclination for risk – the classical model cannot be applied. This explains the necessity for an alternative model, which is used in any economic systems, regardless of their investment & innovative climate and which is effective at all stages of the economic cycle.

Here we offer a hypothesis that private investments are effective not at all stages of the innovative process – because of their drawbacks. The purpose of the chapter is to determine the optimal private stimuli / government expenditures ratio at different stages of the innovative process and to develop an economic model of economic system's innovative development, which ensures the achievement of this ratio for increasing the activity and effectiveness of innovative activities in the conditions of the market economy.

Yuliya A. Agunovich, Kamchatka State Technical University, Petropavlovsk-Kamchatskiy, Russia

https://doi.org/10.1515/9783110643701-007

Materials and Method

The theory and practice of investments in economic system's innovative developments in the conditions of the market economy are studied in the works Atkinsonk and Ezell (2012), García-Quevedo et al. (2018), Gumba and Vlasenko (2017), Haabazoka (2019), Harfst et al. (2017), Kuznetsova et al. (2017), Li et al. (2018), Ramanathan et al. (2018), and Yao et al. (2018).

Inapplicability of the classical model to managing the innovative development in the developing market economy is proved in the works Andronova et al. (2019), Bogoviz and Ragulina (2020), Petrenko and Shevyakova (2019), Popkova (2019), Popkova and Sergi (2020), Popkova et al. (2019), Popkova and Gulzat (2020), Popkova and Parakhina (2019), Popkova et al. (2017), Popkova and Zmiyak (2019), Popkova and Sergi (2018), Popkova and Sergi (2019), Ragulina (2019), Ragulina et al. (2019), Sergi (2003), Sergi (2019), Sergi et al. (2019a), Sergi et al. (2019b), Shulus et al. (2020), Stolyarov et al. (2020), and Zavyalova et al. (2018).

Thus, the existing literature sources acknowledge the necessity for an alternative economic model of investment management of the of modern economic systems' innovative development, but there is no clear idea of this model – in particular, of the preferable private stimuli / government expenditures ratio. This requires further research.

For determining the optimal private stimuli / government expenditures ratio at different stages of the innovative process, the research is performed based on three objects – categories of countries that achieved prominent results at a certain stage of the innovative process. The category of countries with the most innovative universities, which are included in the ranking Reuters (2020) "The World's Most Innovative Universities 2019", includes such developed countries (by the number of universities in top 100) as Germany (9), France (8), China (4) (the only developing country), and Russia (not included in the Reuters ranking, but with innovative universities).

The category of countries with the most innovative entrepreneurial structures, which are includes in the ranking Forbes (2020) "The World's Most Innovative Companies", includes such developed countries as South Korea (9th position) and Japan (32nd position) and such developing countries as India (8th position) and Indonesia (12th position). The category of countries with the highest share of mid-tech and hi-tech industry, including construction, in the structure of added value in industry (medium and high-tech Industry, including construction, % manufacturing value added), according to the World Bank (2020a) ranking, includes such developed countries as Singapore (78%) and Switzerland (65%) and such developing countries as Qatar (48%) and Malaysia (44%).

It should be noted that the USA, which is the leader in all given rankings, is not a research object here; it has not been selected for avoiding the distortion of results and for obtaining the most correct results in view of the distinguished categories of countries. Correlation analysis is used for calculating coefficients of correlation of government expenditures for R&D (as the indicator of government expenditures) and accessibility of venture capital (as the indicator of private stimuli) with the innovation index (as the indicator of result). The initial data for the research are shown in Table 7.1.

Table 7.1: The indicators of private stimuli and government expenditures in innovative development of the distinguished categories of countries in 2020.

Category of countries by the criterion successfulness at a certain stage of the innovative process	Country	Global Innovation Index, score 1–100	Research and development expenditure, % of GDP	9.03. Venture capital availability, score 1–100
Countries with the most innovative universities (Stage 1: R&D)	Germany	58.19	3.02	63.4
	France	54.25	2.19	53.7
	China	54.82	2.15	57.0
	Russia	37.62	1.11	29.3
Countries with the most innovative entrepreneurial structures (Stage 2: implementation of innovations)	South Korea	56.55	4.55	40.5
	Japan	54.68	3.21	55.7
	India	36.58	0.60	52.7
	Indonesia	29.72	0.27	45.9
Countries with the highest share of mid-tech and hi-tech industry (Stage 3: innovative production)	Singapore	58.37	2.17	63.5
	Switzerland	67.24	3.37	56.0
	Qatar	33.86	0.52	63.8
	Malaysia	42.68	1.44	59.5

Source: compiled by the author based on Institute of Scientific Communications (2020), World Bank (2020b), World Economic Forum (2020).

Results

The obtained coefficients of correlation of private stimuli and government expenditures with innovative development in the distinguished categories of countries in 2020 are shown in Figure 7.1.

As shown in Figure 7.1, in all categories of countries the correlation of government expenditures for R&D with the Global Innovation Index is high, exceeding 90%. Correlation of accessibility of venture capital with the Global Innovation Index constitutes 28.83% in countries with the most innovative universities; 37.87% in countries

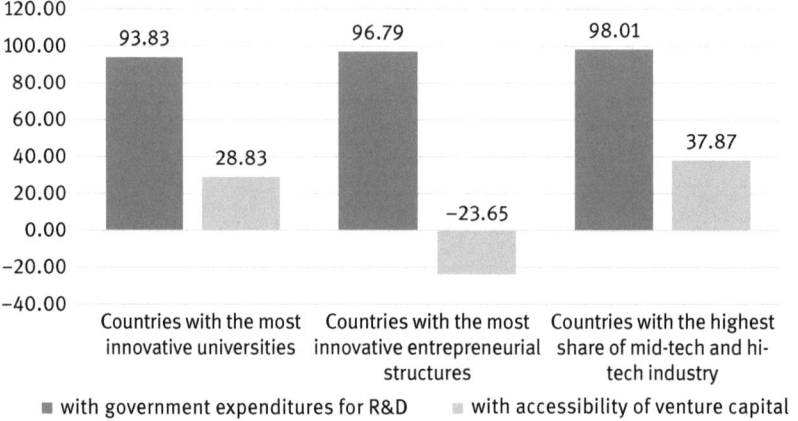

Figure 7.1: Coefficients of correlation of private stimuli and government expenditures with innovative development in the distinguished categories of countries in 2020, %.
Source: developed and compiled by the authors.

with the highest share of mid-tech and hi-tech industry; it is negative in countries with the most innovative entrepreneurial structures (−23.65%).

For establishing the causes of the obtained results of the correlation analysis, a qualitative comparative analysis of private stimuli and government expenditures from the positions of their influence on economic system's innovative development has been performed (Table 7.2).

As shown in Table 7.2, private stimuli (venture investors) offer a narrow list of available objects for investing in R&D, which include only own or private research organizations. Protection of their interests is not guaranteed: negative result of R&D and/or complexity of commercialization of innovations are possible. The requirements to commercialization of innovations are high, commercialization is mandatory, and only applied innovations are in demand. The consequence of unprofitable investing is bankruptcy.

Contrary to them, government expenditures envisage a wide list of available objects for investing in R&D, which include any state-funded universities and private research organizations. Protection of investor's interests is guaranteed by the strict terms of grans and the work of a special committee. The requirements to commercialization of innovations are moderate: commercialization is not mandatory; applied and theoretical innovations with delayed effect are in demand. The consequence of unprofitable investing is reduction of effectiveness of investments in innovations.

Thus, government financing is more flexible and preferable way of financial management of innovations. This is a basis for developing a new economic model of economic system's innovative development based on private stimuli and government expenditures (Figure 7.2).

Table 7.2: Comparative analysis of private stimuli and government expenditures from the positions of their influence on economic system's innovative development.

Comparative criterion	Private stimuli (venture investors)	Government expenditures
Available objects for investing in R&D	Narrow list: only own or private research organizations	Wide list: any state-funded universities and private research organizations
Protection of investor's interests	Protection is not guaranteed: negative result of R&D and/or complexity of innovations' commercialization are possible	Protection is guaranteed by strict conditions of grans and the work of a special committee
Requirements to commercialization of innovations	High, commercialization is mandatory, only applied innovations are of interest	Moderate, commercialization is not mandatory; applied and theoretical innovations with delayed effect are interesting
Consequences of unprofitable investing	bankruptcy	Reduction of effectiveness of investments in innovations

Source: developed and compiled by the authors.

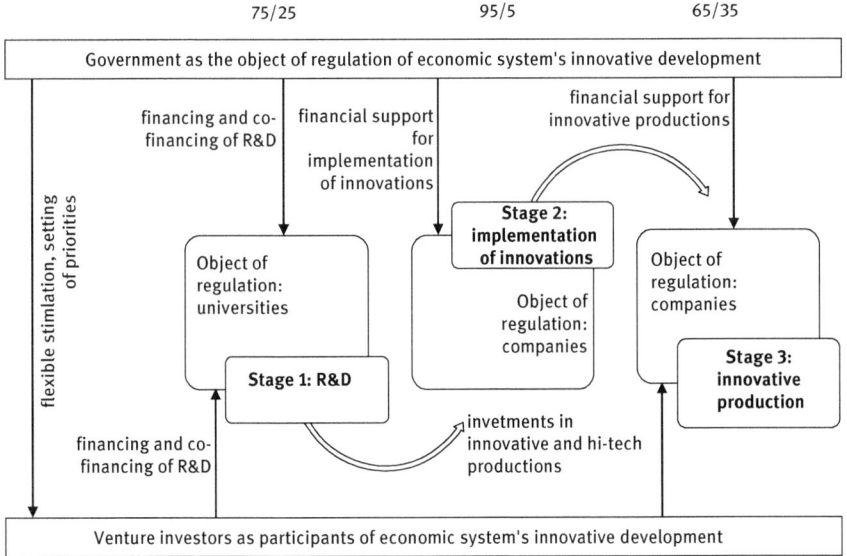

Figure 7.2: The economic model of economic system's innovative development based on private stimuli and government expenditures.
Source: developed and compiled by the authors.

As shown in Figure 7.2, government takes the main burden on financing of economic system's innovative development in the offered new model. The optimal per cent ratio of private stimuli and government expenditures at the R&D stage is 75/25, at the stage of implementation of innovations – 95/5, and at the stage of innovative production – 65/35.

Conclusion

Thus, it has been proved that government financing of the innovative activities is preferable, as, opposite to the existing belief that is based on the experience of developed countries, it is more flexible and effective. The optimal ratio of private stimuli and government expenditures envisages domination of budget financing, while private entrepreneurship should retain the non-financial (organizational & managerial) role in the innovative process. For achieving the established optimal ratio we have developed a new model of economic system's innovative development.

References

Andronova, I.V., Chernova, V.Y., Starostin, V.S., Degtereva (2019). Study of sector-specific innovation efforts: The case from Russian economy. Entrepreneurship and Sustainability Issues, VsI Entrepreneurship and Sustainability Center, 7(1), p. 540–552.

Atkinsonk, R.D., Ezell, S.J. (2012). Innovation Economics: the Race for Global Advantage, New Haven, CT: Yale University Press.

Bogoviz, A.V., Ragulina, Y.V. (2020). Industry competitiveness in the new economy. Lecture Notes in Networks and Systems, 115, p. v–vi.

Forbes (2020). The World's Most Innovative Companies. URL: https://www.forbes.com/innovative-companies/list/#tab:rank (data accessed: 29.03.2020).

García-Quevedo, J., Segarra-Blasco, A., Teruel, M. (2018). Financial constraints and the failure of innovation projects. Technological Forecasting and Social Change, 127, p. 127–140.

Gumba, H.M., Vlasenko, V.A. (2017). Strategy of development of innovative activity in industry and construction: The rationale of the regional dimension. Izvestiya Vysshikh Uchebnykh Zavedenii, Seriya Teknologiya Tekstil'noi Promyshlennosti, 2017-January(2), 2(1), p. 14–18.

Haabazoka, L. (2019). A Study of the Effects of Technological Innovations on the Performance of Commercial Banks in Developing Countries – A Case of the Zambian Banking Industry. In: Popkova E. (eds) The Future of the Global Financial System: Downfall or Harmony. ISC 2018. Lecture Notes in Networks and Systems, vol 57. Springer, Cham, Online ISBN 978-3-030-00102-5, https://doi.org/10.1007/978-3-030-00102-5_132

Harfst, J., Pichler, P., Fischer, W. (2017). Regional Ambassadors-An Innovative Element for the Development of Rural Areas? European Countryside, 9(2), p. 359–374.

Institute of Scientific Communications (2020). Data set "Big data of the modern world economy: digital platform for intelligent analytics – 2020". URL: https://www.archilab.online/en/data/sounting-data-set (data accessed: 17.03.2020).

Kuznetsova, O., Kuznetsova, S., Yumaev, E., Kuznetsov, V., Galtseva, O. (2017). Formation and Development of the Training System for Innovative Development of Regional Industry. E3S Web of Conferences, 15,04019.

Li, X., Subrahmanyam, A., Yang, X. (2018). Can financial innovation succeed by catering to behavioral preferences? Evidence from a callable options market. Journal of Financial Economics, 2(1), p. 34–42.

Petrenko, E.S., Shevyakova, A.L. (2019). Features and perspectives of digitization in Kazakhstan. Studies in Computational Intelligence, 826, p. 889–899.

Popkova, E.G. (2019). Preconditions of formation and development of industry 4.0 in the conditions of knowledge economy. Studies in Systems, Decision and Control, 169(1), 65–72.

Popkova, E.G., Sergi, B.S. (2020). Human Capital and AI in Industry 4.0. Convergence and Divergence in Social Entrepreneurship in Russia. Journal of Intellectual Capital, In press, 2020. https://doi.org/10.1108/JIC-09-2019-0224

Popkova, E.G., Egorova, E.N., Popova, E., Pozdnyakova, U.A. (2019). The model of state management of economy on the basis of the internet of things. Studies in Computational Intelligence, 826, pp. 1137–1144.

Popkova, E.G., Gulzat, K. (2020). Technological Revolution in the 21st Century: Digital Society vs. Artificial Intelligence. Lecture Notes in Networks and Systems, 91, p. 339–345.

Popkova, E.G., Parakhina, V.N. (2019). Managing the global financial system on the basis of artificial intelligence: possibilities and limitations. Lecture Notes in Networks and Systems, 57, pp. 939–946.

Popkova, E.G., Poluyufta, L., Beshanova, Y., Popova, L.V., Kolesnikova, E. (2017). Innovations as a basis for marketing strategies of Russian oil companies in the conditions of oil prices reduction. Contributions to Economics, (9783319606958), p. 449–455.

Popkova, E.G., Zmiyak, K.V. (2019). Priorities of training of digital personnel for industry 4.0: social competencies vs technical competencies. On the Horizon, 27(3–4), p. 138–144.

Popkova, E.G., Sergi, B.S. (2018). Will Industry 4.0 and Other Innovations Impact Russia's Development? In Bruno S. Sergi (Ed.) Exploring the Future of Russia's Economy and Markets: Towards Sustainable Economic Development (pp. 51–68). Bingley, UK: Emerald Publishing Limited.

Popkova, E.G., Sergi, B.S. (Eds.) (2019). Digital Economy: Complexity and Variety vs. Rationality. Berlin: Springer International Publishing.

Ragulina, Y.V. (2019). Priorities of development of industry 4.0 in modern economic systems with different progress in formation of knowledge economy. Studies in Systems, Decision and Control, 169, p. 167–174.

Ragulina, Y.V., Alekseev, A.N., Strizhkina, I.V., Tumanov, A.I. (2019). Methodology of criterial evaluation of consequences of the industrial revolution of the 21st century. Studies in Systems, Decision and Control, 169, p. 235–244.

Ramanathan, R., Ramanathan, U., Bentley, Y. (2018). The debate on flexibility of environmental regulations, innovation capabilities and financial performance – A novel use of DEA. Omega (United Kingdom), 75, p. 131–138.

Reuters (2020). The World's Most Innovative Universities 2019. URL: https://www.reuters.com/innovative-universities-2019 (data accessed: 29. 03.2020).

Sergi, B.S. (2003). Economic Dynamics in Transitional Economies: The Four-P Governments, the EU Enlargement, and the Bruxelles Consensus. New York: Routledge.

Sergi, B.S. (Ed.) (2019). Tech, Smart Cities, and Regional Development in Contemporary Russia. Bingley, UK: Emerald Publishing Limited.

Sergi, B.S., Popkova, E.G. Bogoviz, A.V., Ragulina J.V. (2019a). Costs and Profits of Technological Growth in Russia. In Bruno S. Sergi (Ed.) Tech, Smart Cities, and Regional Development in

Contemporary Russia, pp. 41–54. Bingley, UK: Emerald Publishing Limited. https://doi.org/10.1108/978-1-78973-881-020191005

Sergi, B.S., Popkova, E.G. Bogoviz, A.V., Ragulina J.V. (2019b). Entrepreneurship and Economic Growth: The Experience of Developed and Developing Countries. In Bruno S. Sergi and Cole C. Scanlon (Eds.) Entrepreneurship and Development in the 21st Century (pp. 3–32). Bingley, UK: Emerald Publishing Limited.

Shulus, A.A., Akopova, E.S., Przhedetskaya, N.V., Borzenko, K.V. (2020). Intellectual Production and Consumption: A New Reality of the 21st Century. Lecture Notes in Networks and Systems, 92, pp. 353–359.

Stolyarov, N.O., Petrenko, E.S., Serova, O.A., Umuralieva, A.S. (2020). The Digital Reality of the Modern Economy: New Actors and New Decision-Making Logic. Lecture Notes in Networks and Systems, 87, p. 882–888.

World Bank (2020a). Medium and high-tech Industry (including construction) (% manufacturing value added). URL: https://data.worldbank.org/indicator/NV.MNF.TECH.ZS.UN?most_recent_value_desc=true (data accessed: 29.03.2020).

World Bank (2020b). Research and development expenditure (% of GDP). URL: https://data.worldbank.org/indicator/GB.XPD.RSDV.GD.ZS?view=chart (data accessed: 29. 03.2020).

World Economic Forum (2020). The Global Competitiveness Report 2019. URL: https://www.weforum.org/reports/global-competitiveness-report-2019 (data accessed: 29. 03.2020).

Yao, M., Di, H., Zheng, X., Xu, X. (2018). Impact of payment technology innovations on the traditional financial industry: A focus on China. Technological Forecasting and Social Change, 2(1), p. 22–29.

Zavyalova, E.B. Studenikin, N.V. Starikova, E.A. (2018). Business participation in implementation of socially oriented Sustainable Development Goals in countries of Central Asia and the Caucasus region. Central Asia and the Caucasus, 19(2), p. 56–63.

Part III: The Legal Foundations of Managing The Economic Systems' Innovative Development

Anna V. Bodiako, Svetlana V. Ponomareva, Tatiana M. Rogulenko
and Leonid V. Kolyadov

8 The Modern Institutions of Managing the Economic System's Innovative Development

Introduction

Government machinery covers a lot of institutions, each of which has a certain managerial function. The modern global practice does not distinguish a separate institution for managing the innovative development, which causes uncertainty as to which institutions should be involved in this process. Heterogeneity and the multi-purpose character of state management of sustainable development are arguments in favor of using not one but several institutions. Each of the institutions has to ensure achievement of the three following purposes.

The first goal of state management of sustainable development consists in acceleration of this development as useful activities that create multiple advantages for the economic system – in particular, stimulate the strengthening of its competitive positions in the world markets. The logic of setting this goal is based on the fact that the faster the innovative development of an economic system, the more progressive its society and economy and the more opportunities for participation in the global technological progress, creation and monopolization of new markets, generation of new jobs, and socio-economic development.

The second goal of state management of sustainable development consists in achievement of sustainability of economic activities. The priority of innovative development is stimulating the increase of population's quality of life by creation and implementation of socially-important and "green" innovations. The purpose of state management is to make innovative development follow this priority. The third goal of state management of sustainable development is accelerating the rate of economic

Anna V. Bodiako, Financial University under the Government of the Russian Federation, Moscow, Russia
Svetlana V. Ponomareva, Saint Petersburg State University of Economics, Saint Petersburg, Russia
Tatiana M. Rogulenko, State University of Management, Moscow, Russia
Leonid V. Kolyadov, Federal State Budgetary Educational Institution of Higher Education «Gubkin Russian State University of Oil and Gas (National Research University)», Moscow, Russia

https://doi.org/10.1515/9783110643701-008

growth and ensuring economic crisis management. Innovations could and should perform a counter-cyclic function in economy, which should be stimulated by state management of innovative development.

Absence of a scientific view of the institutions that have to be involved in managing the innovative development causes uncertainty regarding institutional organizations of the government machinery as to distribution of responsibility and resources between the institutions. This problem is to be solved in this chapter.

Materials and Method

The necessity and goals of state management of economic system's innovative development are noted in the works Atkinsonk and Ezell (2012), García-Quevedo et al. (2018), Gumba and Vlasenko (2017), Haabazoka (2019), Harfst et al. (2017), Kuznetsova et al. (2017), Li et al. (2018), Ramanathan et al. (2018), and Yao et al. (2018).

Institutions of managing the economic system's innovative development are studied in the works Andronova et al. (2019), Bogoviz and Ragulina (2020), Petrenko and Shevyakova (2019), Popkova (2019), Popkova and Sergi (2020), Popkova et al. (2019), Popkova and Gulzat (2020), Popkova and Parakhina (2019), Popkova et al. (2017), Popkova and Zmiyak (2019), Popkova and Sergi (2018), Popkova and Sergi (2019), Ragulina (2019), Ragulina et al. (2019), Sergi (2003), Sergi (2019), Sergi et al. (2019a), Sergi et al. (2019b), Shulus et al. (2020), Stolyarov et al. (2020), and Zavyalova et al. (2018).

However, despite the high level of elaboration of this problem, the modern institutions of managing the economic system's innovative development have been studied fragmentarily, and their list is not clear. In this chapter, the research objects are countries with the most effective institutions: "10 Most Politically Stable Countries, Ranked by Perception on Feb. 25, 2020" (Radu and Writer (2020)).

For showing the level of achievement of the goals of sustainable management of innovative development we calculate such indicators as growth of the Global Innovation Index for five years (based on WIPO – as a result of each preceding year), correlation of the Global Innovation Index and the Quality of Life Index (Numbeo) and correlation of the Global Innovation Index with the rate of economic growth (based on the materials of the International Monetary Fund). The basic data for 2016–2020 for further calculation of these indicators are shown in Table 8.1.

Table 8.1: Statistical characteristics of the goals of innovative development management in top 10 countries by effectiveness of institutions in 2016–2020.

Indicator	Year	Canada	Denmark	Netherlands	Austria	Norway	Switzerland	Australia	New Zealand	Sweden	Luxembourg
Global Innovation Index	2016	55.73	57.70	61.58	54.07	53.80	68.30	55.22	55.92	62.40	59.02
	2017	54.71	58.45	58.29	52.65	52.01	66.28	53.07	54.23	63.57	57.11
	2018	53.65	58.70	63.36	53.10	53.14	67.69	51.83	52.87	63.82	56.40
	2019	52.98	58.39	63.32	51.32	52.63	68.40	51.98	51.29	63.08	54.53
	2020	53.88	58.44	61.44	50.94	51.87	67.24	50.34	49.55	63.65	53.47
Quality of Life index	2016	177.23	206.49	192.40	192.40	188.90	208.54	198.79	201.06	185.81	n/a
	2017	167.18	184.92	175.23	190.37	165.93	173.54	176.54	184.74	172.74	n/a
	2018	173.90	197.75	191.25	190.22	176.27	190.81	188.70	182.40	176.81	n/a
	2019	170.32	198.59	188.91	191.05	181.86	195.93	191.13	185.58	178.67	n/a
	2020	163.47	192.67	183.67	182.50	175.19	192.01	186.21	181.02	175.95	n/a
Annual growth rate of GDP, %	2016	1.433	1.137	2.095	1.482	1.024	1.310	2.471	3.956	3.310	3.981
	2017	1.941	1.474	2.144	1.403	1.238	-1.429	3.120	3.076	2.696	3.744
	2018	1.956	1.701	1.840	1.300	1.937	-1.605	2.999	2.940	2.380	3.529
	2019	1.843	1.801	1.732	1.254	2.098	-1.600	2.945	2.563	2.181	3.308
	2020	1.800	1.873	1.682	1.100	2.123	-1.700	2.838	2.561	1.697	3.087

Source: compiled by the authors based on Institute of scientific communications (2020), Numbeo (2020), WIPO (2020), International Monetary Fund (2020).

Regression analysis is used for compiling the models of multiple linear regression dependence of the above indicators of the results of managing the innovative development on the following institutions of state management (World Economic Forum, part 1. "Institutions" of the Global Competitiveness Report 4.0 for 2019):

- security
- social capital
- checks and balances
- public-sector performance
- transparency
- property rights
- corporate governance
- future orientation of government

The selection of data for the above institutions is shown in Table 8.2.

Results

The established characteristics of the models of multiple linear regression are shown in Table 8.3.

As shown in Table 8.3, growth of the Global Innovation Index for five years (y_1) is the highest (1.17%) in case of development of future orientation of government (x_8) by 1 points. Correlation of the Global Innovation Index with the Quality of Life Index (y_1) has the highest growth (0.44%) in case of development of public-sector performance (x_4) by 1 points. Correlation of the Global Innovation Index with the rate of economic growth (y_1) has the highest growth (0.29%) in case of development of security (x_1) by 1 point.

Checks and balances (x_3) creates an "institutional trap" of state management of innovative development, as it stimulates its acceleration (regression coefficient –0.96%), but hinders its contribution into increase of quality of life (regression coefficient –0.12%) and into acceleration of economic growth (regression coefficient –0.38%). Corporate governance (x_7) stimulates simultaneous implementation of all three goals of state management of innovative development (regression coefficients – 0.16%, 0.04%, and 0.08%, accordingly) and thus is a universal institution of regulation of this process.

Based on this, an institutional matrix of managing economic system's innovative development is created (Figure 8.1).

Table 8.2: Institutions of state management of innovative development and its results in top 10 countries, by effectiveness of the institutions in 2020.

Group of indicators	Indicator	Symbol	Canada	Denmark	Netherlands	Austria	Norway	Switzerland	Australia	New Zealand	Sweden	Luxembourg
Results of management, %	Growth of the Global Innovation Index for five years	y_1	−3.32	1.28	−0.23	−5.79	−3.59	−1.55	−8.84	−11.39	2.00	−9.40
	Correlation of the Global Innovation Index with the Quality of Life Index	y_2	0.40	−0.63	0.86	0.70	0.79	0.89	0.42	0.77	−0.89	n/a
	Correlation of the Global Innovation Index with the rate of economic growth	y_3	−0.70	0.80	−0.67	0.89	−0.42	0.42	−0.56	0.91	−0.69	0.99
Managerial institutions, points 1–100	Security	x_1	86.0	87.4	90.1	91.2	90.8	93.8	89.8	92.6	89.9	90.6
	Social capital	x_2	63.3	65.8	64.1	61.6	66.4	62.4	66.8	66.8	59.5	60.5
	Checks and balances	x_3	72.2	77.3	81.1	69.7	79.4	78.8	72.7	83.4	78.0	73.6
	Public-sector performance	x_4	67.0	73.3	77.1	65.6	70.4	76.0	66.0	73.8	69.3	74.4
	Transparency;	x_5	81.0	88.0	82.0	76.0	84.0	85.0	77.0	87.0	85.0	81.0

(continued)

Table 8.2 (continued)

Group of indicators	Indicator	Symbol	Canada	Denmark	Netherlands	Austria	Norway	Switzerland	Australia	New Zealand	Sweden	Luxembourg
	Property rights	x_6	74.5	80.9	88.3	81.5	73.3	85.7	76.6	83.3	81.3	84.8
	Corporate governance	x_7	79.5	71.0	67.9	74.6	77.7	61.6	67.1	82.6	72.9	60.9
	Future orientation of government	x_8	69.1	75.4	78.1	68.2	73.1	76.8	67.5	60.7	71.6	81.3

Source: calculated and compiled by the authors based on World Economic Forum (2020).

Table 8.3: Regression dependence of the results of innovative development on the institutions of state management in top 10 countries by effectiveness of the institutions (2020).

Variable		Dependent variable and its connection to independent variables		
		y_1	y_2	y_3
Multiple R		0.8640	0.9999	0.9465
Constant		−125.47	1.95	−49.72
Coefficient of regression with	x_1 Security	−0.44	0.14	*Key institution for maximization of y_3* 0.29
	x_2	0.39	−0.05	0.18
	x_3 checks and balance	0.96	−0.12	−0.38 *"Institutional trap"*
	x_4 public-sector performance	−2.61	*Key institution for maximization of y_2* 0.44	0.07
	x_5	0.85	−0.22	0.22
	x_6	1.02	−0.16	0.12
	x_7 corporate governance	0.16 *Universal institution for simultaneous maximization of y_3, y_3 and y_3*	0.04	0.08
	x_8 future orientation of government	*Key institution for maximization of y_1* 1.17	−0.07	0.03

Source: calculated and compiled by the authors.

As shown in Figure 8.1, government – as the mega-regulator of innovative development of the economic system – uses the following institutions in this process:
- future orientation of government, public-sector performance, and security for isolated stimulation of achievement of the goals of innovative development, which are most important at present, or the ones that are behind other goals (stimulation of development of these institutions is required);
- corporate governance for simultaneous stimulation of implementation of all goals of innovative development of the economic system (stimulation of development of this institution is required);

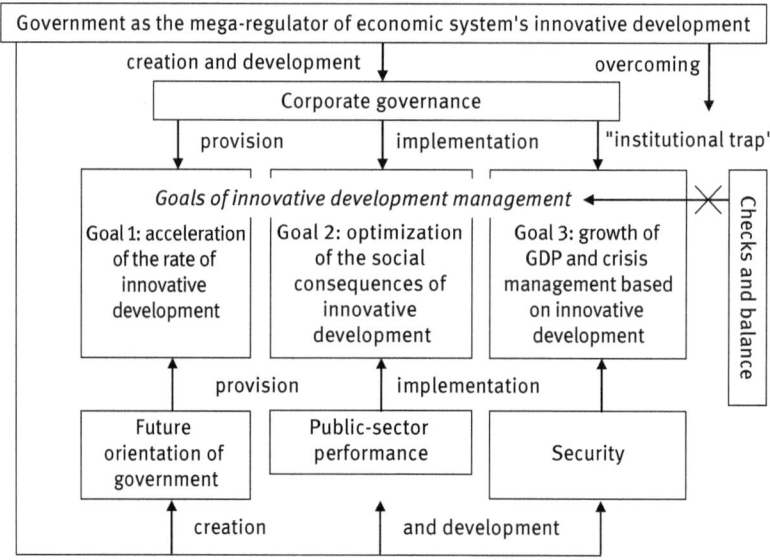

Figure 8.1: The institutional matrix of economic system's innovative development management.
Source: developed and compiled by the authors.

- checks and balances for overcoming the "institutional trap" (institutional barrier) on the path of implementing the goals of economic system's innovative development (it is necessary to restrain the development and/or change the influence of this institution on the process of innovative development).

Conclusion

Thus, the offered hypothesis has been confirmed – state management of economic system's innovative development should not be limited by a narrow institution and should be based on a range of institutions of the government machinery. It has been determined that not all institutions of state management stimulate the implementation of the goals of innovative development of the modern economic systems, and there are "institutional traps", which have to be overcome.

Universal and specific institutions of state management of innovative development have been determined. For a complex approach to use of the whole specter of the necessary institutions, we have developed the institutional matrix of managing the economic system's innovative development, which reflects not only the set of institutes but also the logic of managing them in connection to the goals of innovative development.

References

Andronova, I.V., Chernova, V.Y., Starostin, V.S., Degtereva (2019). Study of sector-specific innovation efforts: The case from Russian economy. Entrepreneurship and Sustainability Issues, VsI Entrepreneurship and Sustainability Center, 7(1), p. 540–552.

Atkinsonk, R.D., Ezell, S.J. (2012). Innovation Economics: the Race for Global Advantage, New Haven, CT: Yale University Press.

Bogoviz, A.V., Ragulina, Y.V. (2020). Industry competitiveness in the new economy. Lecture Notes in Networks and Systems, 115, p. v–vi.

García-Quevedo, J., Segarra-Blasco, A., Teruel, M. (2018). Financial constraints and the failure of innovation projects. Technological Forecasting and Social Change, 127, p. 127–140.

Gumba, H.M., Vlasenko, V.A. (2017). Strategy of development of innovative activity in industry and construction: The rationale of the regional dimension. Izvestiya Vysshikh Uchebnykh Zavedenii, Seriya Teknologiya Tekstil'noi Promyshlennosti, 2017-January(2), 2(1), p. 14–18.

Haabazoka, L. (2019). A Study of the Effects of Technological Innovations on the Performance of Commercial Banks in Developing Countries – A Case of the Zambian Banking Industry. In: Popkova E. (eds) The Future of the Global Financial System: Downfall or Harmony. ISC 2018. Lecture Notes in Networks and Systems, vol 57. Cham: Springer, https://doi.org/10.1007/978-3-030-00102-5_132

Harfst, J., Pichler, P., Fischer, W. (2017). Regional Ambassadors-An Innovative Element for the Development of Rural Areas? European Countryside, 9(2), p. 359–374.

Institute of Scientific Communications (2020). Data set "Big data of the modern world economy: digital platform for intelligent analytics – 2020". URL: https://www.archilab.online/en/data/sounting-data-set (data accessed: 30.03.2020).

International Monetary Fund (2020). World Economic Outlook Database. URL: https://www.imf.org/external/pubs/ft/weo/2017/01/weodata/weoselgr.aspx (data accessed: 30. 03.2020).

Kuznetsova, O., Kuznetsova, S., Yumaev, E., Kuznetsov, V., Galtseva, O. (2017). Formation and Development of the Training System for Innovative Development of Regional Industry. E3S Web of Conferences, 15,04019.

Li, X., Subrahmanyam, A., Yang, X. (2018). Can financial innovation succeed by catering to behavioral preferences? Evidence from a callable options market. Journal of Financial Economics, 2(1), p. 34–42.

Numbeo (2020). Quality of Life Index for Country 2019 Mid-Year. URL: https://www.numbeo.com/quality-of-life/rankings_by_country.jsp (data accessed: 30.03.2020).

Petrenko, E.S., Shevyakova, A.L. (2019). Features and perspectives of digitization in Kazakhstan. Studies in Computational Intelligence, 826, p. 889–899.

Popkova, E.G. (2019). Preconditions of formation and development of industry 4.0 in the conditions of knowledge economy. Studies in Systems, Decision and Control, 169(1), 65–72.

Popkova, E.G., Sergi, B.S. (2020). Human Capital and AI in Industry 4.0. Convergence and Divergence in Social Entrepreneurship in Russia. Journal of Intellectual Capital, In press, 2020. https://doi.org/10.1108/JIC-09-2019-0224

Popkova, E.G., Egorova, E.N., Popova, E., Pozdnyakova, U.A. (2019). The model of state management of economy on the basis of the internet of things. Studies in Computational Intelligence, 826, pp. 1137–1144.

Popkova, E.G., Gulzat, K. (2020). Technological Revolution in the 21st Century: Digital Society vs. Artificial Intelligence. Lecture Notes in Networks and Systems, 91, p. 339–345.

Popkova, E.G., Parakhina, V.N. (2019). Managing the global financial system on the basis of artificial intelligence: possibilities and limitations. Lecture Notes in Networks and Systems, 57, pp. 939–946.

Popkova, E.G., Poluyufta, L., Beshanova, Y., Popova, L.V., Kolesnikova, E. (2017). Innovations as a basis for marketing strategies of Russian oil companies in the conditions of oil prices reduction. Contributions to Economics, (9783319606958), p. 449–455.

Popkova, E.G., Zmiyak, K.V. (2019). Priorities of training of digital personnel for industry 4.0: social competencies vs technical competencies. On the Horizon, 27(3-4), p. 138–144.

Popkova, E.G., Sergi, B.S. (2018). Will Industry 4.0 and Other Innovations Impact Russia's Development? In Bruno S. Sergi (Ed.) Exploring the Future of Russia's Economy and Markets: Towards Sustainable Economic Development (pp. 51–68). Bingley, UK: Emerald Publishing Limited.

Popkova, E.G., Sergi, B.S. (Eds.) (2019). Digital Economy: Complexity and Variety vs. Rationality. Berlin: Springer International Publishing.

Radu, S., Writer, S. (2020). 10 Most Politically Stable Countries, Ranked by Perception on Feb. 25, 2020. URL: https://www.usnews.com/news/best-countries/slideshows/10-most-politically-stable-ountries-ranked-by-perception (data accessed: 30.3.2020).

Ragulina, Y.V. (2019). Priorities of development of industry 4.0 in modern economic systems with different progress in formation of knowledge economy. Studies in Systems, Decision and Control, 169, p. 167–174.

Ragulina, Y.V., Alekseev, A.N., Strizhkina, I.V., Tumanov, A.I. (2019). Methodology of criterial evaluation of consequences of the industrial revolution of the 21st century. Studies in Systems, Decision and Control, 169, p. 235–244.

Ramanathan, R., Ramanathan, U., Bentley, Y. (2018). The debate on flexibility of environmental regulations, innovation capabilities and financial performance – A novel use of DEA. Omega (United Kingdom), 75, p. 131–138.

Sergi, B.S. (2003). Economic Dynamics in Transitional Economies: The Four-P Governments, the EU Enlargement, and the Bruxelles Consensus. New York: Routledge.

Sergi, B.S. (Ed.) (2019). Tech, Smart Cities, and Regional Development in Contemporary Russia. Bingley, UK: Emerald Publishing Limited.

Sergi, B.S., Popkova, E.G. Bogoviz, A.V., Ragulina Y.V. (2019a). The Agro-industrial Complex: Tendencies, Scenarios, and Regulation. In Sergi, Bruno S. (Ed.) Modeling Economic Growth in Contemporary Russia (pp. 233–247). Bingley, UK: Emerald Publishing Limited.

Sergi, B.S., Popkova, E.G., Bogoviz, A.V., Litvinova, T.N. (2019b). Understanding Industry 4.0: AI, the Internet of Things, and the Future of Work. Bingley, UK: Emerald Publishing Limited.

Shulus, A.A., Akopova, E.S., Przhedetskaya, N.V., Borzenko, K.V. (2020). Intellectual Production and Consumption: A New Reality of the 21st Century. Lecture Notes in Networks and Systems, 92, pp. 353–359.

Stolyarov, N.O., Petrenko, E.S., Serova, O.A., Umuralieva, A.S. (2020). The Digital Reality of the Modern Economy: New Actors and New Decision-Making Logic. Lecture Notes in Networks and Systems, 87, p. 882–888.

WIPO (2020). The Global Innovation Index – 2019. URL: https://www.globalinnovationindex.org/Home (data accessed: 30.03.2020).

World Economic Forum (2020). The Global Competitiveness Report 2019. URL: https://www.weforum.org/reports/how-to-end-a-decade-of-lost-productivity-growth (data accessed: 30.03.2020).

Yao, M., Di, H., Zheng, X., Xu, X. (2018). Impact of payment technology innovations on the traditional financial industry: A focus on China. Technological Forecasting and Social Change, 2(1), p. 22–29.

Zavyalova, E.B. Studenikin, N.V. Starikova, E.A. (2018). Business participation in implementation of socially oriented Sustainable Development Goals in countries of Central Asia and the Caucasus region. Central Asia and the Caucasus, 19(2), p. 56–63.

Aleksei Y. Dianov, Leonid F. Malinovskii, AlfiraM. Kumratova,
Lidiya B. Larina and Rustem T. Yuldashev

9 Standards and Norms of Managing the Innovative Development of a Modern Economic System

Introduction

Standards and norms have a traditionally important role in managing the economic systems' innovative development. In the course of the 20th century, industrialization was possible due to state standardization. In countries with the planned model of economy, innovations were the object of government planning. One of the most vivid examples is Soviet Russia, which had clear and detailed norms, which covered also research institutes (e.g., number of scientific personnel, publications, and patents per scientific employees) and companies, which then belonged to the government and the public (e.g., the number of implemented leading technologies).

The modern economic conditions, which are characterized by domination of the market economy, standardization and norming of innovative activities are more flexible and are conducted with the help of the licensing practice, government order, and government grants for R&D, as well as the practice of tax stimulation of entrepreneurship's innovative activity. These practices allow the government to establish the criteria of innovative activity of economic subjects and to implement its norms. At the international level, a lot of attention is paid to standardization of managing the innovative development. The main existing standards include is "ISO 56002-Innovation management" (Itonics, 2020) and "ISO/TC 279. Innovation management" (ISO, 2020).

From the scientific point of view, the practices of standardization and norming of innovative development in the modern economic systems that are implemented in the conditions of the market economy are not sufficiently justified. This causes a problem of opposition of the regulatory approach, within which standards and norms are used, and the market approach, which is based on the mechanism of

Aleksei Y. Dianov, Russian University of Cooperation, Moscow, Russia
Leonid F. Malinovskii, Moscow Region State University, Mytishchi, Russia
Alfira M. Kumratova, "Kuban State Agrarian University named after I.T. Trubilin", Krasnodar, Russia
Lidiya B. Larina, Federal State Budgetary Educational Institution of Higher Education «Gubkin Russian State University of Oil and Gas (National Research University)», Moscow, Russia
Rustem T. Yuldashev, "Moscow State Institute of International Relations (University) of the Ministry of Foreign Affairs Russian Federation", Moscow, Russia

https://doi.org/10.1515/9783110643701-009

competition, as the alternatives of managing the innovative development of a modern economic system. The purpose of this chapter is to compare these approaches and to determine the necessity and expedience of applying the standards and norms of managing the innovative development in modern economic systems.

Materials and Method

Standardization and norming during management of innovative development of modern economic system are studied in the works Atkinsonk and Ezell (2012), García-Quevedo et al. (2018), Gumba and Vlasenko (2017), Haabazoka (2019), Harfst et al. (2017), Kuznetsova et al. (2017), Li et al. (2018), Ramanathan et al. (2018), and Yao et al. (2018).

The specific features of implementation of standards and norms of managing the economic systems' innovative development in the conditions of the market economy are studied in the works Andronova et al. (2019), Bogoviz and Ragulina (2020), Petrenko and Shevyakova (2019), Popkova (2019), Popkova and Sergi (2020), Popkova et al. (2019), Popkova and Gulzat (2020), Popkova and Parakhina (2019), Popkova et al. (2017), Popkova and Zmiyak (2019), Popkova and Sergi (2018), Popkova and Sergi (2019), Ragulina (2019), Ragulina et al. (2019), Sergi (2003), Sergi (2019), Sergi et al. (2019a), Sergi et al. (2019b), Shulus et al. (2020), Stolyarov et al. (2020), and Zavyalova et al. (2018).

For comparing the management of innovative development of a modern economic system based on alternative approaches we use regression and correlation analysis and T.L. Saaty's analytic hierarchy process. At the first stage, regression dependence and correlation of the Innovation Index (Bloomberg) on the Index of Economic Freedom (The Heritage Foundation) are calculated. In order to obtain representative data, we included representatives of different categories by economic freedom in the selection of countries. Also, correlation of these indicators in different categories of countries is calculated. The initial data for 2020 are shown in Table 9.1.

The second stage envisages qualitative research with the help of the expert & analytical method. Significance of each metric of innovations for the modern economic systems is calculated, and weights are assigned. The metrics of innovations are described in Visual Capitalist (2020). Then, score assessment of averaged values of each metric for management based on standards and norms and during market self-management based on competition is performed. As a result, hierarchical synthesis (results of management) is calculated as a sum of products of the values of metrics and their weights.

Table 9.1: Statistics of economic freedom and innovations in 2020.

Category of countries by economic freedom in 2020	Country	Index of economic freedom, points 1–100	Innovation index, points 1–100
Free (100–80)	Singapore	89.4	87.01
	New Zealand	84.1	68.08
	Ireland	80.9	78.65
Mostly free (79.9–70)	Denmark	78.3	83.22
	Canada	78.2	73.11
	USA	76.6	83.17
Moderately free (69.9–60)	France	66.0	82.75
	Chile	76.8	49.58
	Russia	61.0	68.63
Mostly unfree (59.9–50)	China	59.5	78.80
	India	56.5	49.33
	Brazil	53.7	53.65

Source: compiled by the authors based on Bloomberg (2020), The Heritage Foundation (2020).

Results

The obtained results of regression and correlation analysis are shown in Figure 9.1.

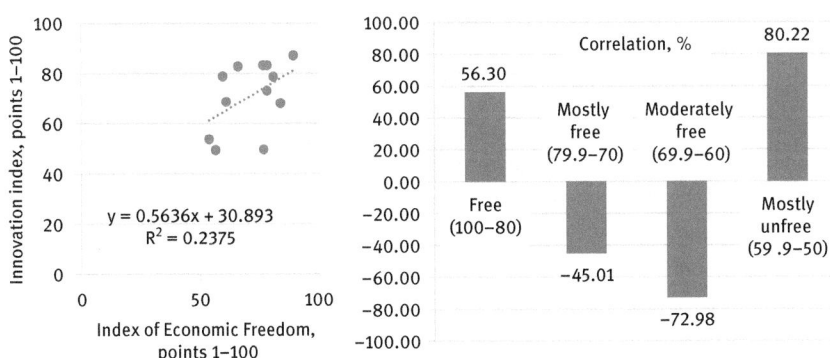

Figure 9.1: Regression curve of dependence of innovations on economic freedom and their correlation in countries of different categories by economic freedom in 2020.
Source: calculated and compiled by the authors.

As shown in Figure 9.1, in the full selection of countries, innovations are explained by the level of economic freedom only by 23.75%. Increase of the level of economic freedom by 1 point leads to increase of the Innovation Index by 0.5636 points. It should be noted that correlation of economic freedom with innovations is positive and high in the category of countries with full economic freedom (56.30%) and the category of countries with minimal economic freedom (80.22%), and in countries with moderate and low economic freedom it is negative, constituting – 45.01% and −72.98%, accordingly.

Significance of metrics of innovations for the modern economic systems is shown in Figure 9.2.

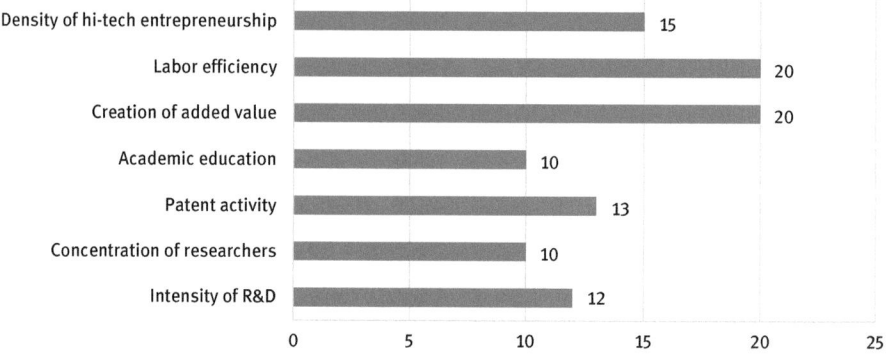

Figure 9.2: Significance of metrics of innovations for the modern economic systems, % (100% in total).
Source: developed and compiled by the authors.

As shown in Figure 9.2, the most significant aspects are labor efficiency (20%) and creation of added value (20%), as well as density of hi-tech entrepreneurship (15%), patent activity (13%), and intensity of R&D (12%). Academic education (10%) and concentration of researchers (10%) are least significant, as they do not reflect the results and could have contradictory influence on them. The possibilities of managing the innovative development of a modern economic system, depending on the managerial approach, are assessed in Table 9.2.

Based on the data of Figure 9.2 and Table 9.2, an evaluation of management of innovative development of a modern economic system with different approaches with the help of analytic hierarchy process is performed (Table 9.3).

As shown in Table 9.3, final evaluation of efficiency of managing the innovative development (hierarchical synthesis) is by 21.21% higher in case of market self-management based on competition (6.00 points) than during management based on standards and norms (4.95 points).

Table 9.2: Possibilities of managing the innovative development of a modern economic system, depending on the managerial approach, points 1–10.

Metrics of innovative development	Management based on standards and norms		Market self management based on competition	
	qualitative characteristics	Score	qualitative characteristics	score
R&D intensity	strictly according to the norm, which ensures rather high indicators	7	unpredictable: depending on the situation in the labor market and educational market, risk of low values	1–10 (on average: 5)
Concentration of researchers		7		1–10 (on average: 5)
Patent activity		7		1–10 (on average: 5)
Academic education		7		1–10 (on average: 7.5)
Creation of added value	strictly according to the norm, without stimuli for exceeding it	3	depending on the situation in the market (on the state of competition) and on the company's capabilities	5–10 (on average: 7.5)
Labor efficiency		3		5–10 (on average: 7.5)
Density of hi-tech entrepreneurship	according to the norm, but its activities are strictly standardized, which restrains its development	4		1–10 (on average: 5)

Source: developed and compiled by the authors.

However, in view of the variability of scores of each indicator and strong dependence of the factual (not estimate) values on the current market situation and the instability of efficiency of managing the innovative development of a modern economic system during market self-management based on competition, it cannot be considered totally preferable, as – in the conditions of a crisis – management based on standards and norms ensures better results, which is also possible – and highly probably – in the period of stability.

Table 9.3: Evaluation of efficiency of managing the innovative development of a modern economic system with the help of analytic hierarchy process with different approaches.

Metrics of innovative development	Weight of metrics	Management based on standards and norms		Market self-management based on competition	
		score	weighted estimate	score	weighted estimate
R&D intensity	0.12	7	7*0.12=0.84	5	5*0.12=0.6
Concentration of researchers	0.1	7	7*0.1=0.7	5	5*0.1=0.5
Patent activity	0.13	7	7*0.13=0.91	5	5*0.13=0.65
Academic education	0.1	7	7*0.1=0.7	5	5*0.1=0.5
Creation of added value	0.2	3	3*0.2=0.6	7.5	7.5*0.2=1.5
Labor efficiency	0.2	3	3*0.2=0.6	7.5	7.5*0.2=1.5
Density of hi-tech entrepreneurship	0.15	4	4*0.15=0.6	5	5*0.15=0.75
Hierarchical synthesis: final evaluation of management efficiency			0.84+0.7+0.91+0.7+ +0.6+0.6+0.6=**4.95**		0.6+0.5+0.65+0.5+ +1.5+1.5+0.75=**6.00**

Source: developed and compiled by the authors.

Conclusion

Thus, the performed research showed that standards and norms of managing the innovative development are important in the modern economic systems. However, efficiency of management with the help of standardization and norming is different in various economic systems and at different stages of the economic cycle. Countries with moderate and low economic freedom should pay more attention to standards and norms of managing the innovative development of a modern economic system, and countries with high and minimal economic freedom should use the market mechanism (competition).

In all economic systems, regardless of the level of economic freedom, it is preferable – in the period of a crisis – to implement norms and standards of innovative activities; and in the period of stability there's a necessity for differentiated state management of innovative development. If market stimuli are sufficient, norms and standards are not required, while they are mandatory in an unfavorable market environment – as market self-management does not allow for a proper level of innovative activity in economy for supporting its effectiveness and competitiveness.

References

Andronova, I.V., Chernova, V.Y., Starostin, V.S., Degtereva (2019). Study of sector-specific innovation efforts: The case from Russian economy. Entrepreneurship and Sustainability Issues, Vsl Entrepreneurship and Sustainability Center, 7(1), p. 540–552.

Atkinsonk, R.D., Ezell, S.J. (2012). Innovation Economics: the Race for Global Advantage, New Haven, CT: Yale University Press.

Bloomberg (2020). Innovation index. URL: https://www.bloomberg.com/news/articles/2020-01-18/germany-breaks-korea-s-six-year-streak-as-most-innovative-nation (data accessed: 30.03.2020)

Bogoviz, A.V., Ragulina, Y.V. (2020). Industry competitiveness in the new economy. Lecture Notes in Networks and Systems, 115, p. v–vi.

García-Quevedo, J., Segarra-Blasco, A., Teruel, M. (2018). Financial constraints and the failure of innovation projects. Technological Forecasting and Social Change, 127, p. 127–140.

Gumba, H.M., Vlasenko, V.A. (2017). Strategy of development of innovative activity in industry and construction: The rationale of the regional dimension. Izvestiya Vysshikh Uchebnykh Zavedenii, Seriya Teknologiya Tekstil'noi Promyshlennosti, 2017-January(2), 2(1), p. 14–18.

Haabazoka, L. (2019). A Study of the Effects of Technological Innovations on the Performance of Commercial Banks in Developing Countries – A Case of the Zambian Banking Industry. In: Popkova E. (eds) The Future of the Global Financial System: Downfall or Harmony. ISC 2018. Lecture Notes in Networks and Systems, vol 57. Springer, Cham, Online ISBN 978-3-030-00102-5, https://doi.org/10.1007/978-3-030-00102-5_132

Harfst, J., Pichler, P., Fischer, W. (2017). Regional Ambassadors-An Innovative Element for the Development of Rural Areas? European Countryside, 9(2), p. 359–374.

ISO (2020). Technical committees. ISO/TC 279. Innovation management. URL: https://www.iso.org/committee/4587737.html (data accessed: 30. 03.2020)

Itonics (2020). ISO 56002 – global guide on innovation management. URL: https://www.itonics-innovation.com/blog/iso-56002-guide-for-innovation-management (data accessed: 30. 03.2020)

Kuznetsova, O., Kuznetsova, S., Yumaev, E., Kuznetsov, V., Galtseva, O. (2017). Formation and Development of the Training System for Innovative Development of Regional Industry. E3S Web of Conferences, 15,04019.

Li, X., Subrahmanyam, A., Yang, X. (2018). Can financial innovation succeed by catering to behavioral preferences? Evidence from a callable options market. Journal of Financial Economics, 2(1), p. 34–42.

Petrenko, E.S., Shevyakova, A.L. (2019). Features and perspectives of digitization in Kazakhstan. Studies in Computational Intelligence, 826, p. 889–899.

Popkova, E.G. (2019). Preconditions of formation and development of industry 4.0 in the conditions of knowledge economy. Studies in Systems, Decision and Control, 169(1),65–72.

Popkova, E.G., Sergi, B.S. (2020). Human Capital and AI in Industry 4.0. Convergence and Divergence in Social Entrepreneurship in Russia. Journal of Intellectual Capital, In press, 2020. https://doi.org/10.1108/JIC-09-2019-0224

Popkova, E.G., Egorova, E.N., Popova, E., Pozdnyakova, U.A. (2019). The model of state management of economy on the basis of the internet of things. Studies in Computational Intelligence, 826, pp. 1137–1144.

Popkova, E.G., Gulzat, K. (2020). Technological Revolution in the 21st Century: Digital Society vs. Artificial Intelligence. Lecture Notes in Networks and Systems, 91, p. 339–345.

Popkova, E.G., Parakhina, V.N. (2019). Managing the global financial system on the basis of artificial intelligence: possibilities and limitations. Lecture Notes in Networks and Systems, 57, pp. 939–946.

Popkova, E.G., Poluyufta, L., Beshanova, Y., Popova, L.V., Kolesnikova, E. (2017). Innovations as a basis for marketing strategies of Russian oil companies in the conditions of oil prices reduction. Contributions to Economics, (9783319606958), p. 449–455.

Popkova, E.G., Zmiyak, K.V. (2019). Priorities of training of digital personnel for industry 4.0: social competencies vs technical competencies. On the Horizon, 27(3–4), p. 138–144.

Popkova, E.G., Sergi, B.S. (2018). Will Industry 4.0 and Other Innovations Impact Russia's Development? In Bruno S. Sergi (Ed.) Exploring the Future of Russia's Economy and Markets: Towards Sustainable Economic Development (pp. 51–68). Bingley, UK: Emerald Publishing Limited.

Popkova, E.G., Sergi, B.S. (Eds.) (2019). Digital Economy: Complexity and Variety vs. Rationality. Berlin: Springer International Publishing.

Ragulina, Y.V. (2019). Priorities of development of industry 4.0 in modern economic systems with different progress in formation of knowledge economy. Studies in Systems, Decision and Control, 169, p. 167–174.

Ragulina, Y.V., Alekseev, A.N., Strizhkina, I.V., Tumanov, A.I. (2019). Methodology of criterial evaluation of consequences of the industrial revolution of the 21st century. Studies in Systems, Decision and Control, 169, p. 235–244.

Ramanathan, R., Ramanathan, U., Bentley, Y. (2018). The debate on flexibility of environmental regulations, innovation capabilities and financial performance – A novel use of DEA. Omega (United Kingdom), 75, p. 131–138.

Sergi, B.S. (2003). Economic Dynamics in Transitional Economies: The Four-P Governments, the EU Enlargement, and the Bruxelles Consensus. New York: Routledge.

Sergi, B.S. (Ed.) (2019). Tech, Smart Cities, and Regional Development in Contemporary Russia. Bingley, UK: Emerald Publishing Limited.

Sergi, B.S., Popkova, E.G. Bogoviz, A.V., Ragulina Y.V. (2019a). The Agro-industrial Complex: Tendencies, Scenarios, and Regulation. In Sergi, Bruno S. (Ed.) Modeling Economic Growth in Contemporary Russia (pp. 233–247). Bingley, UK: Emerald Publishing Limited.

Sergi, B.S., Popkova, E.G., Bogoviz, A.V., Litvinova, T.N. (2019b). Understanding Industry 4.0: AI, the Internet of Things, and the Future of Work. Bingley, UK: Emerald Publishing Limited.

Shulus, A.A., Akopova, E.S., Przhedetskaya, N.V., Borzenko, K.V. (2020). Intellectual Production and Consumption: A New Reality of the 21st Century. Lecture Notes in Networks and Systems, 92, pp. 353–359.

Stolyarov, N.O., Petrenko, E.S., Serova, O.A., Umuralieva, A.S. (2020). The Digital Reality of the Modern Economy: New Actors and New Decision-Making Logic. Lecture Notes in Networks and Systems, 87, p. 882–888.

The Heritage Foundation (2020). Index of economic freedom. URL: https://www.heritage.org/index/ranking (data accessed: 30.03.2020)

Visual Capitalist (2020). Ranked: The Most Innovative Economies in the World. URL: https://www.visualcapitalist.com/world-most-innovative-economies/ (data accessed: 31.03.2020).

Yao, M., Di, H., Zheng, X., Xu, X. (2018). Impact of payment technology innovations on the traditional financial industry: A focus on China. Technological Forecasting and Social Change, 2(1), p. 22–29.

Zavyalova, E.B. Studenikin, N.V. Starikova, E.A. (2018). Business participation in implementation of socially oriented Sustainable Development Goals in countries of Central Asia and the Caucasus region. Central Asia and the Caucasus, 19(2), p. 56–63.

Aleksandr E. Suglobov, Oleg G. Karpovich, Tatyana I. Rudakova,
Daniil M. Pimenov and Inna A. Koryagina

10 The Role of International Organizations in Managing the Modern Economic Systems' Innovative Development

Introduction

Innovative activities of economic systems under the influence of globalization become more international. Leading technologies allow for remote R&D, creation of virtual scientific laboratories, and online exchange of the results of research activities. Selling patented developments in the world markets is attractive, as it allows realizing the rights for objects of intellectual property with the largest profit and maximizing the effectiveness from commercialization of innovations.

Final innovative products are sold around the world and are also produced on the territory of different countries within network business. This ensures diffusion of innovations and maximization of profit of innovations-active and hi-tech entrepreneurship. The principle of international division of labor dictates such scheme of organization of the world economy at which innovative activities are the object of specialization of countries that have competitive advantages – developed human capital and sufficient venture investments.

The transnational character of innovative activities requires its supra-national management. International organizations are one of the leading forces in the system of supra-national management, together with integration unions of countries. This predetermines the importance of studying their role in managing the modern economic systems' innovative development. As supra-national management of innovative activity is not the key goal of most of the modern international organizations, but is one of their multiple tasks, the role of international organizations in managing the modern economic systems' innovative development is not obvious and has to be studied.

This chapter aims at determining the role of international organizations in the process of managing the modern economic systems' innovative development; determining

Aleksandr E. Suglobov, Daniil M. Pimenov, Financial University under the Government of the Russian Federation, Moscow, Russian Federation

Oleg G. Karpovich, Diplomatic Academy of the Ministry of Foreign Affairs of the Russian Federation, Moscow, Russia

Tatyana I. Rudakova, State Educational Institution of Higher Education Moscow Region "University of Technology", Korolev, Russia

Inna A. Koryagina, Plekhanov Russian University of Economics, Moscow, Russia

https://doi.org/10.1515/9783110643701-010

the successfulness of execution of this role; determining the problems and perspectives of overcoming them.

Materials and Method

The international aspect of innovative activities in the modern market economy in the conditions of globalization is studied in the works Atkinsonk and Ezell (2012), García-Quevedo et al. (2018), Gumba and Vlasenko (2017), Haabazoka (2019), Harfst et al. (2017), Kuznetsova et al. (2017), Li et al. (2018), Ramanathan et al. (2018), and Yao et al. (2018).

Certain issues of international organizations' participation in managing the modern economic systems' innovative development are studied in the works Andronova et al. (2019), Bogoviz and Ragulina (2020), Petrenko and Shevyakova (2019), Popkova (2019), Popkova and Sergi (2020), Popkova et al. (2019), Popkova and Gulzat (2020), Popkova and Parakhina (2019), Popkova et al. (2017), Popkova and Zmiyak (2019), Popkova and Sergi (2018), Popkova and Sergi (2019), Ragulina (2019), Ragulina et al. (2019), Sergi (2003), Sergi (2019), Sergi et al. (2019a), Sergi et al. (2019b), Shulus et al. (2020), Stolyarov et al. (2020), and Zavyalova et al. (2018).

However, the role of international organizations in managing the modern economic systems' innovative development has to be further studied. In this chapter, a complex of general scientific methods (systematization of data, induction, deduction, and logical analysis) is used for determining the role; SWOT analysis is used for evaluating the successfulness of international organizations' executing their role in managing the innovative development of the modern economic systems.

Classical SWOT analysis, which envisages generalized qualitative evaluation of the research object, is here supplemented by detailed qualitative evaluation according to the following formula:

$$Xio = \frac{[(S - W)^{\star}O]}{T} \tag{1}$$

where Xio – successfulness of international organizations' executing their role in managing the modern economic systems' innovative development;

S – strengths;

W – weaknesses;

O – opportunities;

T – threats.

Results

For determining the general role that is performed by all international organizations in managing the modern economic systems' innovative development, we consider the functions that are performed by them separately (Table 10.1).

Table 10.1: Functions of international organizations in managing the modern economic systems' innovative development.

Function	International organization	Way of executing the function
International statistics of innovative activities	World Bank (WB)	calculating indicators for all countries, since 1960
Forecasting innovative activities and its influence on the economy	International Monetary Fund (IMF)	forecasting a range of indicators for countries for 2017–2022
Determining the factors and advantages of innovative activities for the economy	World Economic Forum (WEF)	annual indicative evaluation of global competitiveness of countries
Determining the perspective directions of innovative development	International Institute for Management Development (IMD)	compiling the annual ranking of digital competitiveness
Evaluating the social consequences of innovations	United Nations (UN)	setting the goals and compiling the annual sustainable development index
Unifying innovative activities	International Organization for Standardization (ISO)	developing the international standards of innovative activities
Protecting intellectual property rights for innovations	World Intellectual Property Organization (WIPO)	registering international patents and protecting rights for them
Distributing the international flows of venture investments	World Bank (WB)	evaluating the conditions for doing business
	United Nations (UN)	evaluating the investment climate in countries
Ensuring the sale of innovations (free trade)	World Trade Organization (WTO)	regulating international trade of innovations, regulating arguments

Source: developed and compiled by the authors.

As shown in Table 10.1, the function of calculating international statistics of innovative activities is performed by the World Bank, which has been calculating indicators for all countries since 1960. The function of forecasting innovative activities and its influence on the economy is performed by the IMF, which forecasts a range of indicators for 2017–2022. The function of determining the factors and advantages of innovative activities for the economy is performed by the WEF, which performs annual indicative evaluation of countries' global competitiveness.

The function of determining the perspective directions of innovative development is performed by the IMD, which compiled the annual ranking of digital competitiveness. The function of evaluating the social consequences of innovations is performed by the UN, which sets the goals and calculates the sustainable development index. The function of unifying the innovative activities is performed by the ISO, which develops international standards of innovative activities.

The function of protection of intellectual property rights for innovations is performed by the (WIPO), which registers international patents and protects rights for them. The function of distributing the international flows of venture investments is performed by the World Bank, which evaluates the conditions for doing business, and by the UN, which evaluates the investment climate in countries of the world. The function of provision of sales of innovations (free trade) is performed by the WTO, which regulates the international trade of innovations and regulates arguments.

Thus, systematization and generalization of the above functions allows for determining the place and role of the international organizations in managing the modern economic systems' innovative development (Figure 10.1).

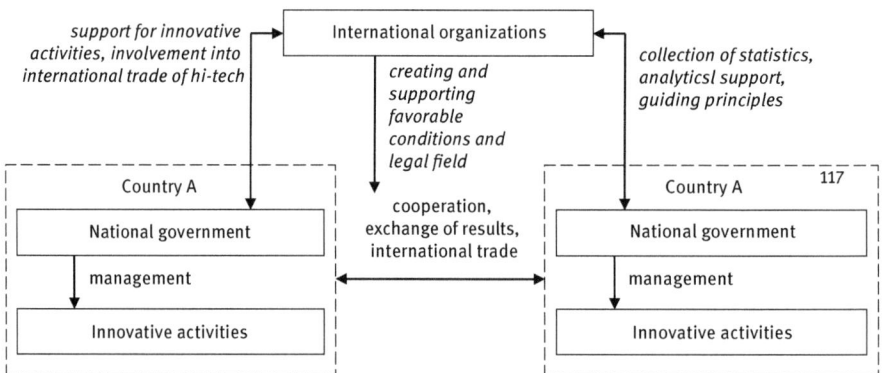

Figure 10.1: The place and role of international organizations in managing the modern economic systems' innovative development.
Source: developed and compiled by the authors.

As shown in Figure 10.1, international organizations are the mega-regulator of managing the modern economic systems' innovative development. They support innovative activities and involve developing countries into international trade of hi-tech, gather statistics, provide analytical support and guiding principles for developed countries, and created and support favorable conditions and legal field for co-operation, exchange of results, and international trade of innovations.

SWOT analysis of successfulness of international organizations' executing their role in managing the modern economic systems' innovative development is shown in Table 10.2.

Based on the data from Table 10.2, the indicator of successfulness of international organizations' performing their role in managing the modern economic systems' innovative development is calculated: $Xio = \frac{[(20-15)*8.5]}{14} = 3.03$. This value exceeds 1, which shows that the international organizations successfully perform their role. However, weaknesses (15 points) and threats (14 points) are vivid and have to be overcome, while opportunities (8.5 points) reflect the perspectives of improving the existing practice of international organizations' participating in managing the modern economic systems' innovative development.

Conclusion

The result of the research is implication of the role of international organizations in managing the modern economic systems' innovative development, which is a complex manifestation of a lot of performed functions. In the generalized form, this role could be formulated as provision of a platform for transnationalization of the innovative activities of countries of the world. The performed evaluation of successfulness of execution of this role of the international organizations (3.03 points) shows that they cope with it.

A threat to the role of international organizations in managing the modern economic systems' innovative development is posed by loss of independence and authority of international organizations, reduction of the resource base of international organizations, and decrease of geography of the influence of international organizations. The perspectives of improving the practice of international organizations' participation in management of modern economic systems' innovative development are connected to expansion of the authorities of international organizations, expansion of the geography of influence of international organizations, and growth of efficiency of international organizations based on digitization.

Table 10.2: SWOT analysis of successfulness of international organizations' executing their role in managing the modern economic systems' innovative development.

Object of analysis	Qualitative characteristics of object of analysis	Quantitative characteristics of object of analysis		
		Score, 1–10	Significance, shares of 1	Weighted score
S: Strengths	independence and high authority of international organizations	scale	8	1.0	8*1.0=8	S= 8+9+3=20
	accumulation of large resources of international organizations		9	1.0	9*1.0=9
	division of labor of international organizations		10	0.3	10*0.3=3
W: Weaknesses	incompleteness of data of statistical reports that are provided by international organizations	urgency	5	1.0	5*1.0=5	W= 5+4+6=15
	assigning a range of recommendations of international organizations to "soft law"		4	1.0	4*1.0=4
	limited rights of international organizations		6	1.0	6*1.0=6
O: Opportunities	expansion of rights of international organizations	probability	2	1.0	2*1.0=2	O= 2+3+3.5=8.5
	expansion of geography of the influence of international organizations		3	1.0	3*1.0=3
	growth of efficiency of international organizations based on digitization		5	0.7	5*0.7=3.5
T: Threats	loss of independence and authority of international and organizations	probability	7	1.0	7*1.0=7	T=7+2+5=14
	reduction of the resources base of international organizations		2	1.0	2*1.0=2
	reduction of the geography of influence of international organizations		5	1.0	5*1.0=5

Source: developed and compiled by the authors.

References

Andronova, I.V., Chernova, V.Y., Starostin, V.S., Degtereva (2019). Study of sector-specific innovation efforts: The case from Russian economy. Entrepreneurship and Sustainability Issues, VsI Entrepreneurship and Sustainability Center, 7(1), p. 540–552.

Atkinsonk, R.D., Ezell, S.J. (2012). Innovation Economics: the Race for Global Advantage, New Haven, CT: Yale University Press.

Bogoviz, A.V., Ragulina, Y.V. (2020). Industry competitiveness in the new economy. Lecture Notes in Networks and Systems, 115, p. v–vi.

García-Quevedo, J., Segarra-Blasco, A., Teruel, M. (2018). Financial constraints and the failure of innovation projects. Technological Forecasting and Social Change, 127, p. 127–140.

Gumba, H.M., Vlasenko, V.A. (2017). Strategy of development of innovative activity in industry and construction: The rationale of the regional dimension. Izvestiya Vysshikh Uchebnykh Zavedenii, Seriya Teknologiya Tekstil'noi Promyshlennosti, 2017-January(2), p. 14–18.

Haabazoka, L. (2019). A Study of the Effects of Technological Innovations on the Performance of Commercial Banks in Developing Countries – A Case of the Zambian Banking Industry. In: Popkova E. (eds</edg>) The Future of the Global Financial System: Downfall or Harmony. ISC 2018. Lecture Notes in <edg>Networks and Systems, vol 57. Springer, Cham, Online ISBN 978-3-030-00102-5, https://doi.org/10.1007/978-3-030-00102-5_132

Harfst, J., Pichler, P., Fischer, W. (2017). Regional Ambassadors-An Innovative Element for the Development of Rural Areas? European Countryside, 9(2), p. 359–374.

Kuznetsova, O., Kuznetsova, S., Yumaev, E., Kuznetsov, V., Galtseva, O. (2017). Formation and Development of the Training System for Innovative Development of Regional Industry. E3S Web of Conferences, 15,04019.

Li, X., Subrahmanyam, A., Yang, X. (2018). Can financial innovation succeed by catering to behavioral preferences? Evidence from a callable options market. Journal of Financial Economics, 2(1), p. 34–42.

Petrenko, E.S., Shevyakova, A.L. (2019). Features and perspectives of digitization in Kazakhstan. Studies in Computational Intelligence, 826, p. 889–899.

Popkova, E.G. (2019). Preconditions of formation and development of industry 4.0 in the conditions of knowledge economy. Studies in Systems, Decision and Control, 169(1), 65–72.

Popkova, E.G., Sergi, B.S. (2020). Human Capital and AI in Industry 4.0. Convergence and Divergence in Social Entrepreneurship in Russia. Journal of Intellectual Capital, In press, 2020. https://doi.org/10.1108/JIC-09-2019-0224

Popkova, E.G., Egorova, E.N., Popova, E., Pozdnyakova, U.A. (2019). The model of state management of economy on the basis of the internet of things. Studies in Computational Intelligence, 826, pp. 1137–1144.

Popkova, E.G., Gulzat, K. (2020). Technological Revolution in the 21st Century: Digital Society vs. Artificial Intelligence. Lecture Notes in Networks and Systems, 91, p. 339–345.

Popkova, E.G., Parakhina, V.N. (2019). Managing the global financial system on the basis of artificial intelligence: possibilities and limitations. Lecture Notes in Networks and Systems, 57, pp. 939–946.

Popkova, E.G., Poluyufta, L., Beshanova, Y., Popova, L.V., Kolesnikova, E. (2017). Innovations as a basis for marketing strategies of Russian oil companies in the conditions of oil prices reduction. Contributions to Economics, (9783319606958), p. 449–455. DOI: 10.1007/978-3-319-60696-5_57

Popkova, E.G., Zmiyak, K.V. (2019). Priorities of training of digital personnel for industry 4.0: social competencies vs technical competencies. On the Horizon, 27(3–4), p. 138–144.

Popkova, E.G., Sergi, B.S. (2018). Will Industry 4.0 and Other Innovations Impact Russia's Development? In Bruno S. Sergi (Ed.) Exploring the Future of Russia's Economy and Markets: Towards Sustainable Economic Development (pp. 51–68). Bingley, UK: Emerald Publishing Limited.

Popkova, E.G., Sergi, B.S. (Eds.) (2019). Digital Economy: Complexity and Variety vs. Rationality. Springer International Publishing.

Ragulina, Y.V. (2019). Priorities of development of industry 4.0 in modern economic systems with different progress in formation of knowledge economy. Studies in Systems, Decision and Control, 169, p. 167–174.

Ragulina, Y.V., Alekseev, A.N., Strizhkina, I.V., Tumanov, A.I. (2019). Methodology of criterial evaluation of consequences of the industrial revolution of the 21st century. Studies in Systems, Decision and Control, 169, p. 235–244.

Ramanathan, R., Ramanathan, U., Bentley, Y. (2018). The debate on flexibility of environmental regulations, innovation capabilities and financial performance – A novel use of DEA. United Kingdom: Omega, 75, p. 131–138.

Sergi, B.S. (2003). Economic Dynamics in Transitional Economies: The Four-P Governments, the EU Enlargement, and the Bruxelles Consensus. New York: Routledge.

Sergi, B.S. (Ed.) (2019). Tech, Smart Cities, and Regional Development in Contemporary Russia. Bingley, UK: Emerald Publishing Limited.

Sergi, B.S., Popkova, E.G. Bogoviz, A.V., Ragulina Y.V. (2019a). The Agro-industrial Complex: Tendencies, Scenarios, and Regulation. In Sergi, Bruno S. (Ed.) Modeling Economic Growth in Contemporary Russia (pp. 233–247). Bingley, UK: Emerald Publishing Limited.

Sergi, B.S., Popkova, E.G., Bogoviz, A.V., Litvinova, T.N. (2019b). Understanding Industry 4.0: AI, the Internet of Things, and the Future of Work. Bingley, UK: Emerald Publishing Limited.

Shulus, A.A., Akopova, E.S., Przhedetskaya, N.V., Borzenko, K.V. (2020). Intellectual Production and Consumption: A New Reality of the 21st Century. Lecture Notes in Networks and Systems, 92, pp. 353–359.

Stolyarov, N.O., Petrenko, E.S., Serova, O.A., Umuralieva, A.S. (2020). The Digital Reality of the Modern Economy: New Actors and New Decision-Making Logic. Lecture Notes in Networks and Systems, 87, p. 882–888.

Yao, M., Di, H., Zheng, X., Xu, X. (2018). Impact of payment technology innovations on the traditional financial industry: A focus on China. Technological Forecasting and Social Change, 2(1), p. 22–29.

Zavyalova, E.B. Studenikin, N.V. Starikova, E.A. (2018). Business participation in implementation of socially oriented Sustainable Development Goals in countries of Central Asia and the Caucasus region. Central Asia and the Caucasus, 19(2), p. 56–63.

Part IV: **The Modern Practical Experience of
Economic and Legal Management of
Economic Systems' Innovative Development**

Yuliya G. Lesnikh, Olga I. Opaleva, Elena N. Akimova,
Valeriy N. Matyukhin and Dzhannet S. Shikhalieva

11 Specific Features of Economic and Legal Management of modern Economic Systems' Innovative Development in Developed Countries

Introduction

Developed countries are an example of successful innovative development. They have the leading positions in various rankings of countries, including the Global Competitiveness Index 4.0 of the World Economic Forum, the IMD World Digital Competitiveness Ranking, and the Global Innovation Index by WIPO and Bloomberg. Uniqueness of experience of developed countries and its usefulness for other participants of the global economic system are due to the fact that developed countries not only achieved the highest level of innovative development but continue their technological progress, supporting high rate of innovative development. This ensures their leadership in the global markets of innovations and hi-tech.

At the same time, developed countries are an artificially created category. This is not an integration union with common interests and policy in the sphere of innovations, but a totality of countries from different geographical regions of the world, which achieved the best results in socio-economic development – in particular, innovative activities. The limits of the category of developed countries are not clearly determined, being flexible and dependent on the point of view. Different expert & analytical organizations offer their lists of developed countries. For example, the IMF distinguishes a sub-category of developed countries – major advanced economies (G7), and the OECD has its own list.

Uncertainty regarding the notion and structure of developed countries does not allow for synthesis and generalization of their experience of managing innovative development or for its use in other countries of the world. The purpose of this chapter is to determine the specific features and to model the economic & legal management of modern economic systems' innovative development in developed countries.

Yuliya G. Lesnikh, "Kuban State Agrarian University named after I.T. Trubilin", Krasnodar, Russia
Olga I. Opaleva, Elena N. Akimova, Valeriy N. Matyukhin, Moscow Region State University, Mytishchi, Russia
Dzhannet S. Shikhalieva, Autonomous Non-profit Organization of Higher Education "Moscow Humanitarian Economic University," North-Caucasian Branch, Mineralnye Vody, Russia

https://doi.org/10.1515/9783110643701-011

Materials and Method

Detailed description of the foundations of economic & legal management of modern economic systems' innovative development is given in the works Atkinsonk and Ezell (2012), García-Quevedo et al. (2018), Gumba and Vlasenko (2017), Haabazoka (2019), Harfst et al. (2017), Kuznetsova et al. (2017), Li et al. (2018), Ramanathan et al. (2018), and Yao et al. (2018).

Experience of developed and developing countries in economic & legal management of modern economic systems' innovative development is given in the works Andronova et al. (2019), Bogoviz and Ragulina (2020), Petrenko and Shevyakova (2019), Popkova (2019), Popkova and Sergi (2020), Popkova et al. (2019), Popkova and Gulzat (2020), Popkova and Parakhina (2019), Popkova et al. (2017), Popkova and Zmiyak (2019), Popkova and Sergi (2018), Popkova and Sergi (2019), Ragulina (2019), Ragulina et al. (2019), Sergi (2003), Sergi (2019), Sergi et al. (2019a), Sergi et al. (2019b), Shulus et al. (2020), Stolyarov et al. (2020), and Zavyalova et al. (2018) (Popkova and Sergi, 2019).

It is possible to see that the specific features of economic & legal management of modern economic systems' innovative development in developed countries are not determined very clearly and are not sufficiently described.

In this chapter, we use the list of developed countries according to OECD (2020), as this is the most detailed list, which includes countries from different regions of the world and is not limited by the most progressive countries (e.g., the USA and Switzerland), covering also recently added countries (e.g., Chile and Mexico).

We classify the OECD countries in three sub-categories by the level of innovative development: Top 3 (the Global Innovation Index – 57–68), Middle 3 (the Global Innovation Index – 46–56), and Low 3 (the Global Innovation Index – 35–45). For determining detailed causal connections of innovative development of developed countries, we analyze a large number of indicators:

- factors of innovative development: expenditures for R&D, Digital Competitiveness Index, Human Development Index, hi-tech export, and mid-tech and hi-tech industry (their cross-correlation with the Global Innovation Index is calculated);
- consequences of innovative development: the Global Competitiveness Index 4.0, rate of economic growth, sustainable development index, happiness index, and the Quality of Life Index (their cross-correlation with the Global Innovation Index is calculated);
- influence of innovations on balance of developed countries (correlation of variation of GDP per capita with the Global Innovation Index for the categories is calculated).

Selection of the statistical data (as of early 2020) is given in Table 11.1.

Table 11.1: Factors, results, and consequences of innovative development of developed countries by the example of the OECD countries, classified into categories by the values of the Global Innovation Index, 2020.

Category	Country	Global Innovation Index points 1–100	Digital Competitiveness Index, points 1–100	Global Competitiveness Index 4.0, points 1–100	Human Development Index, shares of 1	Rate of economic growth, %	Quality of Life Index, points 1–200	Happiness index, points 1–10	Sustainable Development Index, points 1–100	R&D expenditures, % GDP	Hi-tech export, % of industrial export	Mid-tech and hi-tech industry, % of industrial added value	GDP per capita, USD
Top 3 (57–68)	Switzerland	67.24	94.648	82.3	0.946	1.600	196.08	7.480	78.8	3.37	13	65	3,492,879
	Sweden	63.65	96.070	81.2	0.937	2.181	180.52	7.343	85.0	3.33	14	52	55,035.852
	USA	61.73	100.000	83.7	0.920	2.121	176.77	6.892	74.5	2.79	19	47	66,194.406
Middle 3 (46–56)	Australia	50.34	88.897	78.7	0.938	2.945	189.73	7.228	73.9	1.92	17	28	61,038.126
	Belgium	50.18	82.491	76.4	0.919	1.477	160.81	6.923	78.9	2.59	10	50	44,037.533
	Italy	46.30	67.903	71.5	0.883	0.800	143.81	6.223	75.8	1.35	8	43	31,657.755
Low 3 (35–45)	Hungary	44.51	65.472	65.1	0.845	2.600	133.06	5.758	76.9	1.35	17	57	14,435.047
	Slovakia	42.05	62.624	66.8	0.857	3.900	154.53	6.198	76.2	0.88	11	50	19,159.226
	Chile	36.64	66.724	70.5	0.847	2.700	123.80	6.444	75.6	0.36	6	21	15,144.735

Source: compiled by the authors based on Institute of Scientific Communications (2020), World Bank (2020).

Results

Based on the data from Table, the following results of correlation analysis have been obtained (Figures 11.1–11.3).

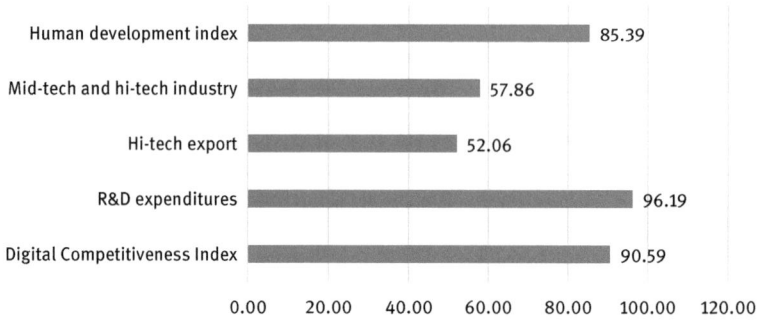

Figure 11.1: Correlation of the Global Innovation Index with the factors of innovative development of developed countries by the example of the OECD countries in 2020, %.
Source: calculated and compiled by the authors.

As shown in Figure 11.1, the key factor of innovative development of developed countries is R&D expenditures (correlation – 96.19%), the Digital Competitiveness Index (correlation – 90.59%), and Human Development Index (correlation – 85.39%). Less significant factors are mid-tech and hi-tech industry (correlation – 57.86%) and hi-tech export (correlation – 52.06%).

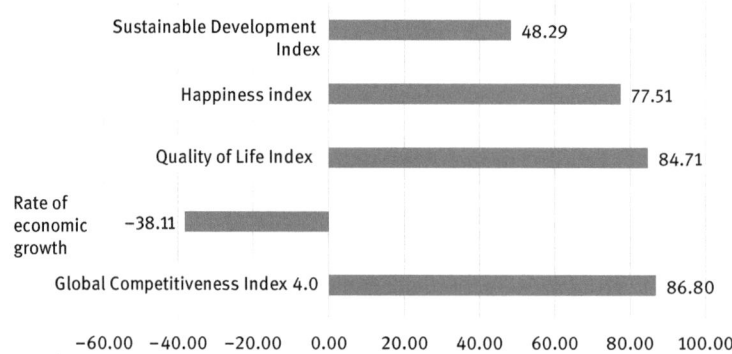

Figure 11.2: Correlation of the Global Innovation Index with the consequences of innovative development of developed countries by the example of the OECD countries in 2020, %.
Source: calculated and compiled by the authors.

As shown in Figure 11.2, the main consequences of innovative development in developed countries are growth of the Global Competitiveness Index 4.0 (correlation – 86.80%), increase of the Quality of Life Index (correlation – 84.1%), and the happiness index (correlation – 77.51%), though its average value in developed countries is relatively low. A negative consequence of innovative development in developed countries is limitation of the rate of economic growth (correlation –38.11%), and the Sustainable Development Index (48.29%) is moderately connected to innovative development.

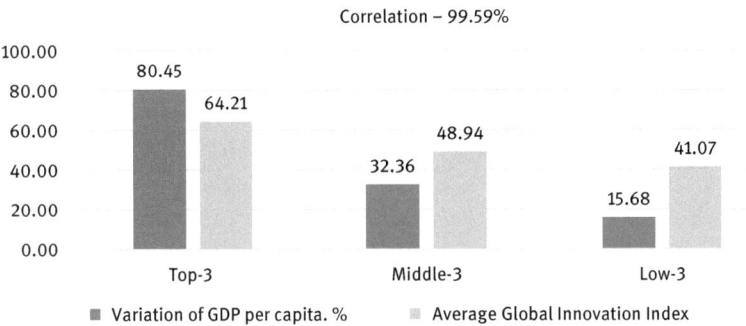

Figure 11.3: Correlation analysis of the consequences of innovative development for the balance of developed countries by the example of the OECD countries in 2020.
Source: calculated and compiled by the authors.

As shown in Figure 11.3, variation of GDP per capita in developed countries decreases significantly in the course of their innovative development. Thus, in the category Low 3 its equals 80.45%, in the category Middle 3–32.36%, and in the category Top 3–15.68%. Correlation of variation of GDP per capita and the average value of the Global Innovation Index in the distinguished categories of developed countries is very high – 99.59%.

Systematization of the obtained results allowed compiling a model of economic & legal management of modern economic systems' innovative development in developed countries (Figure 11.4).

The above model shows that during the economic & legal management of innovative development the modern developed countries use financial, human, and technological resources. They are rather homogeneous. Their innovative activities lead to social advantages (including ecological), but have an economic drawback - slowing down economic growth.

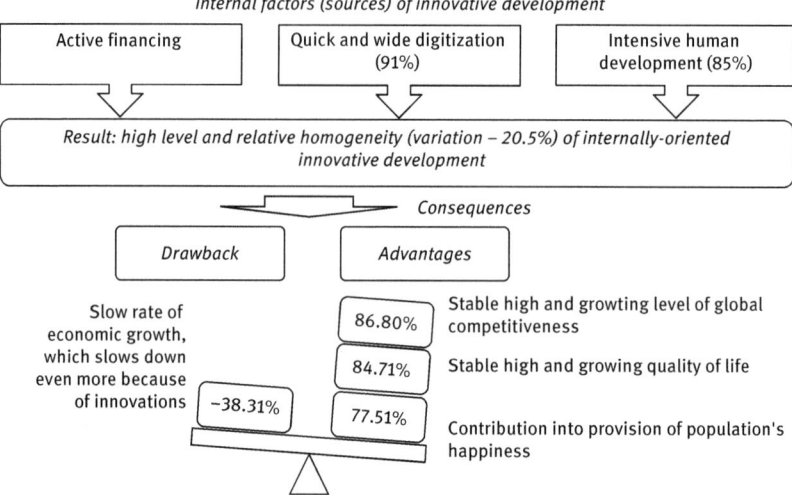

Figure 11.4: The model of economic & legal management of modern economic systems' innovative development in developed countries.
Source: developed and compiled by the authors.

Conclusion

Thus, the specific features of economic & legal management of modern economic systems' innovative development in developed countries have been determined: simultaneous foundation on material (financing R&D) and non-material (development of human resources, development and dissemination of digital technologies) factors and limitation of the influence of globalization on innovations (restrained export).

In developed countries, innovations are a mechanism of well-balanced socioeconomic development, as they allow leveling the disproportions in GDP per capita. The consequences of innovative activities in developed countries are contradictory: on the one hand, they lead to improvement of social indicators, but, on the other hand, slow down the rate of economic growth, which makes the experience of developed countries unattractive for developing countries.

References

Andronova, I.V., Chernova, V.Y., Starostin, V.S., Degtereva (2019). Study of sector-specific innovation efforts: The case from Russian economy. Entrepreneurship and Sustainability Issues, VsI Entrepreneurship and Sustainability Center, 7(1), p. 540–552.
Atkinsonk, R.D., Ezell, S.J. (2012). Innovation Economics: the Race for Global Advantage, New Haven, CT: Yale University Press.

Bogoviz, A.V., Ragulina, Y.V. (2020). Industry competitiveness in the new economy. Lecture Notes in Networks and Systems, 115, p. v–vi.

García-Quevedo, J., Segarra-Blasco, A., Teruel, M. (2018). Financial constraints and the failure of innovation projects. Technological Forecasting and Social Change, 127, p. 127–140.

Gumba, H.M., Vlasenko, V.A. (2017). Strategy of development of innovative activity in industry and construction: The rationale of the regional dimension. Izvestiya Vysshikh Uchebnykh Zavedenii, Seriya Teknologiya Tekstil'noi Promyshlennosti, 2017-January(2), p. 14–18.

Haabazoka, L. (2019). A Study of the Effects of Technological Innovations on the Performance of Commercial Banks in Developing Countries – A Case of the Zambian Banking Industry. In: Popkova E. (eds) The Future of the Global Financial System: Downfall or Harmony. ISC 2018. Lecture Notes in Networks and Systems, vol 57. Springer, Cham, Online ISBN 978-3-030-00102-5, https://doi.org/10.1007/978-3-030-00102-5_132

Harfst, J., Pichler, P., Fischer, W. (2017). Regional Ambassadors-An Innovative Element for the Development of Rural Areas? European Countryside, 9(2), p. 359–374.

Institute of Scientific Communications (2020). Data set "Big data of the modern world economy: digital platform for intelligent analytics – 2020". URL: https://www.archilab.online/en/data/sounting-data-set (data accessed: 17.03.2020).

Kuznetsova, O., Kuznetsova, S., Yumaev, E., Kuznetsov, V., Galtseva, O. (2017). Formation and Development of the Training System for Innovative Development of Regional Industry. E3S Web of Conferences, 15,04019.

Li, X., Subrahmanyam, A., Yang, X. (2018). Can financial innovation succeed by catering to behavioral preferences? Evidence from a callable options market. Journal of Financial Economics, 2(1), p. 34–42.

OECD (2020). Countries. URL: https://www.oecd.org/ (data accessed: 01.04.2020).

Petrenko, E.S., Shevyakova, A.L. (2019). Features and perspectives of digitization in Kazakhstan. Studies in Computational Intelligence, 826, p. 889–899.

Popkova, E.G. (2019). Preconditions of formation and development of industry 4.0 in the conditions of knowledge economy. Studies in Systems, Decision and Control, 169(1), 65–72.

Popkova, E.G., Sergi, B.S. (2020). Human Capital and AI in Industry 4.0. Convergence and Divergence in Social Entrepreneurship in Russia. Journal of Intellectual Capital, In press, 2020. https://doi.org/10.1108/JIC-09-2019-0224

Popkova, E.G., Egorova, E.N., Popova, E., Pozdnyakova, U.A. (2019). The model of state management of economy on the basis of the internet of things. Studies in Computational Intelligence, 826, pp. 1137–1144.

Popkova, E.G., Gulzat, K. (2020). Technological Revolution in the 21st Century: Digital Society vs. Artificial Intelligence. Lecture Notes in Networks and Systems, 91, p. 339–345.

Popkova, E.G., Parakhina, V.N. (2019). Managing the global financial system on the basis of artificial intelligence: possibilities and limitations. Lecture Notes in Networks and Systems, 57, pp. 939–946.

Popkova, E.G., Poluyufta, L., Beshanova, Y., Popova, L.V., Kolesnikova, E. (2017). Innovations as a basis for marketing strategies of Russian oil companies in the conditions of oil prices reduction. Contributions to Economics, (9783319606958), p. 449–455.

Popkova, E.G., Zmiyak, K.V. (2019). Priorities of training of digital personnel for industry 4.0: social competencies vs technical competencies. On the Horizon, 27(3–4), p. 138–144.

Popkova, E.G., Sergi, B.S. (2018). Will Industry 4.0 and Other Innovations Impact Russia's Development? In Bruno S. Sergi (Ed.) Exploring the Future of Russia's Economy and Markets: Towards Sustainable Economic Development (pp. 51–68). Bingley, UK: Emerald Publishing Limited.

Popkova, E.G., Sergi, B.S. (Eds.) (2019). Digital Economy: Complexity and Variety vs. Rationality. Berlin: Springer International Publishing.

Ragulina, Y.V. (2019). Priorities of development of industry 4.0 in modern economic systems with different progress in formation of knowledge economy. Studies in Systems, Decision and Control, 169, p. 167–174.

Ragulina, Y.V., Alekseev, A.N., Strizhkina, I.V., Tumanov, A.I. (2019). Methodology of criterial evaluation of consequences of the industrial revolution of the 21st century. Studies in Systems, Decision and Control, 169, p. 235–244.

Ramanathan, R., Ramanathan, U., Bentley, Y. (2018). The debate on flexibility of environmental regulations, innovation capabilities and financial performance – A novel use of DEA. Omega (United Kingdom), 75, p. 131–138.

Sergi, B.S. (2003). Economic Dynamics in Transitional Economies: The Four-P Governments, the EU Enlargement, and the Bruxelles Consensus. New York: Routledge.

Sergi, B.S. (Ed.) (2019). Tech, Smart Cities, and Regional Development in Contemporary Russia. Bingley, UK: Emerald Publishing Limited.

Sergi, B.S., Popkova, E.G. Bogoviz, A.V., Ragulina Y.V. (2019a). The Agro-industrial Complex: Tendencies, Scenarios, and Regulation. In Sergi, Bruno S. (Ed.) Modeling Economic Growth in Contemporary Russia (pp. 233–247). Bingley, UK: Emerald Publishing Limited.

Sergi, B.S., Popkova, E.G., Bogoviz, A.V., Litvinova, T.N. (2019b). Understanding Industry 4.0: AI, the Internet of Things, and the Future of Work. Bingley, UK: Emerald Publishing Limited.

Shulus, A.A., Akopova, E.S., Przhedetskaya, N.V., Borzenko, K.V. (2020). Intellectual Production and Consumption: A New Reality of the 21st Century. Lecture Notes in Networks and Systems, 92, pp. 353–359.

Stolyarov, N.O., Petrenko, E.S., Serova, O.A., Umuralieva, A.S. (2020). The Digital Reality of the Modern Economy: New Actors and New Decision-Making Logic. Lecture Notes in Networks and Systems, 87, p. 882–888.

World Bank (2020). Indicators. URL: https://data.worldbank.org/indicator (data accessed: 01.04.2020).

Yao, M., Di, H., Zheng, X., Xu, X. (2018). Impact of payment technology innovations on the traditional financial industry: A focus on China. Technological Forecasting and Social Change, 2(1), p. 22–29.

Zavyalova, E.B. Studenikin, N.V. Starikova, E.A. (2018). Business participation in implementation of socially oriented Sustainable Development Goals in countries of Central Asia and the Caucasus region. Central Asia and the Caucasus, 19(2), p. 56–63.

Elena N. Rudakova, Maria V. Zaytseva, Svetlana V. Belyaeva,
Natalia G. Adamchuk and Elena A. Gubareva

12 The Economic and Legal Specifics of Managing the Modern Economic Systems' Innovative Development in Developing Countries

Introduction

Developing countries require innovative development, as it is the basis of the mechanism of overcoming their underrun from developed countries. Innovative activities in developing countries are considered as a method of increasing population's quality of life, but the most important mission of innovations in these countries is acceleration of the rate of economic growth. Quick growth of economy is a specific feature and the key priority of developing countries.

Innovations allow creating and entering new markets, which were inaccessible due to technological barriers, conducting networkization, and gaining effect from the scale. Significance of innovations is so high for developed countries that they are implemented despite the possible undesirable ecological consequences. It is necessary to study the experience of innovative development of developing countries for reconsidering it and finding the methods of its optimization, which allow for harmonization of the interests of acceleration of economic growth with the interests of social development and environment protection.

However, this is a complex scientific and practical problem, as developing countries are too differentiated. They are located in all geographical regions of the world, unlike developed countries – which are concentrated mainly in Western Europe and North America. Developing countries actively form the integration unions, one of which is the EAEU, but integration processes are unequal in the structure of developing countries, which complicates their study. Also, there are

Elena N. Rudakova, Stolypin International Institute of Informatization and Public Administration, Moscow, Russia, Moscow Region State University, Mytishchi, Russia
Maria V. Zaytseva, "Kuban State Agrarian University named after I.T. Trubilin", Krasnodar, Russia
Svetlana V. Belyaeva, Plekhanov Russian University of Economics, Pyatigorsk Branch, Pyatigorsk, Russia
Natalia G. Adamchuk, "Moscow State Institute of International Relations (University) of the Ministry of Foreign Affairs Russian Federation", Moscow, Russia
Elena A. Gubareva, State University of Management, Moscow, Russia

https://doi.org/10.1515/9783110643701-012

quickly developing countries (BRICS), new industrial powers, and underdeveloped countries – though their list constantly changes.

The purpose of this chapter is to study the economic & legal specifics and to model the management of modern economic systems' innovative development in developing countries.

Materials and Method

Foundations of modern economic systems' innovative development are set in the works Andronova et al. (2019), Bogoviz and Ragulina (2020), Petrenko and Shevyakova (2019), Popkova (2019), Popkova and Sergi (2020), Popkova et al. (2019), Popkova and Gulzat (2020), Popkova and Parakhina (2019), Popkova et al. (2017), Popkova and Zmiyak (2019), Popkova and Sergi (2018), Popkova and Sergi (2019), Ragulina (2019), Ragulina et al. (2019), Sergi (2003), Sergi (2019), Sergi et al. (2019a), Sergi et al. (2019b), Shulus et al. (2020), Stolyarov et al. (2020), and Zavyalova et al. (2018).

Specific features of modern economic systems' innovative development in developing countries are studied in the works Atkinsonk and Ezell (2012), García-Quevedo et al. (2018), Gumba and Vlasenko (2017), Haabazoka (2019), Harfst et al. (2017), Kuznetsova et al. (2017), Li et al. (2018), Ramanathan et al. (2018), and Yao et al. (2018). At the same time, the managerial aspect of modern economic systems' innovative development in developing countries requires further scientific elaboration.

For overcoming this gap in the existing research literature, we study the experience of the economic & legal of modern economic systems' innovative development in developing countries with the help of correlation analysis. The research objects are countries from each category of developing countries, distinguished by the economic & geographical principle of the International Monetary Fund (2020). Similarly to the research of developed countries, which was performed in the previous chapter, experience of developing countries is studied through the prism of factors, results, and consequences of innovative development. The statistical basis as of early 2020 is given in Table 12.1.

Results

As a result of processing the data from Table 12.1 with the help of correlation analysis, the following diagrams have been built (Figure 12.1–12.3).

As is show in Figure 12.1, the key – but moderately influencing – factor of innovative development of developed countries is R&D expenditures (correlation – 80.59%). On the whole, innovative development in developing countries could be characterized as spontaneous and with low dependence of the factors that are subject to state

Table 12.1: Factors, results, and consequences of innovative development of developing countries in 2020.

Category	Country	Global Innovation Index, points 1–100	Digital Competitiveness Index, points 1–100	Global Competitiveness Index 4.0, points 1–100	Human Development Index, shares of 1	Rate of economic growth, %	Quality of Life Index, points 1–200	Happiness Index, points 1–10	Sustainable Development Index, points 1–100	R&D expenditures, % of GDP	Hi-tech export, % of industrial export	Mid-tech and hi-tech industry, % of industrial added value	GDP per capita, USD
Commonwealth of Independent States	Russia	37.62	70.406	66.7	0.824	1.500	104.05	5.648	70.9	1.11	11	30	11980.732
	Kazakhstan	31.03	72.623	62.9	0.817	3.210	85.88	5.809	68.7	0.12	22	13	10742.541
Emerging and developing Asia	China	54.82	84.292	73.9	0.758	5.900	99.87	5.191	73.2	2.15	31	41	10643.692
	India	36.58	64.952	61.4	0.647	7.921	115.41	4.015	61.1	0.60	9	43	2357.693
Emerging and developing Europe	Romania	36.76	62.755	64.4	0.816	3.300	135.71	6.070	72.7	0.50	10	44	11966.205
	Serbia	35.71	n/a	60.9	0.799	4.000	117.70	5.603	72.5	0.92	5	27	6579.358
Latin America and the Caribbean	Brazil	33.82	57.346	60.9	0.761	2.000	103.87	6.300	70.6	1.26	13	35	11538.307
	Peru	32.93	54.029	61.7	0.759	3.709	88.14	5.697	71.2	0.13	5	15	7476.934
Middle East, North Africa	Tunisia	32.83	n/a	56.4	0.739	4.200	n/a	4.461	70.0	0.60	7	29	3864.295
	UAE*	42.17	90.295	75.0	0.866	3.451	158.32	6.825	69.7	1.30	14	36	43759.798
Sub-Saharan Africa	Rwanda	27.38	n/a	52.8	0.536	7.500	n/a	3.334	56.0	0.67	13	7	832.511
	Zambia	20.36	n/a	46.5	0.591	4.546	n/a	4.107	52.6	0.28	2	10	1490.294

* UAE – United Arab Emirates.

Source: compiled by the authors based on Institute of Scientific Communications (2020), World Bank (2020).

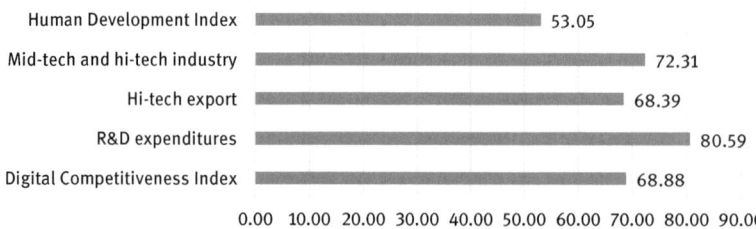

Figure 12.1: Correlation of the Global Innovation Index with the factors of innovative development in developing countries 2020, %.
Source: calculated and compiled by the authors.

management. Also, in order of significance: mid-tech and hi-tech industry (correlation – 72.31%), Digital Competitiveness Index (correlation – 68.88%), and hi-tech export (correlation – 68.39%). The least significant factor is the Human Development Index (correlation 53.05%).

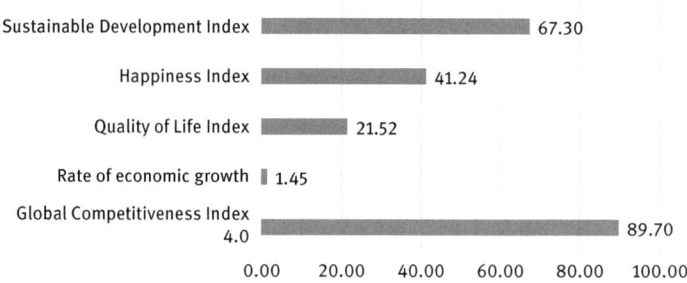

Figure 12.2: Correlation of the Global Innovation Index with the consequences of innovative development of developing countries in 2020, %.
Source: calculated and compiled by the authors.

As is shown in Figure 12.2, the most important consequence of innovative development in developing countries is growth of the Global Competitiveness Index 4.0 (correlation – 89.70%). A moderately significant consequence is growth of the Sustainable Development Index (correlation – 67.30%). Positive influence on the happiness index (correlation – 41.24%), the Quality of Life Index (correlation – 21.52%), and the rate of economic growth (correlation – 1.45%) is very low.

As shown in Figure 12.3, variation of GDP per capita among developing countries is rather high and exceeds 50% in a lot of regions of the world. Correlation of variation of GDP per capita with average value of the Global Innovation Index in the distinguished categories of developing countries is moderate – 53.43%.

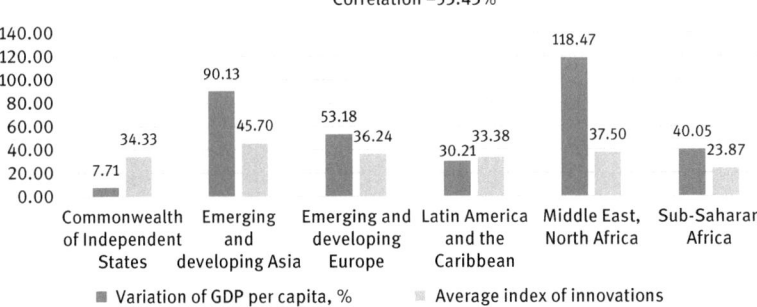

Figure 12.3: Correlation analysis of the consequences of innovative development for balance of developing countries in 2020, %.
Source: calculated and compiled by the authors.

Systematization of the obtained results allows compiling a model of economic & legal management of modern economic systems' innovative development in developing countries (Figure 12.4).

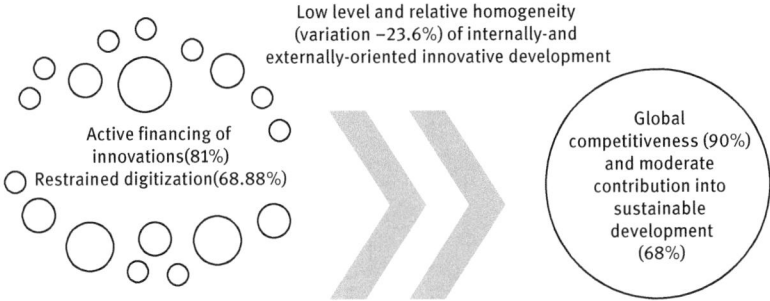

Figure 12.4: The model of economic & legal management of modern economic systems' innovative development in developing countries.
Source: developed and compiled by the authors.

The model in Figure 12.4 shows that during the economic & legal management of innovative development the modern developing countries use financial resources, while technological resources are not used very much, and human resources are barely used. They are rather homogeneous – variation of innovative development constitutes 23.6% – and allow for active export of innovations and hi-tech products. Innovative activities in developing countries allow strengthening their global competitiveness and slightly stimulate their sustainable development.

Conclusion

It should be concluded that experience of developing countries in the sphere of economic & legal management of innovative development differs a lot from experience of developed countries. On the one hand, this explains the remaining disproportions in the global economic system, and, on the other hand, opens a perspective for overcoming them, as developing countries do not conduct "rapid development" based on experience of developed countries, but have their own model of innovative activities. Firstly, the resource basis of developing countries is less diverse – they are based mainly on the financial resources (81%) and digital technologies (69%), while human resources are not that much used in the process of economic & legal management of innovative development.

Secondly, the results of innovative activities are diverse – innovations are used domestically and for export. Due to absence of foreign trade limitations, developing countries gain advantages from the globalization factor, which – paradox as it is – does not lead to loss of their competitive advantages, but, instead, stimulates the growth of their global competitiveness. Thirdly, contrary to the existing beliefs, innovative development of developing countries does not lead to negative consequences, which are observed in developed countries; instead of ecological and social costs it generates advantages for sustainable development. Thus, experience of developing countries is more successful and could be interesting for developed countries.

References

Andronova, I.V., Chernova, V.Y., Starostin, V.S., Degtereva (2019). Study of sector-specific innovation efforts: The case from Russian economy. Entrepreneurship and Sustainability Issues, VsI Entrepreneurship and Sustainability Center, 7(1), p. 540–552.

Atkinsonk, R.D., Ezell, S.J. (2012). Innovation Economics: the Race for Global Advantage, New Haven, CT: Yale University Press.

Bogoviz, A.V., Ragulina, Y.V. (2020). Industry competitiveness in the new economy. Lecture Notes in Networks and Systems, 115, p. v–vi.

García-Quevedo, J., Segarra-Blasco, A., Teruel, M. (2018). Financial constraints and the failure of innovation projects. Technological Forecasting and Social Change, 127, p. 127–140.

Gumba, H.M., Vlasenko, V.A. (2017). Strategy of development of innovative activity in industry and construction: The rationale of the regional dimension. Izvestiya Vysshikh Uchebnykh Zavedenii, Seriya Teknologiya Tekstil'noi Promyshlennosti, 2017-January(2), 2(1), p. 14–18.

Haabazoka, L. (2019). A Study of the Effects of Technological Innovations on the Performance of Commercial Banks in Developing Countries – A Case of the Zambian Banking Industry. In: Popkova E. (eds) The Future of the Global Financial System: Downfall or Harmony. ISC 2018. Lecture Notes in Networks and Systems, vol 57. Springer, Cham, Online ISBN 978-3-030-00102-5, https://doi.org/10.1007/978-3-030-00102-5_132

Harfst, J., Pichler, P., Fischer, W. (2017). Regional Ambassadors-An Innovative Element for the Development of Rural Areas? European Countryside, 9(2), p. 359–374.

Institute of Scientific Communications (2020). Data set "Big data of the modern world economy: digital platform for intelligent analytics – 2020". URL: https://www.archilab.online/en/data/sounting-data-set (data accessed: 02.04.2020).

International Monetary Fund (2020). World Economic Outlook Database. URL: https://www.imf.org/external/pubs/ft/weo/2017/01/weodata/weoselgr.aspx (data accessed: 02. 04.2020).

Kuznetsova, O., Kuznetsova, S., Yumaev, E., Kuznetsov, V., Galtseva, O. (2017). Formation and Development of the Training System for Innovative Development of Regional Industry. E3S Web of Conferences, 15,04019.

Li, X., Subrahmanyam, A., Yang, X. (2018). Can financial innovation succeed by catering to behavioral preferences? Evidence from a callable options market. Journal of Financial Economics, 2(1), p. 34–42.

Petrenko, E.S., Shevyakova, A.L. (2019). Features and perspectives of digitization in Kazakhstan. Studies in Computational Intelligence, 826, p. 889–899.

Popkova, E.G. (2019). Preconditions of formation and development of industry 4.0 in the conditions of knowledge economy. Studies in Systems, Decision and Control, 169(1), 65–72.

Popkova, E.G., Sergi, B.S. (2020). Human Capital and AI in Industry 4.0. Convergence and Divergence in Social Entrepreneurship in Russia. Journal of Intellectual Capital, In press, 2020. https://doi.org/10.1108/JIC-09-2019-0224

Popkova, E.G., Egorova, E.N., Popova, E., Pozdnyakova, U.A. (2019). The model of state management of economy on the basis of the internet of things. Studies in Computational Intelligence, 826, pp. 1137–1144.

Popkova, E.G., Gulzat, K. (2020). Technological Revolution in the 21st Century: Digital Society vs. Artificial Intelligence. Lecture Notes in Networks and Systems, 91, p. 339–345.

Popkova, E.G., Parakhina, V.N. (2019). Managing the global financial system on the basis of artificial intelligence: possibilities and limitations. Lecture Notes in Networks and Systems, 57, pp. 939–946.

Popkova, E.G., Poluyufta, L., Beshanova, Y., Popova, L.V., Kolesnikova, E. (2017). Innovations as a basis for marketing strategies of Russian oil companies in the conditions of oil prices reduction. Contributions to Economics, (9783319606958), p. 449–455.

Popkova, E.G., Zmiyak, K.V. (2019). Priorities of training of digital personnel for industry 4.0: social competencies vs technical competencies. On the Horizon, 27(3–4), p. 138–144.

Popkova, E.G., Sergi, B.S. (2018). Will Industry 4.0 and Other Innovations Impact Russia's Development? In Bruno S. Sergi (Ed.) Exploring the Future of Russia's Economy and Markets: Towards Sustainable Economic Development (pp. 51–68). Bingley, UK: Emerald Publishing Limited.

Popkova, E.G., Sergi, B.S. (Eds.) (2019). Digital Economy: Complexity and Variety vs. Rationality. Berlin: Springer International Publishing.

Ragulina, Y.V. (2019). Priorities of development of industry 4.0 in modern economic systems with different progress in formation of knowledge economy. Studies in Systems, Decision and Control, 169, p. 167–174.

Ragulina, Y.V., Alekseev, A.N., Strizhkina, I.V., Tumanov, A.I. (2019). Methodology of criterial evaluation of consequences of the industrial revolution of the 21st century. Studies in Systems, Decision and Control, 169, p. 235–244.

Ramanathan, R., Ramanathan, U., Bentley, Y. (2018). The debate on flexibility of environmental regulations, innovation capabilities and financial performance – A novel use of DEA. Omega (United Kingdom), 75, p. 131–138.

Sergi, B.S. (2003). Economic Dynamics in Transitional Economies: The Four-P Governments, the EU Enlargement, and the Bruxelles Consensus. New York: Routledge.

Sergi, B.S. (Ed.) (2019). Tech, Smart Cities, and Regional Development in Contemporary Russia. Bingley, UK: Emerald Publishing Limited.

Sergi, B.S., Popkova, E.G. Bogoviz, A.V., Ragulina Y.V. (2019a). The Agro-industrial Complex: Tendencies, Scenarios, and Regulation. In Sergi, Bruno S. (Ed.) Modeling Economic Growth in Contemporary Russia (pp. 233–247). Bingley, UK: Emerald Publishing Limited.

Sergi, B.S., Popkova, E.G., Bogoviz, A.V., Litvinova, T.N. (2019b). Understanding Industry 4.0: AI, the Internet of Things, and the Future of Work. Bingley, UK: Emerald Publishing Limited.

Shulus, A.A., Akopova, E.S., Przhedetskaya, N.V., Borzenko, K.V. (2020). Intellectual Production and Consumption: A New Reality of the 21st Century. Lecture Notes in Networks and Systems, 92, pp. 353–359.

Stolyarov, N.O., Petrenko, E.S., Serova, O.A., Umuralieva, A.S. (2020). The Digital Reality of the Modern Economy: New Actors and New Decision-Making Logic. Lecture Notes in Networks and Systems, 87, p. 882–888.

World Bank (2020). Indicators. URL: https://data.worldbank.org/indicator (data accessed: 02.04.2020).

Yao, M., Di, H., Zheng, X., Xu, X. (2018). Impact of payment technology innovations on the traditional financial industry: A focus on China. Technological Forecasting and Social Change, 2(1), p. 22–29.

Zavyalova, E.B. Studenikin, N.V. Starikova, E.A. (2018). Business participation in implementation of socially oriented Sustainable Development Goals in countries of Central Asia and the Caucasus region. Central Asia and the Caucasus, 19(2), p. 56–63.

Murat A. Bulgarov, Dmitry A. Pashentsev, Mikhail Y. Zakharov,
Denis G. Korovyakovskiy and Sergey K. Kleschev
13 Specifics of Economic and Legal Management of Modern Russia's Economic System's Innovative Development

Introduction

Russia is very interesting for studying innovative development of the modern economic systems due to two reasons. The first reason is the unique international status of Russia due to uncertainty of its position in the system of classification in the modern economic systems. According to the criterion of influence on the global economic processes, Russia is one of the leading economic states of the world, exceeding the OECD countries (e.g., Mexico and Chile) by the indicators of socio-economic development. However, according to the criterion of quick rate of economic growth and due to incompletion of the transitional period of market reformation of economy, Russia is assigned to the category of developing countries – subcategory of the most progressive countries – BRICS.

The second reason consists in the specifics of the organizational & managerial model of state regulation of Russia's socio-economic system. Despite the development of the market relations in most of the commodity markets and markets of production factors, the action of the mechanism of competition in Russia is limited by the institutional gaps. Economic policy of the state is much differentiated and varies in the context of fluctuations of the Russia's economic cycle of transition from liberalism and free trading to planning and protectionism. On the one hand, atypicality of the regulatory practices makes the typical experience of other developed and developed countries inapplicable in Russia – but, on the other hand, the Russian experience is of high interest and could be used in a lot of other countries of the world from both categories.

Murat A. Bulgarov, "Kuban State Agrarian University named after I.T. Trubilin", Krasnodar, Russia
Dmitry A. Pashentsev, The Institute of Legislation and Comparative Law under the Government of the Russian Federation, Moscow, Russia
Mikhail Y. Zakharov, State University of Management, Moscow, Russia
Denis G. Korovyakovskiy, "Moscow State Institute of International Relations (University) of the Ministry of Foreign Affairs Russian Federation", Moscow, Russia
Sergey K. Kleschev, Russian University of Cooperation, Moscow, Russia

https://doi.org/10.1515/9783110643701-013

Thus, an important scientific & practical problem is studying the specifics of the economic & legal management of modern Russia's economic system's innovative development, which predetermines the goal of this chapter – modeling the Russian practice of this management.

Materials and Method

Experience of economic & legal management of innovative development in developing countries is studied in the works Atkinsonk and Ezell (2012), García-Quevedo et al. (2018), Gumba and Vlasenko (2017), Haabazoka (2019), Harfst et al. (2017), Kuznetsova et al. (2017), Li et al. (2018), Ramanathan et al. (2018), and Yao et al. (2018). The Russian practice of innovative development is considered in the works Andronova et al. (2019), Bogoviz and Ragulina (2020), Petrenko and Shevyakova (2019), Popkova (2019), Popkova and Sergi (2020), Popkova et al. (2019), Popkova and Gulzat (2020), Popkova and Parakhina (2019), Popkova et al. (2017), Popkova and Zmiyak (2019), Popkova and Sergi (2018), Popkova and Sergi (2019), Ragulina (2019), Ragulina et al. (2019), Sergi (2003), Sergi (2019), Sergi et al. (2019a), Sergi et al. (2019b), Shulus et al. (2020), Stolyarov et al. (2020), and Zavyalova et al. (2018).

However, the economic & legal issues of economic & legal management of modern Russia's economic system's innovative development are poorly studies and require further independent research. The source of empirical data for this research is Data Set "Interactive Statistics and Intelligent Analytics of the Balanced State of the Regional Economy of Russia in Terms of Big Data and Blockchain – 2020" of the Institute of Scientific Communications. It contains the current statistics of the Russian regional economy (in Russian and English). The data are shown in Table 13.1.

Processing and analysis of the statistical data are performed with the help of variation analysis and correlation analysis – similarly to the previous chapters. Correlation of the potential factors and consequences with the key indicators of the results of economic & legal management of innovative development of Russia's economic system in 2020 – the share of innovative products and share of innovations-active organizations is found.

Results

As a result of complex analysis of the statistical data on the topic of innovative development of the modern Russia's economy, the following results have been obtained (Figures 13.1 and 13.2, Table 13.1).

Table 13.1: Factors, results, and consequences of economic & legal management of innovative development of Russia's economic system in 2020.

Federal District	Share of innovative products, %	Share of innovations-active organizations, %	Level of digitization, points 1–100	Investments in fixed capital per capita, RUB	Balance of regional budget, RUB million	Level of population's employment, %	Balanced financial result of companies' activities, RUB million
Central Federal District	6.70	8.77	47.70	141,030.41	−582,368.93	69.00	872,305.21
Far Eastern Federal District	4.51	6.40	44.66	277,016.68	−44,255.90	68.45	37,093.91
North Caucasus Federal District	4.35	4.27	33.80	56,245.07	26,172.15	58.30	12,559.31
Northwestern Federal District	11.97	9.64	49.66	164,767.83	−142,812.18	68.10	1,610,539.77
Siberian Federal District	1.90	8.68	42.14	91,495.58	125,973.03	60.28	1,310,938.84
South Federal District	11.04	13.84	45.23	150,537.69	152,547.64	63.00	213,120.78
Ural Federal District	8.56	8.20	57.69	283,508.69	64,429.09	65.40	1,031,931.63
Volga Federal District	11.09	8.29	47.48	79,226.23	106,381.85	63.03	6,185.50

Source: compiled by the authors based on Institute of Scientific Communications (2020).

As is shown in Figure 13.1, digitization shows moderate correlation with share of innovative products (53.16%) and share of innovations-active organizations (38.8%). At the same time, investments in fixed capital show low correlation with the both resulting indicators: 9.18% and 6.77%, accordingly.

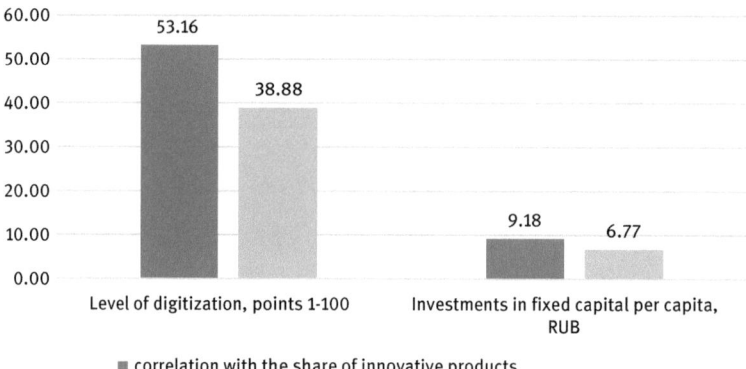

Figure 13.1: Factors of economic & legal management of innovative development of Russia's economic system in 2020 – correlation, %.
Source: calculated and compiled by the authors.

As shown in Figure 13.2, level of population's employment has moderate correlation with share of innovative products (33.02%) and share of innovations-active organizations (19.12%). Balanced financial result of companies' activities shows moderate correlation with share of innovations-active organizations (23.75%), and correlation of balance of regional budget with the both resulting variables is very small.

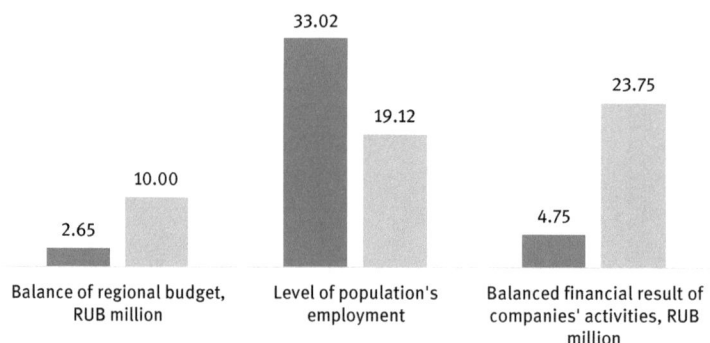

Figure 13.2: The consequences of economic & legal management of innovative development of Russia's economic system in 2020 – correlation, %.
Source: calculated and compiled by the authors.

Table 13.2: Analysis of variation of GDP per capita and results of innovative development of the Russian economic system in 2020.

Indicator	Year	Federal District								Variation, %
		Central	Far Eastern	North Caucasus	Northwestern	Siberian	Southern	Ural	Volga	
Share of innovative products, %	2016	11.6	3.1	6.4	5.1	3.5	8.4	4.4	14.1	56.46
	2017	6.9	3.4	5.8	6.3	3	9	5.2	13.3	50.04
	2018	6.83	3.73	5.26	7.78	2.57	9.64	6.15	12.55	47.13
	2019	6.76	4.1	4.78	9.65	2.21	10.32	7.25	11.79	46.75
	2020	6.7	4.51	4.35	11.97	1.9	11.04	8.56	11.09	49.63
Share of innovations-active organizations, %	2016	10.3	6.4	2.9	8.3	6.9	7.1	8.2	9.4	30.25
	2017	9.9	6.4	3.2	8.6	7.3	8.4	8.2	9.1	27.29
	2018	9.52	6.4	3.53	8.91	7.72	9.94	8.2	8.81	26.32
	2019	9.13	6.4	3.88	9.27	8.19	11.73	8.2	8.55	27.95
	2020	8.77	6.4	4.27	9.64	8.68	13.84	8.2	8.29	32.13
GDP per capita, RUB	2016	616,366	607,004	184,466	562,372	369,150	298,586	758,885	349,885	41.75
	2017	661,535	661,811	196,942	639,081	399,195	320,268	812,674	373,281	42.03
	2018	710,014	721,566	210,262	726,253	431,684	343,524	870,276	398,242	42.46
	2019	762,045	786,716	224,483	825,316	466,818	368,470	931,961	424,872	43.04
	2020	817,890	857,748	239,665	937,892	504,811	395,226	998,018	453,283	43.80

Source: calculated and compiled by the authors based on Institute of Scientific Communications (2020).

The performed correlation analysis (based on the materials of Table 13.2) shows that variation of GDP per capita deceases in the course of increase of share of innovative products (correlation −54.41%), but grows in the course of increase of share of innovations-active organizations (correlation − 46.45%). Based on the obtained results, a model of economic & legal management of modern Russia's economic system's innovative development is compiled (Figure 13.3).

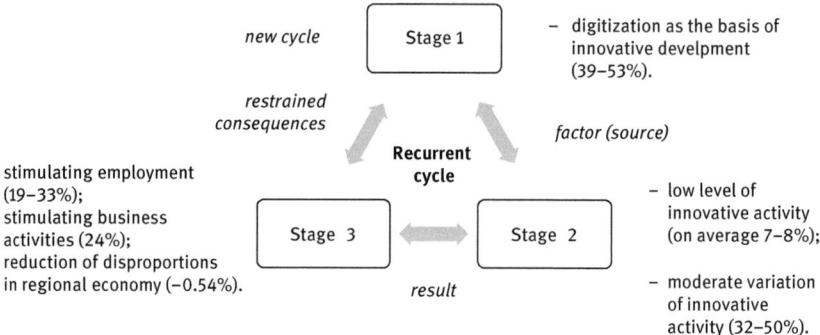

Figure 13.3: The model of economic & legal management of modern Russia's economic system's innovative development.
Source: developed and compiled by the authors.

As shown in Figure 13.3, the process of economic & legal management of modern Russia's economic system's innovative development is cyclical. The first stage envisages digitization, which is the basis of innovative development. It is the factor (source) of innovative results. The general level of innovative activity in the Russian economy is low, but this activity is well-balanced – variation between federal districts is low. The results of innovative development cause positive consequences: stimulate population's employment, stimulate business activity, and reduce disproportions in the regional economy. This ensures socio-economic progress and gives an impulse for the next wave of digitization, with the repeating cycle.

Conclusion

Thus, specifics of economic & legal management of modern Russia's economic system's innovative development consist, firstly, in deficit of financing and foundation on the non-financial factor – digitization. Secondly, in moderate efficiency, but vivid positive consequences for the labor market and balance of the regional economy. The compiled model of economic & legal management of modern Russia's economic system's innovative development shows the cyclic character of this process. This proves that innovative development in Russia is natural and harmonizes with the general socio-economic development, being capable of self-reproduction. This makes Russia's experience in economic & legal management of innovative development attractive for other modern economic systems.

References

Andronova, I.V., Chernova, V.Y., Starostin, V.S., Degtereva (2019). Study of sector-specific innovation efforts: The case from Russian economy. Entrepreneurship and Sustainability Issues, VsI Entrepreneurship and Sustainability Center, 7(1), p. 540–552.

Atkinsonk, R.D., Ezell, S.J. (2012). *Innovation Economics: the Race for Global Advantage*, New Haven, CT: Yale University Press.

Bogoviz, A.V., Ragulina, Y.V. (2020). Industry competitiveness in the new economy. Lecture Notes in Networks and Systems, 115, p. v–vi.

García-Quevedo, J., Segarra-Blasco, A., Teruel, M. (2018). Financial constraints and the failure of innovation projects. Technological Forecasting and Social Change, 127, p. 127–140.

Gumba, H.M., Vlasenko, V.A. (2017). Strategy of development of innovative activity in industry and construction: The rationale of the regional dimension. Izvestiya Vysshikh Uchebnykh Zavedenii, Seriya Teknologiya Tekstil'noi Promyshlennosti, 2017-January(2), 2(1), p. 14–18.

Haabazoka, L. (2019). A Study of the Effects of Technological Innovations on the Performance of Commercial Banks in Developing Countries – A Case of the Zambian Banking Industry. In: Popkova E. (eds) The Future of the Global Financial System: Downfall or Harmony. ISC 2018. Lecture Notes in Networks and Systems, vol 57. Springer, Cham, Online ISBN 978-3-030-00102-5, https://doi.org/10.1007/978-3-030-00102-5_132

Harfst, J., Pichler, P., Fischer, W. (2017). Regional Ambassadors-An Innovative Element for the Development of Rural Areas? European Countryside, 9(2), p. 359–374.

Institute of Scientific Communications (2020). Data Set "Interactive Statistics and Intelligent Analytics of the Balanced State of the Regional Economy of Russia in Terms of Big Data and Blockchain – 2020". URL: http://archilab.online/en/data/date-set-on-the-regional-economy (data accessed: 03.04.2020).

Kuznetsova, O., Kuznetsova, S., Yumaev, E., Kuznetsov, V., Galtseva, O. (2017). Formation and Development of the Training System for Innovative Development of Regional Industry. E3S Web of Conferences, 15,04019.

Li, X., Subrahmanyam, A., Yang, X. (2018). Can financial innovation succeed by catering to behavioral preferences? Evidence from a callable options market. Journal of Financial Economics, 2(1), p. 34–42.

Petrenko, E.S., Shevyakova, A.L. (2019). Features and perspectives of digitization in Kazakhstan. Studies in Computational Intelligence, 826, p. 889–899.

Popkova, E.G. (2019). Preconditions of formation and development of industry 4.0 in the conditions of knowledge economy. Studies in Systems, Decision and Control, 169(1), 65–72.

Popkova, E.G., Sergi, B.S. (2020). Human Capital and AI in Industry 4.0. Convergence and Divergence in Social Entrepreneurship in Russia. Journal of Intellectual Capital, In press, 2020. https://doi.org/10.1108/JIC-09-2019-0224

Popkova, E.G., Egorova, E.N., Popova, E., Pozdnyakova, U.A. (2019). The model of state management of economy on the basis of the internet of things. Studies in Computational Intelligence, 826, pp. 1137–1144.

Popkova, E.G., Gulzat, K. (2020). Technological Revolution in the 21st Century: Digital Society vs. Artificial Intelligence. Lecture Notes in Networks and Systems, 91, p. 339–345.

Popkova, E.G., Parakhina, V.N. (2019). Managing the global financial system on the basis of artificial intelligence: possibilities and limitations. Lecture Notes in Networks and Systems, 57, pp. 939–946.

Popkova, E.G., Poluyufta, L., Beshanova, Y., Popova, L.V., Kolesnikova, E. (2017). Innovations as a basis for marketing strategies of Russian oil companies in the conditions of oil prices reduction. Contributions to Economics, (9783319606958), p. 449–455.

Popkova, E.G., Zmiyak, K.V. (2019). Priorities of training of digital personnel for industry 4.0: social competencies vs technical competencies. On the Horizon, 27(3–4), p. 138–144.

Popkova, E.G., Sergi, B.S. (2018). Will Industry 4.0 and Other Innovations Impact Russia's Development? In Bruno S. Sergi (Ed.) Exploring the Future of Russia's Economy and Markets: Towards Sustainable Economic Development (pp. 51–68). Bingley, UK: Emerald Publishing Limited.

Popkova, E.G., Sergi, B.S. (Eds.) (2019). Digital Economy: Complexity and Variety vs. Rationality. Berlin: Springer International Publishing.

Ragulina, Y.V. (2019). Priorities of development of industry 4.0 in modern economic systems with different progress in formation of knowledge economy. Studies in Systems, Decision and Control, 169, p. 167–174.

Ragulina, Y.V., Alekseev, A.N., Strizhkina, I.V., Tumanov, A.I. (2019). Methodology of criterial evaluation of consequences of the industrial revolution of the 21st century. Studies in Systems, Decision and Control, 169, p. 235–244.

Ramanathan, R., Ramanathan, U., Bentley, Y. (2018). The debate on flexibility of environmental regulations, innovation capabilities and financial performance – A novel use of DEA. Omega (United Kingdom), 75, p. 131–138.

Sergi, B.S. (2003). Economic Dynamics in Transitional Economies: The Four-P Governments, the EU Enlargement, and the Bruxelles Consensus. New York: Routledge.

Sergi, B.S. (Ed.) (2019). Tech, Smart Cities, and Regional Development in Contemporary Russia. Bingley, UK: Emerald Publishing Limited.

Sergi, B.S., Popkova, E.G. Bogoviz, A.V., Ragulina Y.V. (2019a). The Agro-industrial Complex: Tendencies, Scenarios, and Regulation. In Sergi, Bruno S. (Ed.) Modeling Economic Growth in Contemporary Russia (pp. 233–247). Bingley, UK: Emerald Publishing Limited.

Sergi, B.S., Popkova, E.G., Bogoviz, A.V., Litvinova, T.N. (2019b). Understanding Industry 4.0: AI, the Internet of Things, and the Future of Work. Bingley, UK: Emerald Publishing Limited.

Shulus, A.A., Akopova, E.S., Przhedetskaya, N.V., Borzenko, K.V. (2020). Intellectual Production and Consumption: A New Reality of the 21st Century. Lecture Notes in Networks and Systems, 92, pp. 353–359.

Stolyarov, N.O., Petrenko, E.S., Serova, O.A., Umuralieva, A.S. (2020). The Digital Reality of the Modern Economy: New Actors and New Decision-Making Logic. Lecture Notes in Networks and Systems, 87, p. 882–888.

Yao, M., Di, H., Zheng, X., Xu, X. (2018). Impact of payment technology innovations on the traditional financial industry: A focus on China. Technological Forecasting and Social Change, 2(1), p. 22–29.

Zavyalova, E.B. Studenikin, N.V. Starikova, E.A. (2018). Business participation in implementation of socially oriented Sustainable Development Goals in countries of Central Asia and the Caucasus region. Central Asia and the Caucasus, 19(2), p. 56–63.

Part V: **The Current Economic and Legal Problems
of Managing Economic Systems' Innovative
Development**

Liubov I. Soldatova, Anna A. Skomoroshchenko,
Andrey S. Zhurakhovskiy, Aleksandra V. Zakharova
and Sergei B. Chernov

14 Economic and Legal Gaps in Managing Modern Economic Systems' Innovative Development

Introduction

For improving the management of innovative development of the modern economic systems, it is necessary to determine its economic & legal gaps. This is reflected is periodic reconsideration of innovative activities in certain spheres and management of innovations in corporate structures. While certain managerial practices are critically analyzed, a systemic vision of the structure of innovative process in the modern economic systems is absent, which does not allow determining the general perspectives of optimization of economic & legal management of innovative development of the modern economic systems, which are connected to bringing this management in accordance with the modern challenges.

One of them is globalization, which opens diverse opportunities for international cooperation in the sphere of innovations and global sale of innovative products; however, this requires consideration of the global consequences of innovative activities. Another challenge is sustainable development. Innovations should be oriented at solving the current social and ecological problems, not causing negative consequences for society and environment.

The modern challenges include technological progress (digitization). Digital technologies allow raising the efficiency of innovative activities, also being an independent object of innovative activities. The challenges also include economic security. New technologies and innovative products should be safer for the current use and also in the long-term at the global scale.

The purpose of this chapter is to form a systemic vision of economic & legal gaps in managing the innovative development the modern economic systems by determining this management's correspondence to the modern challenges.

Liubov I. Soldatova, Federal State Budgetary Educational Institution of Higher Education "Kostroma State Agricultural Academy", Karavaevo, Russia
Anna A. Skomoroshchenko, "Kuban State Agrarian University named after I.T. Trubilin", Krasnodar, Russia
Andrey S. Zhurakhovskiy, Institute of World Civilizations, Russia
Aleksandra V. Zakharova, Sergei B. Chernov, State University of Management, Moscow, Russia

https://doi.org/10.1515/9783110643701-014

Materials and Method

Imperfection of economic & legal management of innovative development of the modern economic systems is noted by Atkinsonk and Ezell (2012), García-Quevedo et al. (2018), Gumba and Vlasenko (2017), Haabazoka (2019), Harfst et al. (2017), Kuznetsova et al. (2017), Li et al. (2018), Ramanathan et al. (2018), and Yao et al. (2018).

Drawbacks of economic & legal management of innovative development of the modern economic systems by the example of countries, spheres, and companies are given in Andronova et al. (2019), Bogoviz and Ragulina (2020), Petrenko and Shevyakova (2019), Popkova (2019), Popkova and Sergi (2020), Popkova et al. (2019), Popkova and Gulzat (2020), Popkova and Parakhina (2019), Popkova et al. (2017), Popkova and Zmiyak (2019), Popkova and Sergi (2018), Popkova and Sergi (2019), Ragulina (2019), Ragulina et al. (2019), Sergi (2003), Sergi (2019), Sergi et al. (2019a), Sergi et al. (2019b), Shulus et al. (2020), Stolyarov et al. (2020), and Zavyalova et al. (2018).

Despite the large number of publications on this topic, a systemic vision of economic & legal gaps in managing the innovative development of the modern economic systems has not been formed, which requires further complex study of their correspondence to the modern challenges.

For obtaining the fullest, most precise, and most correct results, a qualitative evaluation is performed – it is aimed at determining the signs of mismatch between managing the innovative development and the requirements of each challenge at each stages; qualitative evaluation is combined with quantitative evaluation of each stage's correspondence to each modern challenge. Points are assigned with the help of expert evaluation in the interval 1 (full mismatch) – 10 (full correspondence).

Results

The results of isolated qualitative & quantitative evaluation of the correspondence of economic & legal management of modern economic systems' innovative development to the requirements of different modern challenges in view of the stages of this process are shown in Tables 14.1–14.4.

As shown in Table 14.1, the stage of determining the need for innovations envisages consideration of the narrow segment of the global market and limited marketing mix (stage 1–9 points). At the stage of R&D, international cooperation during R&D is complicated due to the economic & legal barriers (stage 2–6 points). At the stage of registration of rights for innovations, registration of global patents is complicated, and rights for intellectual property are not fully protected at the global level (stage 3–3 points). During commercialization of innovations, the signs of mismatch between management of innovative development and the requirements of

Table 14.1: Qualitative signs of mismatch between economic & legal management of modern economic systems' innovative development and the requirements of globalization in view of the stages of this process.

Stages of innovative development		Signs of mismatch between management of innovative development and the requirements of globalization at each stage	Score
1. Determining the need for innovations		consideration of demand in the narrow segment of the global market, limited marketing mix	9
2. R&D		international cooperation during R&D is complicated due to economic & legal barriers	6
3. Registration of rights for innovations		registration of global patents is complicated, rights for intellectual property are not fully protected at the global level	3
Commercialization of innovations	4. Implementation of innovations, manufacture of innovative products	complexity of organization and management of the network transnational business, high requirements of national governments	7
	5. Realization of innovative products and consumption	customs barriers, complexity of global promotion of innovations	2

Source: developed and compiled by the authors.

globalization is complexity of organization and management of network transnational business, high requirements of national governments (stage 4–7 points), customs barriers, and complexity of global promotion of innovations (stage 5–2 points).

As shown in Table 14.2, at the stage of determination of the need for innovations, the sustainable development goals in a lot of countries belong to the "soft law" (stage 1–7 points). At the stage of R&D there is deficit of "green" and social investments in R&D (stage 2–8 points). At the stage of registration of rights for innovations we see the absence of certain requirements and opportunities for consideration of innovations for sustainable development in the international patent law (stage 3–5 points). During commercialization of innovations, the signs of mismatch between management of innovative development and the requirements of globalization are uncontrollability of corporate social and ecological responsibility (stage 4–9 points); also, the practices of responsible distribution and consumption are at the early stages of institutionalization (stage 5–3 points).

As shown in Table 14.3, at the stage of determination of the need for innovations, digital marketing is complicated by infrastructural barriers (stage 1–8 points).

Table 14.2: Qualitative signs of mismatch between economic & legal management of modern economic systems' innovative development and the requirements of sustainable development in view of the stages of this process.

Stages of innovative development		Signs of mismatch between management of innovative development and the requirements of sustainable development at each stage	Score
1. Determining the need for innovations		goals of sustainable development in a lot of countries belong to "soft law"	7
2. R&D		deficit of "green" and social investments in R&D	8
3. Registration of rights for innovations		absence of separate requirements and opportunities for consideration of consequences of innovations for sustainable development in the international patent law	5
Commercialization of innovations	4. Implementation of innovations, manufacture of innovative products	uncontrollability of corporate social and ecological responsibility	9
	5. Realization of innovative products and consumption	practices of responsible distribution and consumption are at the early stages of institutionalization	3

Source: developed and compiled by the authors.

At the stage of R&D, there are license barriers for digitization of science and the deficit of investments in digital science (stage 2–5 points). At the stage of registration of rights for innovations, online registration of rights is not envisaged by international law (stage 3–2 points). During commercialization of innovations, the signs of mismatch between management of innovative development and the requirements of globalization is deficit of investments in "smart" productions, underdevelopment of their legal field (stage 4–4 points), and digital society's being at the early stage of institutionalization (stage 5–9 points).

As shown in Table 14.4, at the stage of determination of the need for innovations, innovations for provision of economic security belong to public benefits, which are unattractive for venture investors (stage 1–4 points). At the stage of R&D, control of economic security of R&D and their consequences is not envisaged (stage 2–1 point). At the stage of registration of rights for innovations, certain requirements and opportunities for consideration of the consequences of innovations for economic security in the international patent law are absent (stage 3–3 points). During commercialization of innovations, a sign of mismatch between management

Table 14.3: Qualitative signs of mismatch between economic & legal management of modern economic systems' innovative development and the requirements of technological progress in view of the stages of this process.

Stages of innovative development		Signs of mismatch between management of innovative development and the requirements of technological progress	Score
1. Detemrining the need for innovations		Digital marketing is complicated by infrastructural barriers	8
2. R&D		licensed barriers of digitization of science, deficit of investments in digital science	5
3. Registration of rights for innovations		online registration of rights for innovations is not envisaged by international law	2
Commercialization of innovations	4. Implementation of innovations, manufacture of innovative products	deficit of investments in "smart" productions, underdevelopment of their legal field	4
	5. Realization of innovative products and consumption	digital society is at the early stage of institutionalization	9

Source: developed and compiled by the authors.

of innovative development and the requirements of globalization is the fact that interests of economic growth are of higher priority that interests of provision of economic security (stage 4–1 point) and the fact that control over economic security of innovative products is not envisaged (stage 5–1 point).

Based on the data of Tables 14.1–14.4, a generalized quantitative evaluation of the correspondence of economic & legal management of modern economic systems' innovative development to the modern challenges in view of this process's stages is shown in Table 14.5.

As shown in Table 14.5, at the stage of determination of the need for innovations, economic & legal management of innovative development the modern economic systems is up to the modern challenges (7 points), at the stage of R&D – 5 points, at the stage of registration of rights for innovations – 3.25 points, at the stage of implementation of innovations and manufacture of innovative products – 5.25 points, and at the stage of realization of innovative products and consumption – 3.75 points.

On average, the whole innovative process conforms to the requirements of globalization – 5.40 points, requirements of sustainable development – 6.40 points, requirements of technological progress – 5.60 points, and requirements of economic security – 2 points. As a result of systematization of the obtained results, we have

Table 14.4: Qualitative signs of mismatch between economic & legal management of modern economic systems' innovative development and the requirements of economic security in view of the process's stages.

Stages of innovative development		Signs of mismatch between management of innovative development and the requirements of economic security	Score
1. Determination of the need for innovations		innovations for provision of economic security belong to public benefits, which are unattractive for venture investors	4
2. R&D		control of economic security of R&D and their consequences is not envisaged	1
3. Registration of rights for innovations		Absence of separate requirements and possibilities of consideration of the consequences of innovations for economic security in international patent law	3
Commercialization of innovations	4. Implementation of innovations, manufacture of innovative products	Interests of economic growth of are in higher priority that interests of provision of economic security	1
	5. Realization of innovative products and consumption	Control of economic security of innovative products is not envisaged	1

Source: developed and compiled by the authors.

found economic & legal gaps in management of modern economic systems' innovative development (Figure 14.1).

As shown in Figure 14.1, there are three systemic economic & legal gaps in managing the modern economic systems' innovative development: insufficient control in innovations-active countries, underdevelopment of infrastructure and institutions, insufficient protection of the national interests in countries that import new technologies and innovative products, and insufficient control and uncertainty of general "rules of the game" at the global level as a mistake of supra-national regulators and international organizations.

Table 14.5: Quantitative evaluation of the correspondence of economic & legal management of modern economic systems' innovative development to the modern challenges in view of this process's stages.

Modern challenges	Stages of innovative development and evaluation of their correspondence to the challenges					On average for all stages
	1. Determination of the need for innovations	2. R&D	3. Registration of rights for innovations	Commercialization of innovations		
				4. Implementation of innovations, manufacture of innovative products	5. Realization of innovative products and consumption	
Globalization	9	6	3	7	2	5.40
Sustainable development	7	8	5	9	3	6.40
Technological progress (digitization)	8	5	2	4	9	5.60
Economic security	4	1	3	1	1	2.00
On average for all challenges	7.00	5.00	3.25	5.25	3.75	–

Source: developed and compiled by the authors.

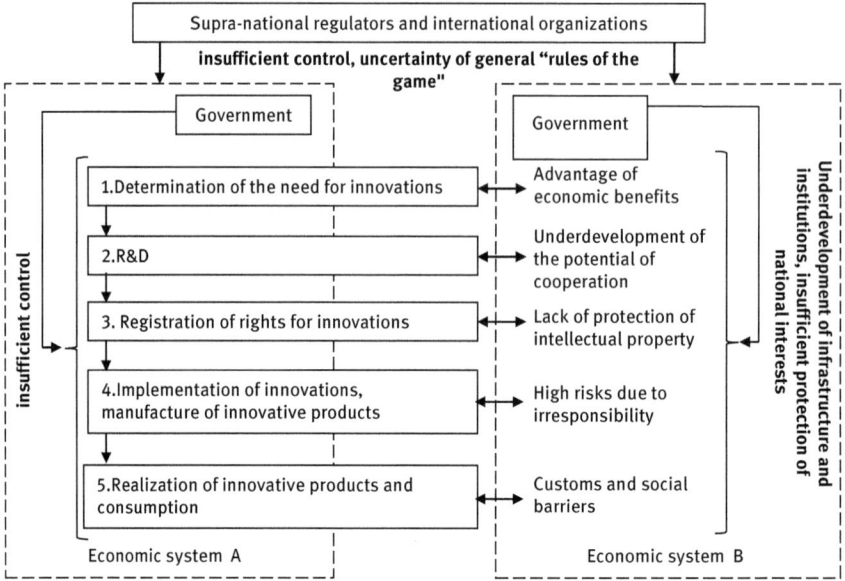

Figure 14.1: Economic & legal gaps in managing the modern economic systems' innovative development.
Source: developed and compiled by the authors.

Conclusion

The results of the research show that economic & legal gaps in managing the modern economic systems' innovative development lead to advantage of economic benefits, underdevelopment of the potential of cooperation during R&D, lack of protection of intellectual property at the global level, high social, ecological, and economic risks due to irresponsibility of innovations-active entrepreneurship, and complexity of selling innovations due to customs and social barriers.

The stage of registration of rights for innovations and the stage of realization of innovative products and consumption are up to the requirements of the modern challenges at the lowest level – 3.25 points out of 10. Economic & legal management of innovative development the modern economic systems is not up to the requirements of economic security. This predetermines the perspectives of improvement of the existing practice of economic & legal management of modern economic systems' innovative development.

References

Andronova, I.V., Chernova, V.Y., Starostin, V.S., Degtereva (2019). Study of sector-specific innovation efforts: The case from Russian economy. Entrepreneurship and Sustainability Issues, VsI Entrepreneurship and Sustainability Center, 7(1), p. 540–552.

Atkinsonk, R.D., Ezell, S.J. (2012). *Innovation Economics: the Race for Global Advantage*, New Haven, CT: Yale University Press.

Bogoviz, A.V., Ragulina, Y.V. (2020). Industry competitiveness in the new economy. Lecture Notes in Networks and Systems, 115, p. v–vi.

García-Quevedo, J., Segarra-Blasco, A., Teruel, M. (2018). Financial constraints and the failure of innovation projects. Technological Forecasting and Social Change, 127, p. 127–140.

Gumba, H.M., Vlasenko, V.A. (2017). Strategy of development of innovative activity in industry and construction: The rationale of the regional dimension. Izvestiya Vysshikh Uchebnykh Zavedenii, Seriya Teknologiya Tekstil'noi Promyshlennosti, 2017-January(2), 2(1), p. 14–18.

Haabazoka, L. (2019). A Study of the Effects of Technological Innovations on the Performance of Commercial Banks in Developing Countries – A Case of the Zambian Banking Industry. In: Popkova E. (eds) The Future of the Global Financial System: Downfall or Harmony. ISC 2018. Lecture Notes in Networks and Systems, vol 57. Springer, Cham, Online ISBN 978-3-030-00102-5, https://doi.org/10.1007/978-3-030-00102-5_132

Harfst, J., Pichler, P., Fischer, W. (2017). Regional Ambassadors-An Innovative Element for the Development of Rural Areas? European Countryside, 9(2), p. 359–374.

Kuznetsova, O., Kuznetsova, S., Yumaev, E., Kuznetsov, V., Galtseva, O. (2017). Formation and Development of the Training System for Innovative Development of Regional Industry. E3S Web of Conferences, 15,04019.

Li, X., Subrahmanyam, A., Yang, X. (2018). Can financial innovation succeed by catering to behavioral preferences? Evidence from a callable options market. Journal of Financial Economics, 2(1), p. 34–42.

Petrenko, E.S., Shevyakova, A.L. (2019). Features and perspectives of digitization in Kazakhstan. Studies in Computational Intelligence, 826, p. 889–899.

Popkova, E.G. (2019). Preconditions of formation and development of industry 4.0 in the conditions of knowledge economy. Studies in Systems, Decision and Control, 169(1), 65–72.

Popkova, E.G., Sergi, B.S. (2020). Human Capital and AI in Industry 4.0. Convergence and Divergence in Social Entrepreneurship in Russia. Journal of Intellectual Capital, In press, 2020. https://doi.org/10.1108/JIC-09-2019-0224

Popkova, E.G., Egorova, E.N., Popova, E., Pozdnyakova, U.A. (2019). The model of state management of economy on the basis of the internet of things. Studies in Computational Intelligence, 826, pp. 1137–1144.

Popkova, E.G., Gulzat, K. (2020). Technological Revolution in the 21st Century: Digital Society vs. Artificial Intelligence. Lecture Notes in Networks and Systems, 91, p. 339–345.

Popkova, E.G., Parakhina, V.N. (2019). Managing the global financial system on the basis of artificial intelligence: possibilities and limitations. Lecture Notes in Networks and Systems, 57, pp. 939–946.

Popkova, E.G., Poluyufta, L., Beshanova, Y., Popova, L.V., Kolesnikova, E. (2017). Innovations as a basis for marketing strategies of Russian oil companies in the conditions of oil prices reduction. Contributions to Economics, (9783319606958), p. 449–455.

Popkova, E.G., Zmiyak, K.V. (2019). Priorities of training of digital personnel for industry 4.0: social competencies vs technical competencies. On the Horizon, 27(3–4), p. 138–144.

Popkova, E.G., Sergi, B.S. (2018). Will Industry 4.0 and Other Innovations Impact Russia's Development? In Bruno S. Sergi (Ed.) Exploring the Future of Russia's Economy and Markets:

Towards Sustainable Economic Development (pp. 51–68). Bingley, UK: Emerald Publishing Limited.

Popkova, E.G., Sergi, B.S. (Eds.) (2019). Digital Economy: Complexity and Variety vs. Rationality. Berlin: Springer International Publishing.

Ragulina, Y.V. (2019). Priorities of development of industry 4.0 in modern economic systems with different progress in formation of knowledge economy. Studies in Systems, Decision and Control, 169, p. 167–174.

Ragulina, Y.V., Alekseev, A.N., Strizhkina, I.V., Tumanov, A.I. (2019). Methodology of criterial evaluation of consequences of the industrial revolution of the 21st century. Studies in Systems, Decision and Control, 169, p. 235–244.

Ramanathan, R., Ramanathan, U., Bentley, Y. (2018). The debate on flexibility of environmental regulations, innovation capabilities and financial performance – A novel use of DEA. Omega (United Kingdom), 75, p. 131–138.

Sergi, B.S. (2003). Economic Dynamics in Transitional Economies: The Four-P Governments, the EU Enlargement, and the Bruxelles Consensus. New York: Routledge.

Sergi, B.S. (Ed.) (2019). Tech, Smart Cities, and Regional Development in Contemporary Russia. Bingley, UK: Emerald Publishing Limited.

Sergi, B.S., Popkova, E.G. Bogoviz, A.V., Ragulina Y.V. (2019a). The Agro-industrial Complex: Tendencies, Scenarios, and Regulation. In Sergi, Bruno S. (Ed.) Modeling Economic Growth in Contemporary Russia (pp. 233–247). Bingley, UK: Emerald Publishing Limited.

Sergi, B.S., Popkova, E.G., Bogoviz, A.V., Litvinova, T.N. (2019b). Understanding Industry 4.0: AI, the Internet of Things, and the Future of Work. Bingley, UK: Emerald Publishing Limited.

Shulus, A.A., Akopova, E.S., Przhedetskaya, N.V., Borzenko, K.V. (2020). Intellectual Production and Consumption: A New Reality of the 21st Century. Lecture Notes in Networks and Systems, 92, pp. 353–359.

Stolyarov, N.O., Petrenko, E.S., Serova, O.A., Umuralieva, A.S. (2020). The Digital Reality of the Modern Economy: New Actors and New Decision-Making Logic. Lecture Notes in Networks and Systems, 87, p. 882–888.

Yao, M., Di, H., Zheng, X., Xu, X. (2018). Impact of payment technology innovations on the traditional financial industry: A focus on China. Technological Forecasting and Social Change, 2(1), p. 22–29.

Zavyalova, E.B. Studenikin, N.V. Starikova, E.A. (2018). Business participation in implementation of socially oriented Sustainable Development Goals in countries of Central Asia and the Caucasus region. Central Asia and the Caucasus, 19(2), p. 56–63.

Andrei V. Berezhnoi, Edem A. Kalafatov, Yana S. Matkovskaya,
Tatyana Y. Mazurina and Ruslan N. Shangaraev
15 Inconsistency and Imbalance of Managing the Modern Economic Systems' Innovative Development

Introduction

For achieving high results during management of modern economic systems' innovative development, it should conform to two criteria. 1st criterion: consistency. The managerial measures should be built logically and performed in a predicted and confirmed order. The managerial measures should also ensure the target list and order of stages of the innovative process. Consistent state management allows reducing the risks and increasing the advantages of innovative activities for all market participants.

2nd criterion: balance. Management of innovative development should stimulate the establishment and support for balance of interests of concerned parties and avoid creation of preferential conditions for some market players and unfavorable conditions for other market players. Management should also stimulate the balance of the innovative process, which stages should be effective and should contribute equally into final results. Special attention should be paid to harmonization of social and economic interests in the process of innovative activities, as they often contradict each other.

A generalized view at the modern global innovative practice shows that not all entrepreneurial structures are inclined to innovative activities even in case of favorable conditions in the market and internal opportunities (e.g., if there are resources). The results of innovative activities often have an advantage in favor of economic benefits and could be connected to negative social consequences. An example could be financial innovations that caused the 2008 crisis.

Andrei V. Berezhnoi, "Kuban State Agrarian University named after I.T. Trubilin", Krasnodar, Russia
Edem A. Kalafatov, Federal State Budgetary Educational Institution of Higher Education "V.I. Vernadsky Crimean Federal University" Institute of economics and management, Simferopol, Republic of Crimea, Russia
Yana S. Matkovskaya, Federal State Budgetary Institution of Science V.A. Trapeznikov Institute of Control Sciences Russian Academy of Sciences, Moscow, Russia
Tatyana Y. Mazurina, State University of Management, Moscow, Russia
Ruslan N. Shangaraev, Diplomatic Academy of the Ministry of Foreign Affairs of the Russian Federation, Moscow, Russia

https://doi.org/10.1515/9783110643701-015

Based on this, we offer a hypothesis that the modern practice of state management of innovative development of economic systems does not fully conform to the criteria of consistency and balance and requires correction. The purpose of this chapter is to determine consistency and balance of this practice and to substantiate the perspectives of its improvement.

Materials and Method

The essence and significance of the criteria of consistency and balance during assessment of efficiency of the practice of state management of the of modern economic systems' innovative development are considered in Atkinsonk and Ezell (2012), García-Quevedo et al. (2018), Gumba and Vlasenko (2017), Haabazoka (2019), Harfst et al. (2017), Kuznetsova et al. (2017), Li et al. (2018), Ramanathan et al. (2018), and Yao et al. (2018).

Evaluation of consistency and balance of certain separate practices of state management of modern economic systems' innovative development is performed in the works Andronova et al. (2019), Bogoviz and Ragulina (2020), Petrenko and Shevyakova (2019), Popkova (2019), Popkova and Sergi (2020), Popkova et al. (2019), Popkova and Gulzat (2020), Popkova and Parakhina (2019), Popkova et al. (2017), Popkova and Zmiyak (2019), Popkova and Sergi (2018), Popkova and Sergi (2019), Ragulina (2019), Ragulina et al. (2019), Sergi (2003), Sergi (2019), Sergi et al. (2019a), Sergi et al. (2019b), Shulus et al. (2020), Stolyarov et al. (2020), and Zavyalova et al. (2018).

The performed overview of the existing research literature shows that though the theory of consistency and balance of state management of the modern economic systems' innovative development has been elaborated, the practical aspects of the set problem require further research. In this chapter, in order to fill the gap in the existing scientific knowledge, the authors use logical analysis, economic modeling of organizational & managerial processes structural & functional, and regression analysis.

Results

A scheme of the existing modern international practice of state management of innovative development of economic systems is shown in Figure 15.1.

As shown in Figure 15.1, in the existing scheme of managing the modern economic systems' innovative development government does not manage business's innovative activities, but conducts its own innovative practices. The innovative activities of business and government are separated.

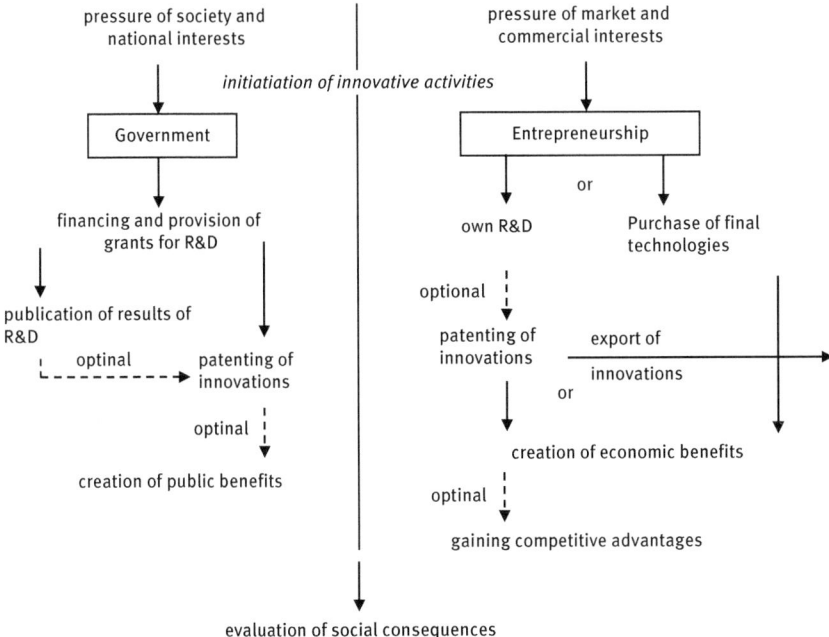

Figure 15.1: The existing scheme of managing the modern economic systems' innovative development.
Source: developed and compiled by the authors.

Under the pressure of society and national interests, government finances and gives grants for R&D. The results of R&D could be published, but patenting of innovations is optimal (not mandatory). Commercialization of innovations is complicated, and creation of public benefits is optional.

Under the pressure of the market and commercial interests, entrepreneurship conducts its own R&D or purchases final innovations. Own R&D could be inefficient; patenting of their results is optimal. Patented technologies could be exported or used during creation of economic benefits. Thus, entrepreneurial innovations are always commercialized. However, they ensure creation of competitive advantages only in case of their independent use by domestic business structures, which created them. Social consequences of innovations are evaluated in the end.

Thus, the existing practice of managing the modern economic systems' innovative development has three drawbacks:

- Inconsistency: evaluation of social consequences of innovations, especially entrepreneurial (economic benefits) is conducted not at the beginning, at the stage of planning of innovations and R&D, as the priority of the innovative activities, but in the end – as a limitation on the path of gaining profit from the innovations;

- Imbalance of the interests of society/government and entrepreneurship and limitation of public and economic benefits, created as a result of the innovative activities;
- Imbalance of the fundamental and applied innovations, scattered character of the innovative activities and their results – which complicates commercialization of innovations.

For showing these drawbacks, let us consider the structure of the leading production technologies in Russia in 2014–2018 (Figure 15.2).

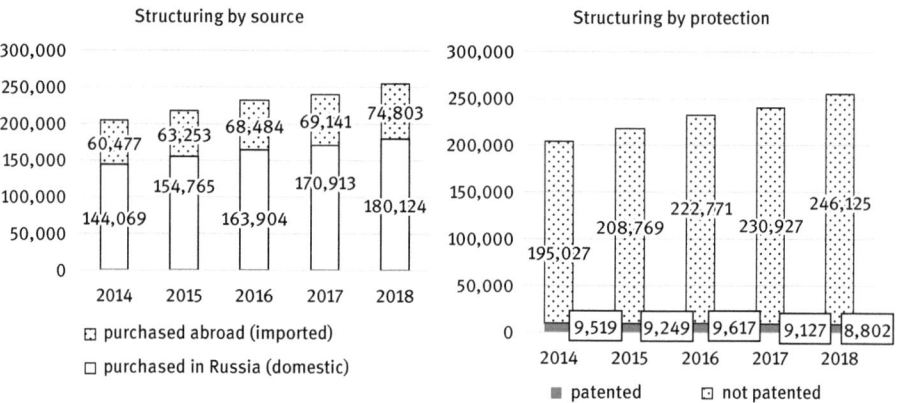

Figure 15.2: Structuring of the leading production technologies in Russia in 2014–2018.
Source: calculated and built by the authors based on Federal State Statistics Service (2020).

As shown in Figure 15.2, in 2014–2018 almost 30% of the leading production technologies that were used in Russia were purchased abroad, and 96% of all data were not patented – i.e., not protected by intellectual property rights. Active import of innovations does not allow Russian entrepreneurship to form competitive advantages by means of innovative activities. A similar situation is observed in the world practice (Figure 15.3).

As shown in Figure 15.3, the publication and patent activity in the world has been growing in 2000–2018. Dependence of the number of patents in the world is by 86.03% explained by the number of publications in scientific and technical journals. Increase of the number of publications by 1 leads to increase of the number of patents by 0.9428. Though this regression dependence is strong, for the studied indicators it should strive to 100%. For overcoming the determined drawbacks, we offer an optimization scheme of managing the modern economic systems' innovative development (Figure 15.4).

As shown in Figure 15.4, the offered scheme allows overcoming the barrier (a line in Figure 15.1) between society's interests and entrepreneurship's interests.

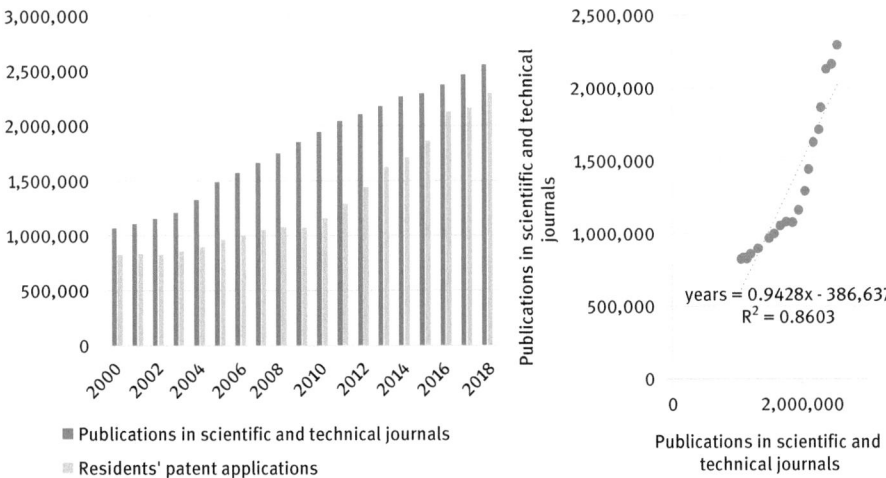

Figure 15.3: Dynamic and regression analysis of dependence of the patent activity in the world on the publication activity in 2000–2018.
Source: calculated and built by the authors based on World Bank (2020).

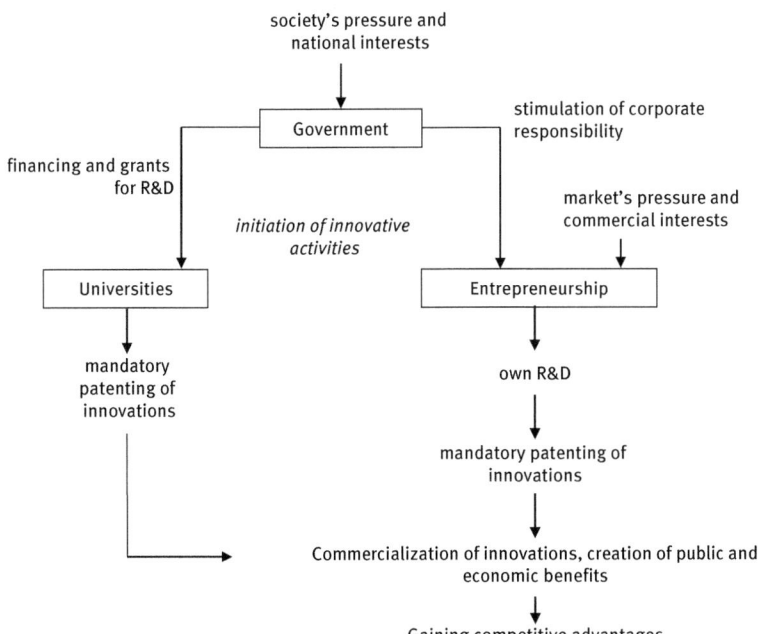

Figure 15.4: The offered optimization scheme of managing the modern economic systems' innovative development.
Source: developed and compiled by the authors.

Government is at the peak of the innovative system. Under the pressure of society and national interests, it initiates innovative activities – on the one hand, through universities, with financing and grant support for R&D with mandatory patenting of their results; on the other hands, through stimulation of their corporate responsibility. Companies conduct their own R&D with mandatory patenting of innovations. The result is commercialization of innovations, creation of public and economic benefits, and receipt of competitive advantages.

Conclusion

Thus, the offered hypothesis has been confirmed. It has been substantiated that state management of modern economic systems' innovative development is inconsistent and unbalanced. This is seen in three drawbacks of this management: absence of preliminary evaluation of the social consequences of innovations, imbalance of the interests of society/government and entrepreneurship, and imbalance of fundamental and applied innovations.

For overcoming the determined drawbacks, we have developed an optimization scheme of managing the modern economic systems' innovative development. A new treatment of innovative activities as an object of state management is offered – it envisages mandatory observation of the following conditions: patenting of the R&D results, commercialization of innovations, creation of public and economic benefits, and gaining competitive advantages. Thus, R&D that did not lead to any results that are subject to patenting should not be considered an object of state management, and technologies that do not ensure competitive advantages should not be considered innovations.

References

Andronova, I.V., Chernova, V.Y., Starostin, V.S., Degtereva (2019). Study of sector-specific innovation efforts: The case from Russian economy. Entrepreneurship and Sustainability Issues, Vsl Entrepreneurship and Sustainability Center, 7(1), p. 540–552.

Atkinsonk, R.D., Ezell, S.J. (2012). *Innovation Economics: the Race for Global Advantage*, New Haven, CT: Yale University Press.

Bogoviz, A.V., Ragulina, Y.V. (2020). Industry competitiveness in the new economy. Lecture Notes in Networks and Systems, 115, p. v–vi.

García-Quevedo, J., Segarra-Blasco, A., Teruel, M. (2018). Financial constraints and the failure of innovation projects. Technological Forecasting and Social Change, 127, p. 127–140.

Gumba, H.M., Vlasenko, V.A. (2017). Strategy of development of innovative activity in industry and construction: The rationale of the regional dimension. Izvestiya Vysshikh Uchebnykh Zavedenii, Seriya Teknologiya Tekstil'noi Promyshlennosti, 2017-January(2), 2(1), p. 14–18.

Haabazoka, L. (2019). A Study of the Effects of Technological Innovations on the Performance of Commercial Banks in Developing Countries – A Case of the Zambian Banking Industry. In: Popkova E. (eds) The Future of the Global Financial System: Downfall or Harmony. ISC 2018. Lecture Notes in Networks and Systems, vol 57. Springer, Cham, https://doi.org/10.1007/978-3-030-00102-5_132

Harfst, J., Pichler, P., Fischer, W. (2017). Regional Ambassadors-An Innovative Element for the Development of Rural Areas? European Countryside, 9(2), p. 359–374.

Kuznetsova, O., Kuznetsova, S., Yumaev, E., Kuznetsov, V., Galtseva, O. (2017). Formation and Development of the Training System for Innovative Development of Regional Industry. E3S Web of Conferences, 15,04019. DOI: 10.1051/e3sconf/20171504019

Li, X., Subrahmanyam, A., Yang, X. (2018). Can financial innovation succeed by catering to behavioral preferences? Evidence from a callable options market. Journal of Financial Economics, 2(1), p. 34–42.

Petrenko, E.S., Shevyakova, A.L. (2019). Features and perspectives of digitization in Kazakhstan. Studies in Computational Intelligence, 826, p. 889–899.

Popkova, E.G. (2019). Preconditions of formation and development of industry 4.0 in the conditions of knowledge economy. Studies in Systems, Decision and Control, 169(1), 65–72.

Popkova, E.G., Sergi, B.S. (2020). Human Capital and AI in Industry 4.0. Convergence and Divergence in Social Entrepreneurship in Russia. Journal of Intellectual Capital, In press, 2020. https://doi.org/10.1108/JIC-09-2019-0224

Popkova, E.G., Egorova, E.N., Popova, E., Pozdnyakova, U.A. (2019). The model of state management of economy on the basis of the internet of things. Studies in Computational Intelligence, 826, pp. 1137–1144.

Popkova, E.G., Gulzat, K. (2020). Technological Revolution in the 21st Century: Digital Society vs. Artificial Intelligence. Lecture Notes in Networks and Systems, 91, p. 339–345.

Popkova, E.G., Parakhina, V.N. (2019). Managing the global financial system on the basis of artificial intelligence: possibilities and limitations. Lecture Notes in Networks and Systems, 57, pp. 939–946.

Popkova, E.G., Poluyufta, L., Beshanova, Y., Popova, L.V., Kolesnikova, E. (2017). Innovations as a basis for marketing strategies of Russian oil companies in the conditions of oil prices reduction. Contributions to Economics, (9783319606958), p. 449–455.

Popkova, E.G., Zmiyak, K.V. (2019). Priorities of training of digital personnel for industry 4.0: social competencies vs technical competencies. On the Horizon, 27(3–4), p. 138–144.

Popkova, E.G., Sergi, B.S. (2018). Will Industry 4.0 and Other Innovations Impact Russia's Development? In Bruno S. Sergi (Ed.) Exploring the Future of Russia's Economy and Markets: Towards Sustainable Economic Development (pp. 51–68). Bingley, UK: Emerald Publishing Limited.

Popkova, E.G., Sergi, B.S. (Eds.) (2019). Digital Economy: Complexity and Variety vs. Rationality. Springer International Publishing.

Ragulina, Y.V. (2019). Priorities of development of industry 4.0 in modern economic systems with different progress in formation of knowledge economy. Studies in Systems, Decision and Control, 169, p. 167–174.

Ragulina, Y.V., Alekseev, A.N., Strizhkina, I.V., Tumanov, A.I. (2019). Methodology of criterial evaluation of consequences of the industrial revolution of the 21st century. Studies in Systems, Decision and Control, 169, p. 235–244.

Ramanathan, R., Ramanathan, U., Bentley, Y. (2018). The debate on flexibility of environmental regulations, innovation capabilities and financial performance – A novel use of DEA. Omega (United Kingdom), 75, p. 131–138.

Sergi, B.S. (2003). Economic Dynamics in Transitional Economies: The Four-P Governments, the EU Enlargement, and the Bruxelles Consensus. New York: Routledge.

Sergi, B.S. (Ed.) (2019). Tech, Smart Cities, and Regional Development in Contemporary Russia. Bingley, UK: Emerald Publishing Limited.

Sergi, B.S., Popkova, E.G. Bogoviz, A.V., Ragulina Y.V. (2019a). The Agro-industrial Complex: Tendencies, Scenarios, and Regulation. In Sergi, Bruno S. (Ed.) Modeling Economic Growth in Contemporary Russia (pp. 233–247). Bingley, UK: Emerald Publishing Limited.

Sergi, B.S., Popkova, E.G., Bogoviz, A.V., Litvinova, T.N. (2019b). Understanding Industry 4.0: AI, the Internet of Things, and the Future of Work. Bingley, UK: Emerald Publishing Limited.

Shulus, A.A., Akopova, E.S., Przhedetskaya, N.V., Borzenko, K.V. (2020). Intellectual Production and Consumption: A New Reality of the 21st Century. Lecture Notes in Networks and Systems, 92, pp. 353–359.

Stolyarov, N.O., Petrenko, E.S., Serova, O.A., Umuralieva, A.S. (2020). The Digital Reality of the Modern Economy: New Actors and New Decision-Making Logic. Lecture Notes in Networks and Systems, 87, p. 882–888.

World Bank (2020). Indicators. URL: https://data.worldbank.org/indicator (data accessed: 05.04.2020).

Yao, M., Di, H., Zheng, X., Xu, X. (2018). Impact of payment technology innovations on the traditional financial industry: A focus on China. Technological Forecasting and Social Change, 2(1), p. 22–29.

Zavyalova, E.B. Studenikin, N.V. Starikova, E.A. (2018). Business participation in implementation of socially oriented Sustainable Development Goals in countries of Central Asia and the Caucasus region. Central Asia and the Caucasus, 19(2), p. 56–63.

Federal State Statistics Service. Russia in numbers: short statistical yearbook – 2019. URL: https://www.gks.ru/bgd/regl/b19_11/Main.htm (data accessed: 05. 04.2020).

Aleksei V. Bogoviz, Erastus Mwanaumo and Lubinda Haabazoka

16 The Global Disproportions in Managing the Innovative Development of Developed and Developing Countries

Introduction

Innovative development in different economic systems is always specific, as it is determined by the conditions in which it takes place – the initial level of technological provision, resource provision of further innovative activities, and preparation and susceptibility of the social environment. Therefore, variation of the level and rate of innovative development of economic systems should be treated as a norm.

At the same time, vivid differences and total imbalance of innovative development at the global scale are connected to a range of negative effects. One of these is lack of realization of the potential of acceleration of the global technological progress. Involvement of certain countries into creation of the leading technologies and separation of other countries from this process hinder it – which could be treated as a destructive ("unhealthy") competition.

Another negative effect consists in close connection between innovations and socio-economic position of economic systems. Presence of hi-tech economic with progressive societies, in which high living standards have been achieved, with simultaneous preservation of low-tech economies with low living standards could lead to aggravation of contradictions between countries and increase the socio-economic tension at the global scale.

Another negative effect from the global disproportions in managing the innovative development of developed and developing countries is limitations for international trade and international movement of production factors. Economies in different technological modes cannot be integrated, which hinders the international division of labor and reduces effectiveness of the global economy.

The risk of emergence of the above negative effects predetermines the necessity of regulating the innovative development – implementation of transnational initiatives on leveling the global disproportions of this development and correction of the national strategies of innovative activities. The purpose of this chapter is to determine the global disproportions in managing the innovative development of developed and developing countries and to determine the perspectives of overcoming them.

Aleksei V. Bogoviz, Independent researcher, Moscow, Russia
Erastus Mwanaumo, Department of Civil and Environmental Engineering, School of Engineering, University of Zambia, Lusaka, Zambia
Lubinda Haabazoka, Director of The University of Zambia Graduate School of Business, Zambia

https://doi.org/10.1515/9783110643701-016

Materials and Method

The specifics of the innovative development in developed and developing countries are studied in the works Atkinsonk and Ezell (2012), García-Quevedo et al. (2018), Gumba and Vlasenko (2017), Haabazoka (2019), Harfst et al. (2017), Kuznetsova et al. (2017), Li et al. (2018), Ramanathan et al. (2018), and Yao et al. (2018).

The problem of balance of the global economic system and contribution of innovative development into its solution are considered in the works Andronova et al. (2019), Bogoviz and Ragulina (2020), Bogoviz and Sergi (2018), Petrenko and Shevyakova (2019), Popkova (2019), Popkova and Sergi (2020), Popkova et al. (2019), Popkova and Gulzat (2020), Popkova and Parakhina (2019), Popkova et al. (2017), Popkova and Zmiyak (2019), Popkova and Sergi (2018), Popkova and Sergi (2019), Ragulina (2019), Ragulina et al. (2019), Sergi (2003), Sergi (2019), Sergi et al. (2019), Shulus et al. (2020), Stolyarov et al. (2020), and Zavyalova et al. (2018).

However, the global disproportions in managing the innovative development of developed and developing countries have not been defined strictly by the modern economics and require further research. For finding these disproportions, we study the whole specter of statistical indicators on the topic of innovative development, which are accessible based on the official data of the World Bank. The research is performed based on the 2020 data.

The modern experience of innovative development of economic systems is analyzed in comparison with developed countries, which representatives are advanced economies (G7) and developing countries (BRICS). For the most vivid contrast between the selected categories of countries, we use average values of the indicators. The statistical characteristics of innovative development of the given countries are shown in Table 16.1.

Results

The average indicators of resource efficiency of the innovative development of developed and developing countries in 2020 are shown in Figure 16.1.

As shown in Figure 16.1, R&D expenditures in developed countries (2.25% of GDP) are by 1.89 times higher than in developing countries (1.19% of GDP). Number of R&D researchers per 1 million people in developed countries (4,265) is by 3.75 times higher than in developing countries (1,136). This means that resource intensity of R&D in developed countries is much higher than in developing countries.

Charge for intellectual property in developed countries (0.45% of GDP) is by 1.45 times higher than in developing countries (0.31% of GDP). Export of hi-tech products in developed countries (17.71% of industrial export) is by 1.28 times higher than in developing countries (13.80% of industrial export). This shows that developed

Table 16.1: Statistical characteristics of innovative development of developed and developing countries in 2020.

Category	Country	Research and development expenditure, % of GDP	Charges for the use of intellectual property, payments, BoP, current US$	Gross domestic product, current prices, billions U.S. dollars	High-technology exports, % of manufactured exports	Patent applications, residents	Researchers in R&D per million people	The Global Competitiveness Index, score 1–100
Advanced economies (G7)	Canada	1.55	1,1824,788.46	1,783.360	16	4,349	4,264	79.6
	France	2.19	15,938,476.81	2,650.237	26	14,303	4,450	78.8
	Germany	3.02	15,630,232.20	3,727.659	16	46,617	5,003	81.8
	Italy	1.35	5,141,287.99	1,922.214	8	8,921	2,245	71.5
	Japan	3.21	21,725,592.92	5,163.766	17	253,630	5,304	82.3
	UK	1.66	13,545,558.59	2,689.841	22	12,865	4,341	81.2
	USA	2.79	56,117,000.00	22,063.044	19	285,095	4,245	83.7
BRICS	Brazil	1.26	5,124,101.63	2,447.245	13	4,980	888	60.9
	China	2.15	35,782,953.95	15,066.667	31	1,393,815	1,225	73.9
	India	0.60	7,905,957.78	3,252.721	9	16,289	253	61.4
	Russia	1.11	6,288,170.00	1,712.024	11	24,926	2,822	66.7
	South Africa	0.82	1,817,432.56	353.409	5	657	492	62.4

Source: compiled by the authors based on Institute of Scientific Communications (2020), World Bank (2020).

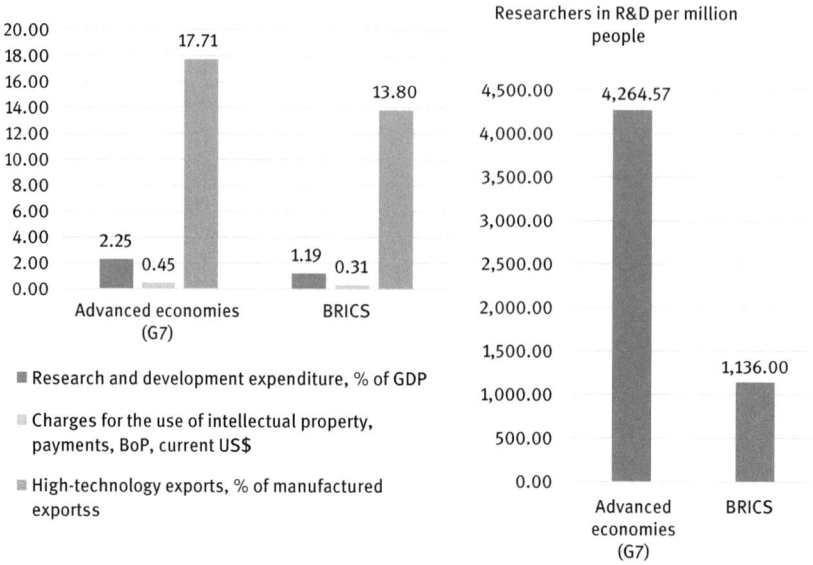

Figure 16.1: Average indicators of resource efficiency of the innovative development of developed and developing countries in 2020.
Source: calculated and compiled by the authors.

countries actively conduct export of their innovative products and technologies – the spheres of science and hi-tech productions play an important role in formation of GDP and acceleration of economic growth of developed countries.

The average statistics of patenting and regression analysis of its contribution into provision of competitiveness of developed and developing countries in 2020 shown in Figure 16.2.

As shown in Figure 16.2, residents' patent activity in developing countries (288,133.40) is by 3.22 higher than in developed countries (89,397.14). This is especially peculiar in view of large resource intensity of R&D in developed countries, where effectiveness of innovative activities (number of researchers and expenditures for R&D / number of patents ratio) is much lower than in developing countries.

Regression analysis has shown that increase of patent activity by 1 in developing countries leads to slight increase of the Global Competitiveness Index 4.0. Correlation of these indicators is rather high – 83.18%. In developed countries, correlation of patent activity with the Global Competitiveness Index 4.0 is much lower – 33.74%. The obtained conclusions allow compiling a model of the modern global economic system's innovative development (Figure 16.3).

As shown in Figure 16.3, innovative development of the modern global economic system is not well-balanced. It is characterized by an imbalance – a strong advantage in favor of developed countries, which move technological progress.

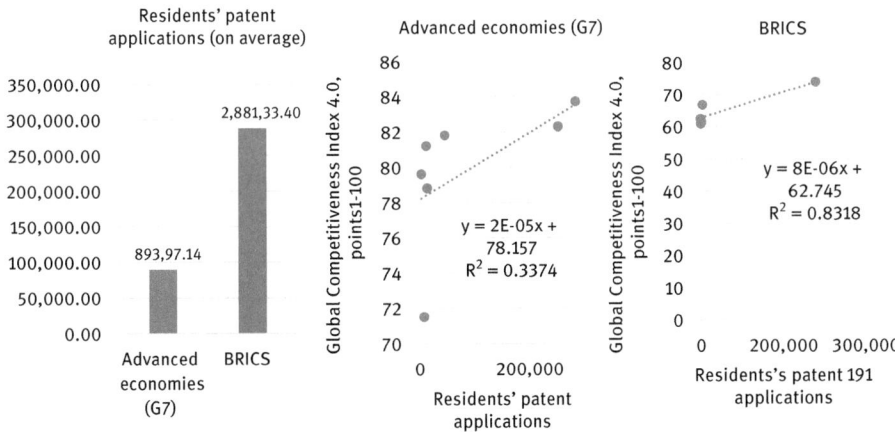

Figure 16.2: Patenting and regression analysis of its contribution into provision of competitiveness of developed and developing countries in 2020.
Source: calculated and compiled by the authors.

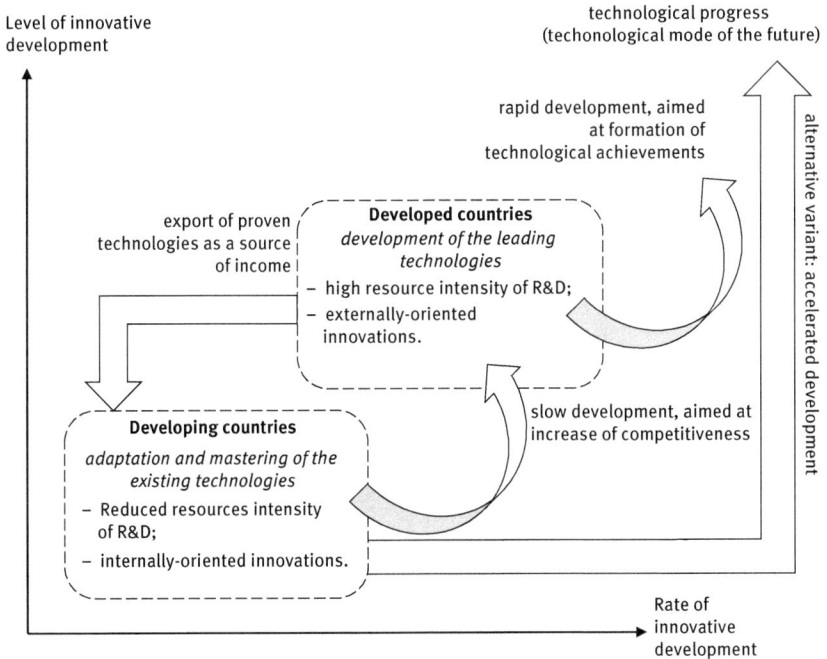

Figure 16.3: The model of the modern global economic system's development.
Source: developed and compiled by the authors.

Development of leading technologies requires high resource intensity of R&D, but, due to external orientation of innovations the proven technologies become a source of national income, collected based on export. Rapid development, aimed at formation of technological achievement, defines the leadership of developed countries in the global markets of innovations.

Developing countries import the proven technologies and hi-tech products. Their innovative development is connected to adaptation and mastering of the existing technologies. In this case, resource intensity of R&D is reduced, and innovations are internally-oriented. Slow development, aimed at increase of competitiveness, allows developing countries to improve their positions in the world markets due to innovations – but as peripheral participants, while developed countries preserve the leadership.

The perspective of balancing the global innovative development of economy is connected to developing countries' using the alternative variant of managing their innovative activities, which envisages accelerated development, which allows them overtaking developed countries and forming own technological achievements, as well as performing a transfer to the future technological mode together with developed countries.

Conclusion

Thus, global disproportions in managing the innovative development of developed and developing countries are manifested in all aspects of innovative activities of the countries of these categories: resource intensity, resource efficiency, and consequences of the studied activities. Slow diffusion of innovations leads to the fact that developed countries have sustainable technological achievements. Their R&D is more complex and expensive, but allow for export of hi-tech products, thus returning investments in creation of hi-tech products.

Developing countries do not have access to progressive technologies, but receive only obsolete technologies and have to import hi-tech products. Their R&D is specific and is aimed at increase of global competitiveness, but not for overtaking the developed countries but for reaching their current level – while the developed countries quickly develop and perform a transfer to the future technological mode. Overcoming the determined disproportions envisages the change of the approach to managing the innovative development in developing countries.

References

Andronova, I.V., Chernova, V.Y., Starostin, V.S., Degtereva (2019). Study of sector-specific innovation efforts: The case from Russian economy. Entrepreneurship and Sustainability Issues, VsI Entrepreneurship and Sustainability Center, 7(1), p. 540–552.

Atkinsonk, R.D., Ezell, S.J. (2012). *Innovation Economics: the Race for Global Advantage*, New Haven, CT: Yale University Press.

Bogoviz, A.V., Ragulina, Y.V. (2020). Industry competitiveness in the new economy. Lecture Notes in Networks and Systems, 115, p. v–vi.

Bogoviz, A.V., Sergi, B.S. (2018). Will the Circular Economy Be the Future of Russia's Growth Model? In Bruno S. Sergi (Ed.). Exploring the Future of Russia'sEconomy and Markets: Towards Sustainable Economic Development, Bingley, UK: Emerald Publishing, pp. 125–141.

García-Quevedo, J., Segarra-Blasco, A., Teruel, M. (2018). Financial constraints and the failure of innovation projects. Technological Forecasting and Social Change, 127, p. 127–140.

Gumba, H.M., Vlasenko, V.A. (2017). Strategy of development of innovative activity in industry and construction: The rationale of the regional dimension. Izvestiya Vysshikh Uchebnykh Zavedenii, Seriya Teknologiya Tekstil'noi Promyshlennosti, 2017-January(2), p. 14–18.

Haabazoka, L. (2019). A Study of the Effects of Technological Innovations on the Performance of Commercial Banks in Developing Countries – A Case of the Zambian Banking Industry. In: Popkova E. (eds) The Future of the Global Financial System: Downfall or Harmony. ISC 2018. Lecture Notes in Networks and Systems, vol 57. Springer, Cham, Online ISBN 978-3-030-00102-5, https://doi.org/10.1007/978-3-030-00102-5_132

Harfst, J., Pichler, P., Fischer, W. (2017). Regional Ambassadors-An Innovative Element for the Development of Rural Areas? European Countryside, 9(2), p. 359–374.

Institute of Scientific Communications (2020). Data set "Big data of the modern world economy: digital platform for intelligent analytics – 2020". URL: https://www.archilab.online/en/data/sounting-data-set (data accessed: 06.04.2020).

Kuznetsova, O., Kuznetsova, S., Yumaev, E., Kuznetsov, V., Galtseva, O. (2017). Formation and Development of the Training System for Innovative Development of Regional Industry. E3S Web of Conferences, 15,04019.

Li, X., Subrahmanyam, A., Yang, X. (2018). Can financial innovation succeed by catering to behavioral preferences? Evidence from a callable options market. Journal of Financial Economics, 2(1), p. 34–42.

Petrenko, E.S., Shevyakova, A.L. (2019). Features and perspectives of digitization in Kazakhstan. Studies in Computational Intelligence, 826, p. 889–899.

Popkova, E.G. (2019). Preconditions of formation and development of industry 4.0 in the conditions of knowledge economy. Studies in Systems, Decision and Control, 169(1), 65–72.

Popkova, E.G., Sergi, B.S. (2020). Human Capital and AI in Industry 4.0. Convergence and Divergence in Social Entrepreneurship in Russia. Journal of Intellectual Capital, In press, 2020.

Popkova, E.G., Egorova, E.N., Popova, E., Pozdnyakova, U.A. (2019). The model of state management of economy on the basis of the internet of things. Studies in Computational Intelligence, 826, pp. 1137–1144.

Popkova, E.G., Gulzat, K. (2020). Technological Revolution in the 21st Century: Digital Society vs. Artificial Intelligence. Lecture Notes in Networks and Systems, 91, p. 339–345.

Popkova, E.G., Parakhina, V.N. (2019). Managing the global financial system on the basis of artificial intelligence: possibilities and limitations. Lecture Notes in Networks and Systems, 57, pp. 939–946.

Popkova, E.G., Poluyufta, L., Beshanova, Y., Popova, L.V., Kolesnikova, E. (2017). Innovations as a basis for marketing strategies of Russian oil companies in the conditions of oil prices reduction. Contributions to Economics, (9783319606958), p. 449–455.

Popkova, E.G., Zmiyak, K.V. (2019). Priorities of training of digital personnel for industry 4.0: social competencies vs technical competencies. On the Horizon, 27(3–4), p. 138–144.

Popkova, E.G., Sergi, B.S. (2018). Will Industry 4.0 and Other Innovations Impact Russia's Development? In Bruno S. Sergi (Ed.) Exploring the Future of Russia's Economy and Markets: Towards Sustainable Economic Development (pp. 51–68). Bingley, UK: Emerald Publishing Limited.

Popkova, E.G., Sergi, B.S. (Eds.) (2019). Digital Economy: Complexity and Variety vs. Rationality. Berlin: Springer International Publishing.

Ragulina, Y.V. (2019). Priorities of development of industry 4.0 in modern economic systems with different progress in formation of knowledge economy. Studies in Systems, Decision and Control, 169, p. 167–174.

Ragulina, Y.V., Alekseev, A.N., Strizhkina, I.V., Tumanov, A.I. (2019). Methodology of criterial evaluation of consequences of the industrial revolution of the 21st century. Studies in Systems, Decision and Control, 169, p. 235–244.

Ramanathan, R., Ramanathan, U., Bentley, Y. (2018). The debate on flexibility of environmental regulations, innovation capabilities and financial performance – A novel use of DEA. Omega (United Kingdom), 75, p. 131–138.

Sergi, B.S. (2003). Economic Dynamics in Transitional Economies: The Four-P Governments, the EU Enlargement, and the Bruxelles Consensus. New York: Routledge.

Sergi, B.S. (Ed.) (2019). Tech, Smart Cities, and Regional Development in Contemporary Russia. Bingley, UK: Emerald Publishing Limited.

Sergi, B.S., Popkova, E.G. Bogoviz, A.V., Litvinova, T.N. (2019). Understanding Industry 4.0: AI, the Internet of Things, and the Future of Work. Bingley, UK: Emerald Publishing Limited.

Shulus, A.A., Akopova, E.S., Przhedetskaya, N.V., Borzenko, K.V. (2020). Intellectual Production and Consumption: A New Reality of the 21st Century. Lecture Notes in Networks and Systems, 92, pp. 353–359.

Stolyarov, N.O., Petrenko, E.S., Serova, O.A., Umuralieva, A.S. (2020). The Digital Reality of the Modern Economy: New Actors and New Decision-Making Logic. Lecture Notes in Networks and Systems, 87, p. 882–888.

World Bank (2020). Indicators. URL: https://data.worldbank.org/indicator (data accessed: 06.04.2020).

Yao, M., Di, H., Zheng, X., Xu, X. (2018). Impact of payment technology innovations on the traditional financial industry: A focus on China. Technological Forecasting and Social Change, 2(1), p. 22–29.

Zavyalova, E.B. Studenikin, N.V. Starikova, E.A. (2018). Business participation in implementation of socially oriented Sustainable Development Goals in countries of Central Asia and the Caucasus region. Central Asia and the Caucasus, 19(2), p. 56–63.

Part VI: **Recommendations for Economic and Legal Management of Economic Systems' Innovative Development**

Vladimir S. Osipov, Elena L. Gulkova, Larisa O. Velikanova,
Marina V. Bogdanova and Tatiana V. Tkachenko

17 The Concept of Consistent and Well-Balanced Economic and Legal Management of the Modern Economic Systems' Innovative Development

Introduction

Adoption of the global goals of sustainable development increased the important of the issues of consistency and balance during management of economic systems' development. The approach to solving these issues depends on the priorities that are set before a specific economic practice. During consideration of the practice of economic & legal management of the modern economic systems' innovative development, consistency means timely consideration of the social consequences of innovations, which is performed at each stage of the innovative process with elimination of innovations that bring increased social risks and/or do not provide the expected social advantages.

Balance of economic & legal management of the modern economic systems' innovative development envisages integrity of the innovative process, balance of theoretical developments, their application in practice, and efficiency of the innovative activities. The innovative process could be characterized as well-balanced only if all its stages are successfully passed – from R&D to commercialization of innovations and receipt of advantages in the form of return of investments and strengthening of the market positions. Advantage of theoretical R&D, which do not ensure the formalized positive results that are subject to patenting and are high demand in the market, shows an imbalance of innovative development.

The existing concept of economic & legal management of the modern economic systems' innovative development does not conform to the requirements of consistency, as it treats the consequences of innovations for society as secondary and less significant, as compared to private and commercial advantages, which are obtained due to the innovative activities of entrepreneurship. It does not conform to the requirements of balance, as it shares a wide treatment of innovations, which allows

Vladimir S. Osipov, "Moscow State Institute of International Relations (University) of the Ministry of Foreign Affairs Russian Federation", Moscow, Russia
Elena L. Gulkova, Marina V. Bogdanova, State University of Management, Moscow, Russia
Larisa O. Velikanova, "Kuban State Agrarian University named after I.T. Trubilin", Krasnodar, Russia
Tatiana V. Tkachenko, Moscow Aviation Institute (National Research University), Moscow, Russia

https://doi.org/10.1515/9783110643701-017

passing not all stages of the innovative process but only certain of them (e.g., during theoretical developments that are not subject to commercialization).

The purpose of this chapter is developing a new concept of the practice of economic & legal management of the modern economic systems' innovative development that fully conforms to the requirements of consistency and balance.

Materials and Method

The theoretical idea of consistency and balance of economic & legal management of the modern economic systems' innovative development is given in the works Atkinsonk and Ezell (2012), García-Quevedo et al. (2018), Gumba and Vlasenko (2017), Haabazoka (2019), Harfst et al. (2017), Kuznetsova et al. (2017), Li et al. (2018), Ramanathan et al. (2018), and Yao et al. (2018).

The applied issues of consistent and well-balanced economic & legal management of the modern economic systems' innovative development are studied in the works Andronova et al. (2019), Bogoviz and Ragulina (2020), Bogoviz and Sergi (2018), Petrenko and Shevyakova (2019), Popkova (2019), Popkova and Sergi (2020), Popkova et al. (2019), Popkova and Gulzat (2020), Popkova and Parakhina (2019), Popkova et al. (2017), Popkova and Zmiyak (2019), Popkova and Sergi (2018), Popkova and Sergi (2019), Ragulina (2019), Ragulina et al. (2019), Sergi (2003), Sergi (2019), Sergi et al. (2019)

Shulus et al. (2020), Stolyarov et al. (2020), and Zavyalova et al. (2018).

Content analysis of the existing research literature shows the main existing practices of economic & legal management of the modern economic systems' innovative development. The results of evaluation of their correspondence to the requirements of consistency and balance are shown in Table 17.1.

As shown in Table 17.1, the existing practices of economic & legal management of the modern economic systems' innovative development do not fully conform to the requirements of consistency and balance. Thus, the practice of foundation on government financing of R&D and the practice of limitation of hi-tech export only slightly conform to the requirements of consistency of management. The practice of support for the initiatives of integration of universities with business – e.g., based on clustering – conforms to the requirements of balance of management only to a certain extent.

The practices of introduction of strict criteria of resource efficiency of R&D (reduction of the number of researchers and the volume of financing with the similar target results), high requirements to international translation (publications) of the results of R&D and tax stimulation of the innovative activity of entrepreneurship do not conform to the requirements of consistency or balance. This confirms the necessity for developing a new concept, which would ensure consistent and well-balanced economic & legal management of modern economic systems' innovative development.

Table 17.1: Correspondence of the existing practices of economic & legal management of the modern economic systems' innovative development to the requirements of consistency and balance.

Existing practices of innovative development management	Correspondence to the requirements of consistency	Correspondence to the requirements of balance
Foundation on government financing of R&D	+ socially important R&D is financed	− requirements to commercialization of innovations are not envisaged
Introduction of strict criteria of resource efficiency of R&D (reduction of the number of researchers and the volume of financing with the similar target results)	− insufficient attention to the social consequences due to high burden on researchers	− For supporting resource efficiency, theoretical efficiency without commercialization innovations is enough
High requirements to international translation (publications) of the results of R&D	− instead of care for the internal social consequences, a research is worried about external adoption of innovations	− purely theoretical innovations are supported
Limitation of export of the leading technologies	+ possibility to focus on the internal social consequences	− high complexity of commercialization of innovations (limited demand)
Tax stimulation of innovative activity of entrepreneurship	− support for innovations, regardless of their social consequences	− support for innovations, regardless of their advantages for business
Support for initiatives of integration of universities with business – e.g., based on clustering	− commercial benefits come to the foreground	+ expanded opportunities for commercialization innovations

"+" – conforms;
"−" – does not conform.
Source: developed and compiled by the authors.

Results

Here we offer a concept of economic & legal management of the modern economic systems' innovative development, in which consistency of management is treated from the positions of social effectiveness, and balance – from the positions of economic effectiveness. The conceptual schemes of the recommended managerial practices are shown in Figures 17.1 and 17.2.

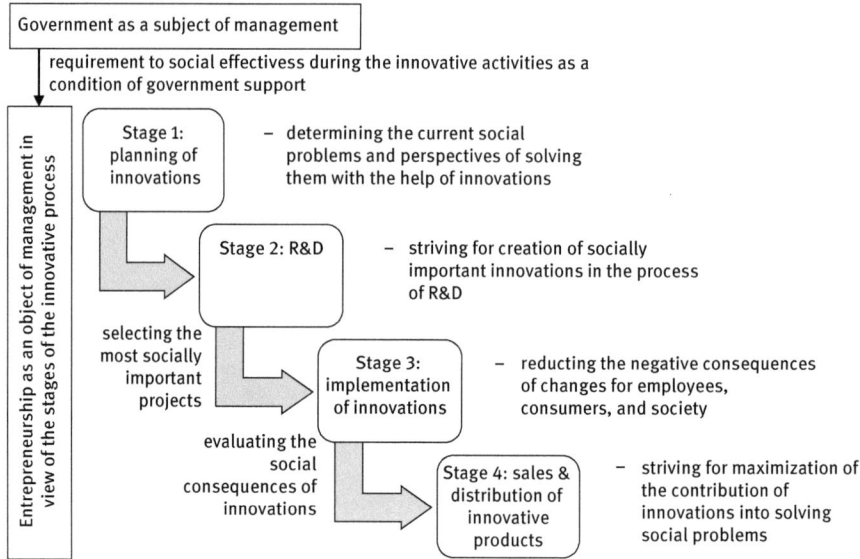

Figure 17.1: The conceptual scheme of managing the consistency of innovative activities in the modern economic systems.
Source: developed and compiled by the authors.

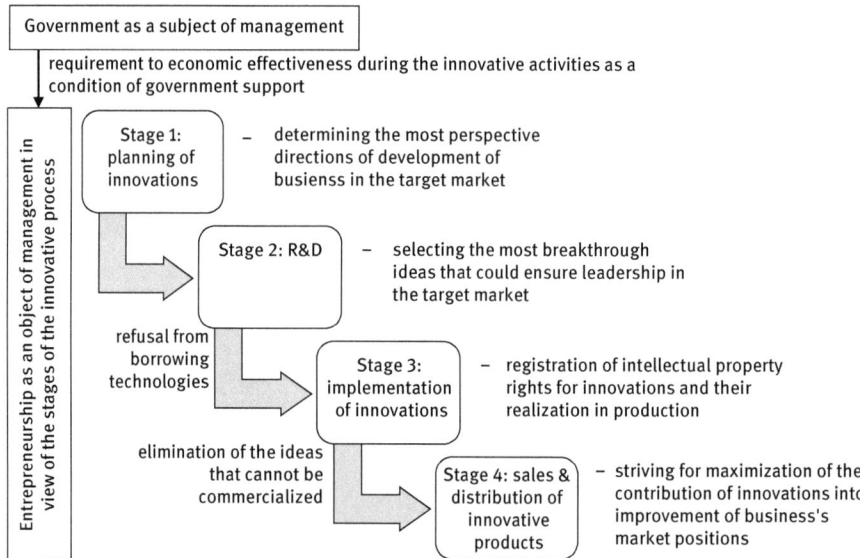

Figure 17.2: The conceptual scheme of managing the balance of innovative activities in modern economic systems.
Source: developed and compiled by the authors.

As is shown in Figure 17.1, government – as the subject of management – sets a requirement to social effectiveness during innovative activities as a condition of government support for entrepreneurship as the object of management. At each stage of the innovative process, there have to be certain results of management. The stage of planning of innovations should envisage determination of the important social problems and perspectives of solving them with the help of innovations. As a result of this stage, the most socially important innovative projects are selected.

At the stage of R&D, companies should strive for creation of socially important innovations. As a result of this stage, the social consequences of innovations are evaluated. The stage of patenting of innovations is omitted in this scheme, as it does not require specific results in the sphere of social effectiveness. At the stage of implementation of innovations, it is necessary to reduce the negative consequences of changes for employees, consumers, and society. At the stage of sales & distribution of innovative products, business has to strive for maximization of the contribution of innovations into solving social problems.

As shown in Figure 17.2, government – as the subject of management – sets a requirement to economic effectiveness during innovative activities as a condition of government support for entrepreneurship as the object of management. At each stage of the innovative process, there should be certain results of management. At the state of planning of innovations, the most perspective directions of business's development in the target market should be determined. As a result of this stage, it is necessary to refuse from borrowing technologies.

At the stage of R&D, the most breakthrough ideas should be selected – which can ensure leadership in the target market. As a result of this stage, the ideas that cannot be commercialized are eliminated. At the stage of implementation of innovations, intellectual property rights for innovations should be registered, and their realization in production should be ensured. At the stage of sales & distribution of innovative products, it is necessary to strive for maximization of the contribution of innovations into improvement of business's market positions.

The developed concept of consistent and well-balanced economic & legal management of the modern economic systems' innovative development also envisages systemic (e.g., once a year) monitoring of social and economic effectiveness of this management. For this, the corresponding indicators and their framework values are offered (Table 17.2).

As shown in Table 17.1, the objects of monitoring (indicators) should be corporate social reports, social treatment of innovations, quality of life, inflow of venture investments, economic growth, and competitiveness of business. Depending on the correspondence to the framework values, corrections into state management of innovative development should be made, or its successfulness should be acknowledged.

Table 17.2: The indicators and their framework values for monitoring of consistency and balance economic & legal management of the modern economic systems' innovative development.

Sphere of monitoring	Object of monitoring (indicator)	Successful management	Normal management	Critical management
Monitoring of consistency	Corporate social reports	more than 70% of innovations-active companies publish	31–69%% of innovations-active companies publish	less than 30% of innovations-active companies publish
	Social treatment of innovations	vivid positive	contradictory, heterogeneous	very negative
	Quality of life	grows	unchanged	decreases
Monitoring of balance	Inflow of venture investments	active inflow of investments	restrained inflow or unchanged volume of investments	outflow of investments
	Economic growth	quick (more than 10% annually)	moderate (3–9%)	slow (less than 3%)
	Competitiveness of business	grows	unchanged	decreases

Source: developed and compiled by the authors.

Conclusion

Thus, it has been proved that inconsistency and imbalance of economic & legal management of the modern economic systems' innovative development are explained by fundamental gaps. The existing managerial practices are not oriented at provision of consistency and balance and do not conform to their requirements. For solving this problem, the proprietary concept of consistent and well-balanced economic & legal management of the modern economic systems' innovative development is offered – it treats them from the positions of social and economic effectiveness and offers framework recommendations for management and monitoring of its results.

References

Andronova, I.V., Chernova, V.Y., Starostin, V.S., Degtereva (2019). Study of sector-specific innovation efforts: The case from Russian economy. Entrepreneurship and Sustainability Issues, Vsl Entrepreneurship and Sustainability Center, 7(1), p. 540–552.
Atkinsonk, R.D., Ezell, S.J. (2012). *Innovation Economics: the Race for Global Advantage*, New Haven, CT: Yale University Press.

Bogoviz, A.V., Ragulina, Y.V. (2020). Industry competitiveness in the new economy. Lecture Notes in Networks and Systems, 115, p. v–vi.

Bogoviz, A.V., Sergi, B.S. (2018). Will the Circular Economy Be the Future of Russia's Growth Model? In Bruno S. Sergi (Ed.). Exploring the Future of Russia'sEconomy and Markets: Towards Sustainable Economic Development, Bingley, UK: Emerald Publishing, pp. 125–141.

García-Quevedo, J., Segarra-Blasco, A., Teruel, M. (2018). Financial constraints and the failure of innovation projects. Technological Forecasting and Social Change, 127, p. 127–140.

Gumba, H.M., Vlasenko, V.A. (2017). Strategy of development of innovative activity in industry and construction: The rationale of the regional dimension. Izvestiya Vysshikh Uchebnykh Zavedenii, Seriya Teknologiya Tekstil'noi Promyshlennosti, 2017-January(2), p. 14–18.

Haabazoka, L. (2019). A Study of the Effects of Technological Innovations on the Performance of Commercial Banks in Developing Countries – A Case of the Zambian Banking Industry. In: Popkova E. (eds) The Future of the Global Financial System: Downfall or Harmony. ISC 2018. Lecture Notes in Networks and Systems, vol 57. Springer, Cham, Online ISBN 978-3-030-00102-5, https://doi.org/10.1007/978-3-030-00102-5_132

Harfst, J., Pichler, P., Fischer, W. (2017). Regional Ambassadors-An Innovative Element for the Development of Rural Areas? European Countryside, 9(2), p. 359–374.

Kuznetsova, O., Kuznetsova, S., Yumaev, E., Kuznetsov, V., Galtseva, O. (2017). Formation and Development of the Training System for Innovative Development of Regional Industry. E3S Web of Conferences, 15,04019.

Li, X., Subrahmanyam, A., Yang, X. (2018). Can financial innovation succeed by catering to behavioral preferences? Evidence from a callable options market. Journal of Financial Economics, 2(1), p. 34–42.

Petrenko, E.S., Shevyakova, A.L. (2019). Features and perspectives of digitization in Kazakhstan. Studies in Computational Intelligence, 826, p. 889–899.

Popkova, E.G. (2019). Preconditions of formation and development of industry 4.0 in the conditions of knowledge economy. Studies in Systems, Decision and Control, 169(1),65–72.

Popkova, E.G., Sergi, B.S. (2020). Human Capital and AI in Industry 4.0. Convergence and Divergence in Social Entrepreneurship in Russia. Journal of Intellectual Capital, In press, 2020.

Popkova, E.G., Egorova, E.N., Popova, E., Pozdnyakova, U.A. (2019). The model of state management of economy on the basis of the internet of things. Studies in Computational Intelligence, 826, pp. 1137–1144.

Popkova, E.G., Gulzat, K. (2020). Technological Revolution in the 21st Century: Digital Society vs. Artificial Intelligence. Lecture Notes in Networks and Systems, 91, p. 339–345.

Popkova, E.G., Parakhina, V.N. (2019). Managing the global financial system on the basis of artificial intelligence: possibilities and limitations. Lecture Notes in Networks and Systems, 57, pp. 939–946.

Popkova, E.G., Poluyufta, L., Beshanova, Y., Popova, L.V., Kolesnikova, E. (2017). Innovations as a basis for marketing strategies of Russian oil companies in the conditions of oil prices reduction. Contributions to Economics, (9783319606958), p. 449–455.

Popkova, E.G., Zmiyak, K.V. (2019). Priorities of training of digital personnel for industry 4.0: social competencies vs technical competencies. On the Horizon, 27(3–4), p. 138–144.

Popkova, E.G., Sergi, B.S. (2018). Will Industry 4.0 and Other Innovations Impact Russia's Development? In Bruno S. Sergi (Ed.) Exploring the Future of Russia's Economy and Markets: Towards Sustainable Economic Development (pp. 51–68). Bingley, UK: Emerald Publishing Limited.

Popkova, E.G., Sergi, B.S. (Eds.) (2019). Digital Economy: Complexity and Variety vs. Rationality. Berlin: Springer International Publishing.

Ragulina, Y.V. (2019). Priorities of development of industry 4.0 in modern economic systems with different progress in formation of knowledge economy. Studies in Systems, Decision and Control, 169, p. 167–174.

Ragulina, Y.V., Alekseev, A.N., Strizhkina, I.V., Tumanov, A.I. (2019). Methodology of criterial evaluation of consequences of the industrial revolution of the 21st century. Studies in Systems, Decision and Control, 169, p. 235–244.

Ramanathan, R., Ramanathan, U., Bentley, Y. (2018). The debate on flexibility of environmental regulations, innovation capabilities and financial performance – A novel use of DEA. Omega (United Kingdom), 75, p. 131–138.

Sergi, B.S. (2003). Economic Dynamics in Transitional Economies: The Four-P Governments, the EU Enlargement, and the Bruxelles Consensus. New York: Routledge.

Sergi, B.S. (Ed.) (2019). Tech, Smart Cities, and Regional Development in Contemporary Russia. Bingley, UK: Emerald Publishing Limited.

Sergi, B.S., Popkova, E.G. Bogoviz, A.V., Litvinova, T.N. (2019). Understanding Industry 4.0: AI, the Internet of Things, and the Future of Work. Bingley, UK: Emerald Publishing Limited.

Shulus, A.A., Akopova, E.S., Przhedetskaya, N.V., Borzenko, K.V. (2020). Intellectual Production and Consumption: A New Reality of the 21st Century. Lecture Notes in Networks and Systems, 92, pp. 353–359.

Stolyarov, N.O., Petrenko, E.S., Serova, O.A., Umuralieva, A.S. (2020). The Digital Reality of the Modern Economy: New Actors and New Decision-Making Logic. Lecture Notes in Networks and Systems, 87, p. 882–888.

Yao, M., Di, H., Zheng, X., Xu, X. (2018). Impact of payment technology innovations on the traditional financial industry: A focus on China. Technological Forecasting and Social Change, 2(1), p. 22–29.

Zavyalova, E.B. Studenikin, N.V. Starikova, E.A. (2018). Business participation in implementation of socially oriented Sustainable Development Goals in countries of Central Asia and the Caucasus region. Central Asia and the Caucasus, 19(2), p. 56–63.

Leonid V. Stolyarov, Dina N. Savinskaya, Camila I. Weisman,
Tatiana P. Saraldaeva and Ekaterina S. Safronova

18 A Perspective Algorithm of Economic and Legal Management of the Modern Economic Systems' Innovative Development

Introduction

Imperfection of the existing algorithm of economic & legal management of the modern economic systems' innovative development causes a range of problems, which hinder the development and reduce its effectiveness. One of the problems is excessive or deficit financing of the innovative activities in economy. Financial support for innovative activities is often considered separately from the general process of innovations management.

In the course of emergence of new problems of socio-economic development, the volume of financing of innovative activities changes. Financing of innovations is also a part of the state budget, and the volume of this financing is determined by deficit or surplus of the budget. If the budget assets are sufficient, the means for grant support for R&D without clear priorities of innovative development could be allocated. In this case, expenditures for R&D are a tool of improving the country's position in international rankings of innovative development, and innovations are considered as a goal in itself.

Another problem is unjustified application of the measures of state regulation, when the set managerial goals could be achieved based on market self-management. Without a clear idea of the order of management of innovative development, the need for correcting the innovative activities could appear unexpectedly. Absence of preliminary assessment of the market situation and planning of the managerial measures cause a high risk of regulation of the innovative activities, which is connected to excessive expenditure of managerial resources and limitation of the market mechanism.

Randomness of the existing managerial algorithm should be overcome by ordering its stages. This is an important scientific and practical problem, which is to be solved

Leonid V. Stolyarov, Moscow Region State University, Mytishchi, Russia
Dina N. Savinskaya, "Kuban State Agrarian University named after I.T. Trubilin", Krasnodar, Russia
Camila I. Weisman, Ekaterina S. Safronova, State Educational Institution of Higher Education
Moscow Region "University of Technology", Korolev, Russia
Tatiana P. Saraldaeva, State University of Management, Moscow, Russia

https://doi.org/10.1515/9783110643701-018

in this chapter. The purpose is to develop a perspective algorithm of economic & legal management of the modern economic systems' innovative development.

Materials and Method

Stages of the process of economic & legal management of the modern economic systems' innovative development are discussed in the works Atkinsonk and Ezell (2012), García-Quevedo et al. (2018), Gumba and Vlasenko (2017), Haabazoka (2019), Harfst et al. (2017), Kuznetsova et al. (2017), Li et al. (2018), Ramanathan et al. (2018), and Yao et al. (2018).

The existing algorithm of economic & legal management of the modern economic systems' innovative development is studied in the works Andronova et al. (2019), Bogoviz and Ragulina (2020), Bogoviz and Sergi (2018)6 Petrenko and Shevyakova (2019), Popkova (2019), Popkova and Sergi (2020), Popkova et al. (2019), Popkova and Gulzat (2020), Popkova and Parakhina (2019), Popkova et al. (2017), Popkova and Zmiyak (2019), Popkova and Sergi (2018), Popkova and Sergi (2019), Ragulina (2019), Ragulina et al. (2019), Sergi (2003), Sergi (2019), Sergi et al. (2019)

Shulus et al. (2020), Stolyarov et al. (2020), and Zavyalova et al. (2018).

Analysis of the contents of the above literature sources show that there is no clear and comprehensive idea of the algorithm of economic & legal management of modern economic systems' innovative development in the modern economic science. There is no generally accepted totality of stages of this algorithm either.

However, systematization of the materials of the existing publications and the performed overview of the national and international normative & legal materials on the topic of innovative development shows that the algorithm of economic & legal management of innovative development is treated as a linear process, which is not repeated. Each new innovative project for company and the time period of innovative development for a country is considered separately.

Results

The developed perspective algorithm of economic & legal management of the modern economic systems' innovative development is shown in Figure 18.1.

The offered algorithm is of the cyclic – not linear – character. This ensures accumulation of experience and constant improvement of the managerial practice, as well as succession of goals and priorities of innovative development. The algorithm contains six consecutive stages, each of which is mandatory.

At the first stage, priorities of innovative development are determined. The priorities could be social (solving certain social tasks or increasing the general quality

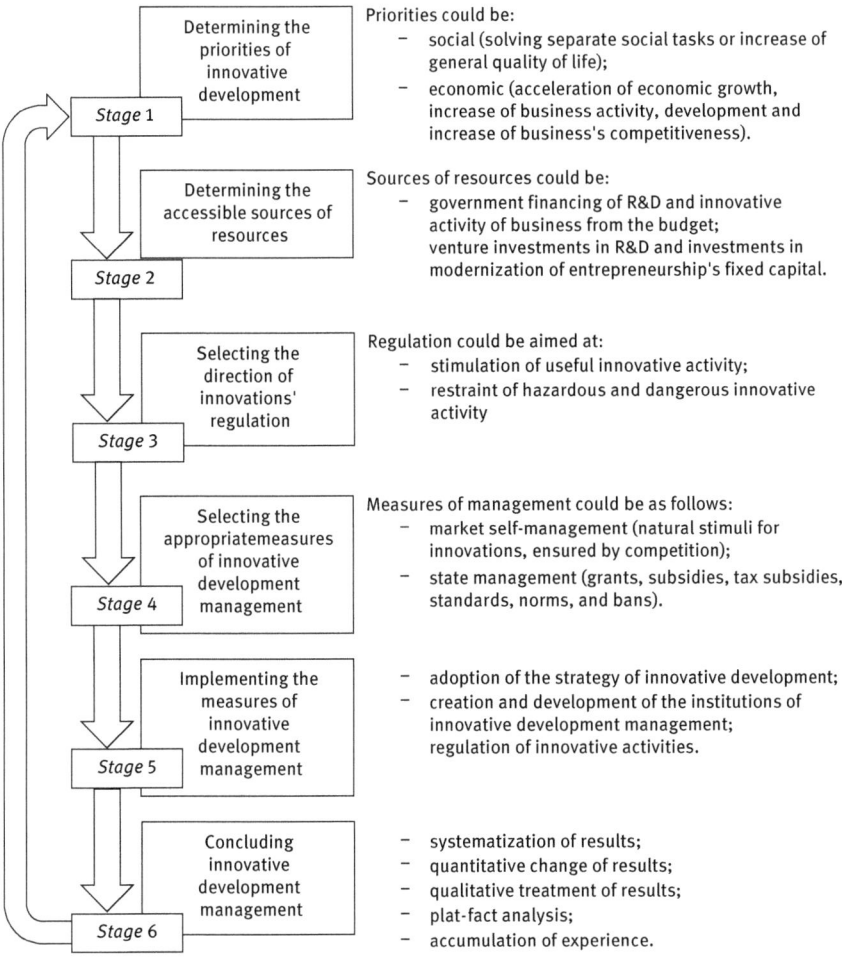

		Priorities could be:
Determining the priorities of innovative development **Stage 1**		– social (solving separate social tasks or increase of general quality of life); – economic (acceleration of economic growth, increase of business activity, development and increase of business's competitiveness).
Determining the accessible sources of resources **Stage 2**		Sources of resources could be: – government financing of R&D and innovative activity of business from the budget; venture investments in R&D and investments in modernization of entrepreneurship's fixed capital.
Selecting the direction of innovations' regulation **Stage 3**		Regulation could be aimed at: – stimulation of useful innovative activity; – restraint of hazardous and dangerous innovative activity
Selecting the appropriatemeasures of innovative development management **Stage 4**		Measures of management could be as follows: – market self-management (natural stimuli for innovations, ensured by competition); – state management (grants, subsidies, tax subsidies, standards, norms, and bans).
Implementing the measures of innovative development management **Stage 5**		– adoption of the strategy of innovative development; – creation and development of the institutions of innovative development management; regulation of innovative activities.
Concluding innovative development management **Stage 6**		– systematization of results; – quantitative change of results; – qualitative treatment of results; – plat-fact analysis; – accumulation of experience.

Figure 18.1: A perspective algorithm of economic & legal management of the modern economic systems' innovative development.
Source: developed and compiled by the authors.

of life) and economic (acceleration of economic growth, increase of business activity, and development and increase of business's competitiveness). The priorities are determined based on the general strategy of socio-economic development of the economic system and based on the current situation in the internal and external (global) environments.

At the second stage, accessible sources of resources are determined. The sources could be government financing of R&D and innovative activity of business, as well as venture investments in R&D and investments in modernization of entrepreneurship's fixed capital. Preference should be given to private venture investments, and government financing should be provided only is there is no alternative.

At the third stage, the direction of innovations' regulation is selected. Regulation could be aimed at stimulation of useful innovative activity or at restraint of hazardous or dangerous innovative activity. The accumulated experience and the current practice of innovative activities in economy are taken into account here. In in the previous period, innovations ensured social advantages, and current R&D is conducted by socially-responsible business – thus, innovations require support. If the economic system has an experience of negative consequences of innovations, and social responsibility of business, which conducts R&D and implements innovations, is low, innovations could cause high risks and require limitation and thorough control by the government.

The fourth stage envisages selection of the appropriate measures of innovative development management. The management measures could be market self-management (natural stimuli for innovations, ensured by competition) or state management (grants, subsidies, tax subsidies, standards, norms, and bans). As in the case with financing, preference should be given to market self-management.

However, even in this case government has an important role in innovative development management. State management should be indirect and should be aimed at supporting effectiveness and sufficient strength of the market mechanism for executing the task of stimulation or restraint of innovations. Indirect regulation could also envisage support for social progress and institutionalization of responsible consumption.

The fifth stage envisages implementation of the management measures of innovative development: adoption of the strategy of innovative development, creation and development of the institutions of innovative development management, and regulation of the innovative activities. In the existing algorithm, this state is sometimes seen as the only one. We think that implementation of the managerial measures should be preceded by thorough preparation, for ensuring the effectiveness of these measures.

The sixth stage envisages conclusion of the results of innovative development management. It includes systematization of results, quantitative measuring of results, qualitative treatment of results, plan-fact analysis, and accumulation of experience. The following scale is offered for monitoring of the results of economic & legal management of the modern economic systems' innovative development (Table 18.1).

As is shown in Table 18.1, four evaluation criteria for monitoring of the results of economic & legal management of the modern economic systems' innovative development are offered. 1st criterion: economic effectiveness. For the results of management to be considered positive according to this criterion, return of investments in innovations should be achieved, and economic advantages (micro-economic – e.g., profit from commercialization innovations and sales of innovative products) should exceed the factual expenditures (e.g., investments in restoration of fixed capital).

2nd criterion: consistency. For the results of management to be considered positive according to this criterion, the current social problems should be solved with the help of innovations. 3rd criterion: balance. For the results of management to be considered positive according to this criterion, successful commercialization of innovations and

Table 18.1: The scale for monitoring of the results of economic & legal management of the modern economic systems' innovative development.

Evaluation criterion	Treatment of the management results by the set criterion		
	Positive results	**Neutral results**	**Negative results**
Economic effectiveness	return of investments in innovations is achieved	investments are returned, but no profit	return of investments is not achieved
	economic advantages exceed the factual expenditures	economic advantages are at the level of factual expenditures	factual expenditures exceed economic advantages
Consistency	innovations allow solving the current social problems	innovations are not connected to vivid social consequences	social consequences of innovations are negative
Balance	successful commercialization of innovations, strengthening of competitiveness of entrepreneurship	commercialization of innovations does not stimulate strengthening of entrepreneurship's competitiveness	commercialization of innovations is not achieved
Macro-economic consequences	goals of innovative development are achieved	gals of innovative development are not fully achieved	goals of innovative development are not achieved
	non-target macro-economic advantages from innovations are gained		non-target advantages are not gained

Source: developed and compiled by the authors.

strengthening of competitiveness of entrepreneurship should be performed. 4th criterion: macro-economic consequences. For the results of management to be considered positive according to this criterion, the goals of innovative development should be achieved, and non-target macro-economic advantages from innovations should be reached.

Conclusion

It should be noted that the developed perspective algorithm economic & legal management of the modern economic systems' innovative development is recommended for application at the national and regional levels – i.e., it could be useful for the purposes of territorial planning and management. The new algorithm ensures the following advantages of economic & legal management of the modern economic systems' innovative development:

- cyclic character of innovative development management: each innovative process and each innovative strategy is considered a new loop of the cycle of innovative development. This allows forming traditions of innovative development, achieving its goals at the current or next loop of development and formulating the priorities of the innovative activities with higher precision, based on past experience;
- order, regularity, and timeliness of management, absence of gaps: the offered algorithm is detailed and includes all the necessary stages. Due to this, the risks of the innovative activities are brought down to the minimum. The offered recommendations for managerial decisions allow reducing the burden on the government machine and realizing the potential of market self-management.

References

Andronova, I.V., Chernova, V.Y., Starostin, V.S., Degtereva (2019). Study of sector-specific innovation efforts: The case from Russian economy. Entrepreneurship and Sustainability Issues, Vsl Entrepreneurship and Sustainability Center, 7(1), p. 540–552.

Atkinsonk, R.D., Ezell, S.J. (2012). *Innovation Economics: the Race for Global Advantage*, New Haven, CT: Yale University Press.

Bogoviz, A.V., Ragulina, Y.V. (2020). Industry competitiveness in the new economy. Lecture Notes in Networks and Systems, 115, p. v–vi.

Bogoviz, A.V., Sergi, B.S. (2018). Will the Circular Economy Be the Future of Russia's Growth Model? In Bruno S. Sergi (Ed.). Exploring the Future of Russia'sEconomy and Markets: Towards Sustainable Economic Development, Bingley, UK: Emerald Publishing, pp. 125–141.

García-Quevedo, J., Segarra-Blasco, A., Teruel, M. (2018). Financial constraints and the failure of innovation projects. Technological Forecasting and Social Change, 127, p. 127–140.

Gumba, H.M., Vlasenko, V.A. (2017). Strategy of development of innovative activity in industry and construction: The rationale of the regional dimension. Izvestiya Vysshikh Uchebnykh Zavedenii, Seriya Teknologiya Tekstil'noi Promyshlennosti, 2017-January(2), p. 14–18.

Haabazoka, L. (2019). A Study of the Effects of Technological Innovations on the Performance of Commercial Banks in Developing Countries – A Case of the Zambian Banking Industry. In: Popkova E. (eds) The Future of the Global Financial System: Downfall or Harmony. ISC 2018. Lecture Notes in Networks and Systems, vol 57. Springer, Cham, https://doi.org/10.1007/978-3-030-00102-5_132

Harfst, J., Pichler, P., Fischer, W. (2017). Regional Ambassadors-An Innovative Element for the Development of Rural Areas? European Countryside, 9(2), p. 359–374.

Kuznetsova, O., Kuznetsova, S., Yumaev, E., Kuznetsov, V., Galtseva, O. (2017). Formation and Development of the Training System for Innovative Development of Regional Industry. E3S Web of Conferences, 15,04019.

Li, X., Subrahmanyam, A., Yang, X. (2018). Can financial innovation succeed by catering to behavioral preferences? Evidence from a callable options market. Journal of Financial Economics, 2(1), p. 34–42.

Petrenko, E.S., Shevyakova, A.L. (2019). Features and perspectives of digitization in Kazakhstan. Studies in Computational Intelligence, 826, p. 889–899.

Popkova, E.G. (2019). Preconditions of formation and development of industry 4.0 in the conditions of knowledge economy. Studies in Systems, Decision and Control, 169(1), 65–72.

Popkova, E.G., Sergi, B.S. (2020). Human Capital and AI in Industry 4.0. Convergence and Divergence in Social Entrepreneurship in Russia. Journal of Intellectual Capital, In press, 2020. https://doi.org/10.1108/JIC-09-2019-0224

Popkova, E.G., Egorova, E.N., Popova, E., Pozdnyakova, U.A. (2019). The model of state management of economy on the basis of the internet of things. Studies in Computational Intelligence, 826, pp. 1137–1144.

Popkova, E.G., Gulzat, K. (2020). Technological Revolution in the 21st Century: Digital Society vs. Artificial Intelligence. Lecture Notes in Networks and Systems, 91, p. 339–345.

Popkova, E.G., Parakhina, V.N. (2019). Managing the global financial system on the basis of artificial intelligence: possibilities and limitations. Lecture Notes in Networks and Systems, 57, pp. 939–946.

Popkova, E.G., Poluyufta, L., Beshanova, Y., Popova, L.V., Kolesnikova, E. (2017). Innovations as a basis for marketing strategies of Russian oil companies in the conditions of oil prices reduction. Contributions to Economics, (9783319606958), p. 449–455.

Popkova, E.G., Zmiyak, K.V. (2019). Priorities of training of digital personnel for industry 4.0: social competencies vs technical competencies. On the Horizon, 27(3–4), p. 138–144.

Popkova, E.G., Sergi, B.S. (2018). Will Industry 4.0 and Other Innovations Impact Russia's Development? In Bruno S. Sergi (Ed.) Exploring the Future of Russia's Economy and Markets: Towards Sustainable Economic Development (pp. 51–68). Bingley, UK: Emerald Publishing Limited.

Popkova, E.G., Sergi, B.S. (Eds.) (2019). Digital Economy: Complexity and Variety vs. Rationality. Berlin: Springer International Publishing.

Ragulina, Y.V. (2019). Priorities of development of industry 4.0 in modern economic systems with different progress in formation of knowledge economy. Studies in Systems, Decision and Control, 169, p. 167–174.

Ragulina, Y.V., Alekseev, A.N., Strizhkina, I.V., Tumanov, A.I. (2019). Methodology of criterial evaluation of consequences of the industrial revolution of the 21st century. Studies in Systems, Decision and Control, 169, p. 235–244.

Ramanathan, R., Ramanathan, U., Bentley, Y. (2018). The debate on flexibility of environmental regulations, innovation capabilities and financial performance – A novel use of DEA. Omega (United Kingdom), 75, p. 131–138.

Sergi, B.S. (2003). Economic Dynamics in Transitional Economies: The Four-P Governments, the EU Enlargement, and the Bruxelles Consensus. New York: Routledge.

Sergi, B.S. (Ed.) (2019). Tech, Smart Cities, and Regional Development in Contemporary Russia. Bingley, UK: Emerald Publishing Limited.

Sergi, B.S., Popkova, E.G. Bogoviz, A.V., Litvinova, T.N. (2019). Understanding Industry 4.0: AI, the Internet of Things, and the Future of Work. Bingley, UK: Emerald Publishing Limited.

Shulus, A.A., Akopova, E.S., Przhedetskaya, N.V., Borzenko, K.V. (2020). Intellectual Production and Consumption: A New Reality of the 21st Century. Lecture Notes in Networks and Systems, 92, pp. 353–359.

Stolyarov, N.O., Petrenko, E.S., Serova, O.A., Umuralieva, A.S. (2020). The Digital Reality of the Modern Economy: New Actors and New Decision-Making Logic. Lecture Notes in Networks and Systems, 87, p. 882–888.

Yao, M., Di, H., Zheng, X., Xu, X. (2018). Impact of payment technology innovations on the traditional financial industry: A focus on China. Technological Forecasting and Social Change, 2(1), p. 22–29.

Zavyalova, E.B. Studenikin, N.V. Starikova, E.A. (2018). Business participation in implementation of socially oriented Sustainable Development Goals in countries of Central Asia and the Caucasus region. Central Asia and the Caucasus, 19(2), p. 56–63.

Ekaterina S. Vasiutina, Olga G. Kryukova, Oksana E. Ivanova,
Elena V. Popova and Olga A. Ageeva

19 The Model of Leveling the Global Disproportions in Modern Economic Systems' Innovative Development Management

Introduction

Imbalance of the world markets of innovations is one of the important problems on the path of provision of well-balanced development of the global economic system. Imperfection of the approaches to managing the modern economic systems' innovative development is one of the main reasons of differentiation of countries of the world, together with provision with resources and natural & climate and socio-cultural conditions, which are not subject to state management.

Though innovative development is the most manageable cause (out of the causes listed above), there are no visible results yet – moreover, it is possible to observe the increase of disproportions in the world markets of leading technologies and hi-tech products. Developed countries show stable leadership in these markets, possessing top universities, prominent production capacities in R&D, and licenses and patents for the key developments, which form the basis for the future research.

Based on the experience of the recent decades, there formed a hypothesis that underdeveloped countries cannot accelerate the rate of their innovative development and completely depend on external support from developed countries and international organizations. According to this hypothesis, reduction of the gap between developing and developed countries is seen in the context of diffusion of innovations and international technological exchange, as well as movement of hi-tech productions on the territory of underdeveloped countries.

However, there are no scientific proofs of this hypothesis. What is more important, the measures that are implemented according to this hypothesis lead to an opposite

Ekaterina S. Vasiutina, Federal State Budgetary Institution of Higher Education «Russian State Social University», Moscow, Russia
Olga G. Kryukova, Financial University under the Government of the Russian Federation, Moscow, Russia
Oksana E. Ivanova, Federal State Budgetary Educational Institution of Higher Education «Kostroma State Agricultural Academy», Karavaevo, Russia
Elena V. Popova, "Kuban State Agrarian University named after I.T. Trubilin", Krasnodar, Russia
Olga A. Ageeva, State University of Management, Moscow, Russia

https://doi.org/10.1515/9783110643701-019

result: instead of an impulse for development, underdeveloped countries are losing the ability for innovative development and turn into production departments of developed countries. That's why we offer an alternative hypothesis – underdeveloped countries could and should change the approach to managing the innovative development and master a new role in the world markets of innovations; the key to overcoming the disproportions in these markets lies not in the sphere of developed countries, which protect their leadership, but in the sphere of underdeveloped countries, which should become their rivals.

The purpose of this chapter is to model the current dynamics of the world markets of innovations and the perspectives of leveling of the global disproportions in managing the modern economic systems' innovative development based on modernization of management in underdeveloped countries.

Materials and Method

The problem of the global differentiation of the level of modern economic systems' innovative development and inequality of the world markets of innovations and hi-tech is considered in the works Atkinsonk and Ezell (2012), García-Quevedo et al. (2018), Gumba and Vlasenko (2017), Haabazoka (2019), Harfst et al. (2017), Kuznetsova et al. (2017), Li et al. (2018), Ramanathan et al. (2018), and Yao et al. (2018).

The existing approach to solving the problem of disproportions in modern economic systems' innovative development with the help of managerial measures that are used in developed countries and in the activities of international organizations is shown in the works Andronova et al. (2019), Bogoviz and Ragulina (2020), Bogoviz and Sergi (2018), Petrenko and Shevyakova (2019), Popkova (2019), Popkova and Sergi (2020), Popkova et al. (2019), Popkova and Gulzat (2020), Popkova and Parakhina (2019), Popkova et al. (2017), Popkova and Zmiyak (2019), Popkova and Sergi (2018), Popkova and Sergi (2019), Ragulina (2019), Ragulina et al. (2019), Sergi (2003), Sergi (2019), Sergi et al. (2019), Shulus et al. (2020), Stolyarov et al. (2020), and Zavyalova et al. (2018).

The existing literature's description of the perspectives of leveling of the global disproportions in the modern economic systems' innovative development based on the measures that could be implemented in underdeveloped countries is not sufficient. Modeling of the process of emergence of the global disproportions in managing the modern economic systems' innovative development, which shows the drawbacks of the existing approach, is performed in Figure 19.1.

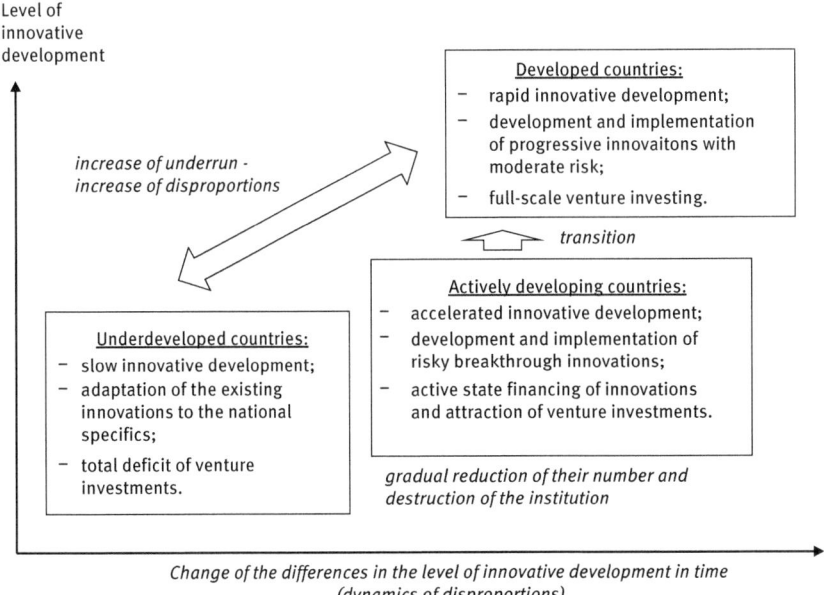

Figure 19.1: Modeling of the process of emergence of the global disproportions in managing the modern economic systems' innovative development.
Source: developed and compiled by the authors.

As shown in Figure 19.1, there are three players in the world markets of innovations and hi-tech:

- Underdeveloped countries, which innovative development is slow and which adapt the existing innovations to the national specifics, with total deficit of venture investments;
- Actively developing countries, with quick innovative development, which develop and implement risky breakthrough innovations, perform active state financing of innovations, and attract venture investments;
- Developed countries, with rapid innovative development, which develop and implement progressive innovations with moderate risk and conduct full-scale venture investing.

Under the existing managerial approach to managing the innovative development in economic systems, actively developing countries perform a gradual transition to the category of developed countries. Their number is reduced, and the institution of periphery of the world markets of innovations is destroyed, as underdeveloped countries are not developing. The change of differences in the level of innovative development in time, envisages increase of underrun – growth of disproportions. Thus, dynamics of the disproportions is negative.

Results

Here we offer a new model of managing the modern economic systems' innovative development at the global scale. Its comparative analysis (compared to the existing model) is performed in Table 19.1.

Table 19.1: Comparative analysis of the existing and offered new model of managing the modern economic systems' innovative development at the global scale.

Characteristics of management		Existing model	Offered new model
Conditions	Dominating method of supporting the underdeveloped countries (role of international organizations)	transfer of obsolete technologies for delayed implementation	provision of venture investments for independent development
	Approach to managing the innovative development in underdeveloped countries	orientation at adaptation of the existing technologies	active attraction of venture investments, orientation at breakthrough innovations
	Social environment (consumer preferences) in underdeveloped countries	preferring the imported innovations, mistrust to domestic production	import substitution, preferring domestic innovations
Results	Role of underdeveloped countries in the world markets of innovations and hi-tech	passive development: production departments of developed countries	active development: own R&D and hi-tech productions
	Structure of world markets of innovations	two-component structure: only leaders and outsiders	poly-component structures: leaders, outsiders, and developed periphery
	Disproportions in the level of innovative development at the global scale	large and increasing with time	moderate and decreasing with time

Source: developed and compiled by the authors.

As shown in Table 19.1, the dominating method of supporting the underdeveloped countries (role of international organizations) in the existing model consists in transfer of obsolete technologies for delayed implementation, and in the offered new model – in provision of venture investments for independent development. The approach to managing the innovative development in underdeveloped countries envisages orientation at adaptation of the existing technologies, and in the recommended model – at active attraction of venture investments and orientation at breakthrough innovations. The social environment (consumer preferences) in underdeveloped countries is characterized by preference for imported innovations and mistrust to domestic production – this should be replaced by import substitution and preference for domestic innovations.

Observation of the above conditions allows achieving the following results. The role of underdeveloped countries in the world markets of innovations and hi-tech in the existing model is brought down to passive development as production departments of developed countries – according to the authors' recommendations, it should change to active development, which envisages own R&D and development of hi-tech productions.

The structure of the world markets of innovations in the existing model has two components – it should have only leaders and outsiders, and in the new model there should be leaders, outsiders, and periphery. Disproportions in the level of innovative development at the global scale are large and increase with time, and in the new model they will be moderate and will decrease with time. The recommended new model of leveling the global disproportions in management of modern economic systems' innovative development is shown in Figure 19.2.

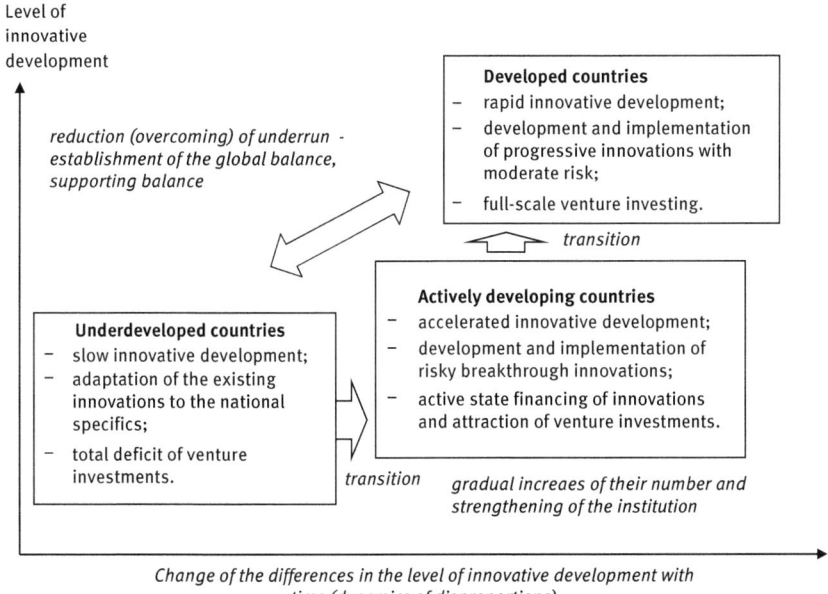

Figure 19.2: The model of leveling the global disproportions in management of modern economic systems' innovative development.
Source: developed and compiled by the authors.

As shown in Figure 19.2, in the offered new model actively developing countries and underdeveloped countries perform a transition (underdeveloped countries become actively developing countries). This allows filling and preventing the void in the global markets of innovations and hi-tech. The number of actively developing countries grows gradually, and their institution is strengthening. Reduction (overcoming) of the underrun is achieved – establishment of the global balance of in the global economy.

Conclusion

The research results have provided the theoretical arguments in favor of the offered hypothesis on perspectives of the alternative practice of overcoming of disproportions in the global markets of innovations and hi-tech. It has been shown that implementation of the existing managerial model leads to increase of disproportions – due to actively developing countries' transition to the category of developed countries and emergence of void in their place, while underdeveloped countries do not have opportunities for independent innovative development.

The new developed model of leveling the global disproportions in management of modern economic systems' innovative development allows underdeveloped countries to develop independently and pass into the category of actively developing countries. In this case, the gap between them and developed countries will be gradually decreasing, and the disproportion will be becoming less significant. During further studies, it is recommended to approbate the developed model in the practice of underdeveloped countries and discuss them for verification of the offered scientific hypothesis.

References

Andronova, I.V., Chernova, V.Y., Starostin, V.S., Degtereva (2019). Study of sector-specific innovation efforts: The case from Russian economy. Entrepreneurship and Sustainability Issues, Vsl Entrepreneurship and Sustainability Center, 7(1), p. 540–552.

Atkinsonk, R.D., Ezell, S.J. (2012). *Innovation Economics: the Race for Global Advantage*, New Haven, CT: Yale University Press.

Bogoviz, A.V., Ragulina, Y.V. (2020). Industry competitiveness in the new economy. Lecture Notes in Networks and Systems, 115, p. v–vi.

Bogoviz, A.V., Sergi, B.S. (2018). Will the Circular Economy Be the Future of Russia's Growth Model? In Bruno S. Sergi (Ed.). Exploring the Future of Russia'sEconomy and Markets: Towards Sustainable Economic Development, Bingley, UK: Emerald Publishing, pp. 125–141.

García-Quevedo, J., Segarra-Blasco, A., Teruel, M. (2018). Financial constraints and the failure of innovation projects. Technological Forecasting and Social Change, 127, p. 127–140.

Gumba, H.M., Vlasenko, V.A. (2017). Strategy of development of innovative activity in industry and construction: The rationale of the regional dimension. Izvestiya Vysshikh Uchebnykh Zavedenii, Seriya Teknologiya Tekstil'noi Promyshlennosti, 2017-January(2), p. 14–18.

Haabazoka, L. (2019). A Study of the Effects of Technological Innovations on the Performance of Commercial Banks in Developing Countries – A Case of the Zambian Banking Industry. In: Popkova E. (eds) The Future of the Global Financial System: Downfall or Harmony. ISC 2018. Lecture Notes in Networks and Systems, vol 57. Springer, Cham, Online ISBN 978-3-030-00102-5, https://doi.org/10.1007/978-3-030-00102-5_132

Harfst, J., Pichler, P., Fischer, W. (2017). Regional Ambassadors-An Innovative Element for the Development of Rural Areas? European Countryside, 9(2), p. 359–374.

Kuznetsova, O., Kuznetsova, S., Yumaev, E., Kuznetsov, V., Galtseva, O. (2017). Formation and Development of the Training System for Innovative Development of Regional Industry. E3S Web of Conferences, 15,04019.

Li, X., Subrahmanyam, A., Yang, X. (2018). Can financial innovation succeed by catering to behavioral preferences? Evidence from a callable options market. Journal of Financial Economics, 2(1), p. 34–42.

Petrenko, E.S., Shevyakova, A.L. (2019). Features and perspectives of digitization in Kazakhstan. Studies in Computational Intelligence, 826, p. 889–899.

Popkova, E.G. (2019). Preconditions of formation and development of industry 4.0 in the conditions of knowledge economy. Studies in Systems, Decision and Control, 169(1), 65–72.

Popkova, E.G., Sergi, B.S. (2020). Human Capital and AI in Industry 4.0. Convergence and Divergence in Social Entrepreneurship in Russia. Journal of Intellectual Capital, In press, 2020.

Popkova, E.G., Egorova, E.N., Popova, E., Pozdnyakova, U.A. (2019). The model of state management of economy on the basis of the internet of things. Studies in Computational Intelligence, 826, pp. 1137–1144.

Popkova, E.G., Gulzat, K. (2020). Technological Revolution in the 21st Century: Digital Society vs. Artificial Intelligence. Lecture Notes in Networks and Systems, 91, p. 339–345.

Popkova, E.G., Parakhina, V.N. (2019). Managing the global financial system on the basis of artificial intelligence: possibilities and limitations. Lecture Notes in Networks and Systems, 57, pp. 939–946.

Popkova, E.G., Poluyufta, L., Beshanova, Y., Popova, L.V., Kolesnikova, E. (2017). Innovations as a basis for marketing strategies of Russian oil companies in the conditions of oil prices reduction. Contributions to Economics, (9783319606958), p. 449–455.

Popkova, E.G., Zmiyak, K.V. (2019). Priorities of training of digital personnel for industry 4.0: social competencies vs technical competencies. On the Horizon, 27(3–4), p. 138–144.

Popkova, E.G., Sergi, B.S. (2018). Will Industry 4.0 and Other Innovations Impact Russia's Development? In Bruno S. Sergi (Ed.) Exploring the Future of Russia's Economy and Markets: Towards Sustainable Economic Development (pp. 51–68). Bingley, UK: Emerald Publishing Limited.

Popkova, E.G., Sergi, B.S. (Eds.) (2019). Digital Economy: Complexity and Variety vs. Rationality. Berlin: Springer International Publishing.

Ragulina, Y.V. (2019). Priorities of development of industry 4.0 in modern economic systems with different progress in formation of knowledge economy. Studies in Systems, Decision and Control, 169, p. 167–174.

Ragulina, Y.V., Alekseev, A.N., Strizhkina, I.V., Tumanov, A.I. (2019). Methodology of criterial evaluation of consequences of the industrial revolution of the 21st century. Studies in Systems, Decision and Control, 169, p. 235–244.

Ramanathan, R., Ramanathan, U., Bentley, Y. (2018). The debate on flexibility of environmental regulations, innovation capabilities and financial performance – A novel use of DEA. Omega (United Kingdom), 75, p. 131–138.

Sergi, B.S. (2003). Economic Dynamics in Transitional Economies: The Four-P Governments, the EU Enlargement, and the Bruxelles Consensus. New York: Routledge.

Sergi, B.S. (Ed.) (2019). Tech, Smart Cities, and Regional Development in Contemporary Russia. Bingley, UK: Emerald Publishing Limited.

Sergi, B.S., Popkova, E.G. Bogoviz, A.V., Litvinova, T.N. (2019). Understanding Industry 4.0: AI, the Internet of Things, and the Future of Work. Bingley, UK: Emerald Publishing Limited.

Shulus, A.A., Akopova, E.S., Przhedetskaya, N.V., Borzenko, K.V. (2020). Intellectual Production and Consumption: A New Reality of the 21st Century. Lecture Notes in Networks and Systems, 92, pp. 353–359.

Stolyarov, N.O., Petrenko, E.S., Serova, O.A., Umuralieva, A.S. (2020). The Digital Reality of the Modern Economy: New Actors and New Decision-Making Logic. Lecture Notes in Networks and Systems, 87, p. 882–888.

Yao, M., Di, H., Zheng, X., Xu, X. (2018). Impact of payment technology innovations on the traditional financial industry: A focus on China. Technological Forecasting and Social Change, 2(1), p. 22–29.

Zavyalova, E.B. Studenikin, N.V. Starikova, E.A. (2018). Business participation in implementation of socially oriented Sustainable Development Goals in countries of Central Asia and the Caucasus region. Central Asia and the Caucasus, 19(2), p. 56–63.

Aleksandr E. Suglobov, Ekaterina A. Orlova, Oleg G. Karpovich,
Evgeny V. Vologdin and Irina P. Drachena

20 Future Scenarios of Innovative Development of the Global Economic System Depending on the Economic and Legal Features of Managing this Process

Introduction

Forecasting of the perspectives of development of the world markets of innovations and hi-tech is very important in the process of strategic development of these markets. According to the current approach to scenario analysis of the studied markets' future, the decisive factor is economic & legal management of innovative development of developed countries as the driver of technological progress. This allows seeing the horizons of the global economy's innovative development. At present, developed countries (OECD) already have a digital society and robotization, with expected creation of "smart" companies and cities.

At the same time, the existing approach has two serious drawbacks. Firstly, surface study – even specialized scientific works pay attention not only to developed but also to actively developing countries (e.g., BRICS) in the aspect of acceleration of their modernization. Little attention is thus paid to underdeveloped countries, in which the process of creation of a digital society is complicated by the institutional and infrastructural barriers, and further innovative development is not clear. It cannot be similar to developed countries, and underdeveloped countries cannot form their own model of innovative development due to insufficient research basis.

Secondly, unsystematic character – the level of differentiation of countries in the global markets of innovations and hi-tech cannot be determined during unilateral research of these markets from the positions of their leaders or reduced in case of absence of recommendations for underdeveloped countries. A new approach is necessary for overcoming these drawbacks – it should focus on underdeveloped countries and aim at overcoming their underrun from developed countries. Such approach is

Aleksandr E. Suglobov, Financial University under the Government of the Russian Federation, Moscow, Russian Federation
Ekaterina A. Orlova, State University of Management, Moscow, Russia
Oleg G. Karpovich, Diplomatic Academy of the Ministry of Foreign Affairs of the Russian Federation», Moscow, Russia
Evgeny V. Vologdin, Altai State University, Barnaul, Russia
Irina P. Drachena, State Educational Institution of Higher Education Moscow Region "University of Technology", Korolev, Russia

https://doi.org/10.1515/9783110643701-020

developed in this chapter, which purpose is to compile future scenarios of innovative development of the global economic system depending on economic & legal features of this process management, with emphasis on underdeveloped countries.

Materials and Method

General perspectives of innovative development of the global economic system with emphasis on progress in developed countries are shown in the works Andronova et al. (2019), Bogoviz and Ragulina (2020), Bogoviz and Sergi (2018), Petrenko and Shevyakova (2019), Popkova (2019), Popkova and Sergi (2020), Popkova et al. (2019), Popkova and Gulzat (2020), Popkova and Parakhina (2019), Popkova et al. (2017), Popkova and Zmiyak (2019), Popkova and Sergi (2018), Popkova and Sergi (2019), Ragulina (2019), Ragulina et al. (2019), Sergi (2003), Sergi (2019), Sergi et al. (2019), Shulus et al. (2020), Stolyarov et al. (2020), and Zavyalova et al. (2018).

Forecasting and foresight of innovative development of the global economic system depending on the economic & legal features of this process management in actively developing countries are presented in the works Atkinsonk and Ezell (2012), García-Quevedo et al. (2018), Gumba and Vlasenko (2017), Haabazoka (2019), Harfst et al. (2017), Kuznetsova et al. (2017), Li et al. (2018), Ramanathan et al. (2018), and Yao et al. (2018). As the perspectives of innovative development of underdeveloped countries are poorly studied, they require further research.

For determining the initial point of forecasting, the authors analyze the dynamics of change of the disproportions in the global economic system. For reflecting the consequences of innovative development, the key indicator is not the traditionally used Global Innovation Index but the Global Competitiveness Index. The authors calculate the difference of direct average of the Global Competitiveness Index among top 10 (developed) counties in the 2010 ranking and direct average of this index among underdeveloped countries from the lower part of the WIPO Global Innovation Index for 2019. The obtained result is compared to the similar result in 2010, for determining the dynamics for the recent ten years. The data are visualized in Figure 20.1.

Based on the data of Figure 20.1, direct average of top 10 developed countries in 2010 has been calculated – it equals 54.18 points, which is by 17.69 points higher than direct average for 10 underdeveloped countries (36.49 points). In 2020, the gap between the countries of these categories increased by 1.83 times and reached 32.40 points – direct average in developed countries equals 82.1 points, and in underdeveloped countries – 49.71 points. This tendency shows increase of the disproportions in the global economic system and the necessity to overcome them. For this, the authors perform scenario modeling with the help of regression analysis and simplex method (when solving the optimization tasks of forecasting). The selection of statistical data for the research is shown in Table 20.1.

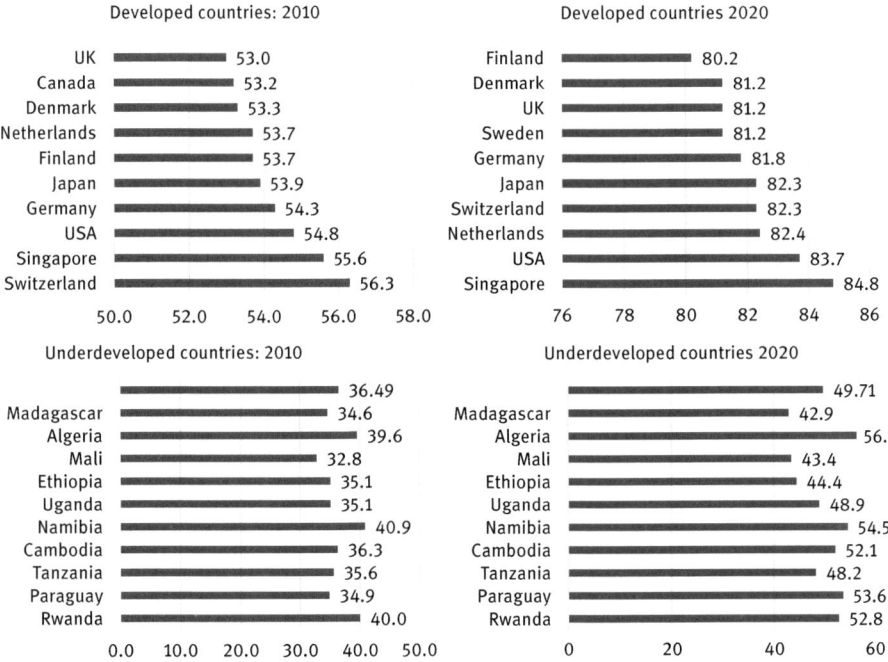

Figure 20.1: The Global Competitiveness Index in developed countries (top 10) and in underdeveloped countries in 2010 and 2020, points 1–100.
Source: compiled by the authors based on Institute of Scientific Communications (2020), World Economic Forum (2020).

Results

Based on the data from Table 20.1, the following models of multiple linear regression have been compiled:

- $y = 39.029 + 0.008*x1 - 0.14*x2 + 0.1*x3 + 0.07*x4 + 0.25**x5$, which shows dependence of the Global Competitiveness Index on the whole totality of the managerial factors;
- $x3 = -6.07 - 0.01*x1 + 5.32*x2 + 0.30*x3$, which shows dependence of hi-tech export on the number of researchers in R&D, R&D expenditures, and availability of venture investments;
- $x4 = 2.49 - 0.003*x1 - 9.95*x2 + 0.25*x3$, which shows dependence of hi-tech internally oriented production on the number of researchers in R&D, R&D expenditures, and availability of venture investments.

Table 20.1: Statistics of economic & legal management of innovative development in underdeveloped countries in 2020.

Country	Researchers in R&D (per million people)	Research and development expenditure (% of GDP)	High-technology exports (% of manufactured exports)	Medium and high-tech Industry (including construction) (% manufacturing value added)	Venture capital availability	Global Competitiveness Index, score 1–100
	x_1	x_2	x_3	x_4	x_5	Y
Rwanda	12	0.67	13	7	44.4	52.8
Paraguay	135	0.15	10	22	31.7	53.6
Tanzania	19	0.51	7	6	34.4	48.2
Cambodia	30	0.12	2	0	36.5	52.1
Namibia	149	0.34	0	7	33.4	54.5
Uganda	28	0.17	4	11	25	48.9
Ethiopia	91	0.27	6	16	38.2	44.4
Mali	33	0.29	1	n/a	28.1	43.4
Algeria	819	0.54	1	3	41.4	56.3
Madagascar	34	0.01	1	4	25	42.9
Average	135.00	0.31	4.50	8.44	33.81	49.71

Source: compiled by the authors based on Institute of Scientific Communications (2020), World Bank (2020), World Economic Forum (2020).

According to the determined dependencies, we have compiled three alternative forecasting scenarios of economic & legal management of innovative development in underdeveloped countries (until 2025) (Figures 20.2–20.4).

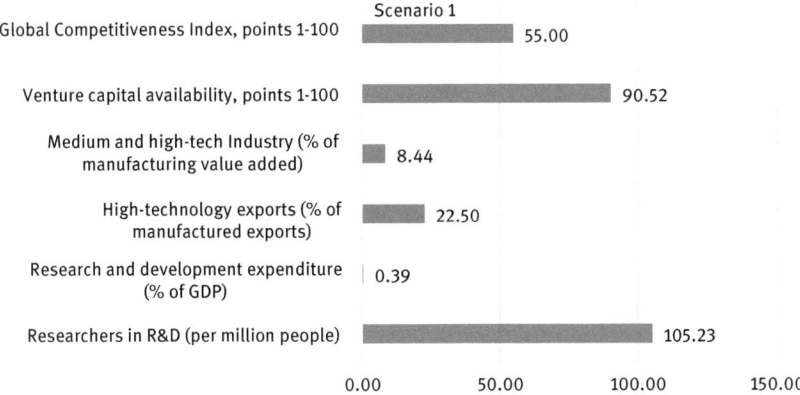

Figure 20.2: Scenario of externally oriented economic & legal management of innovative development in underdeveloped countries.
Source: developed and compiled by the authors.

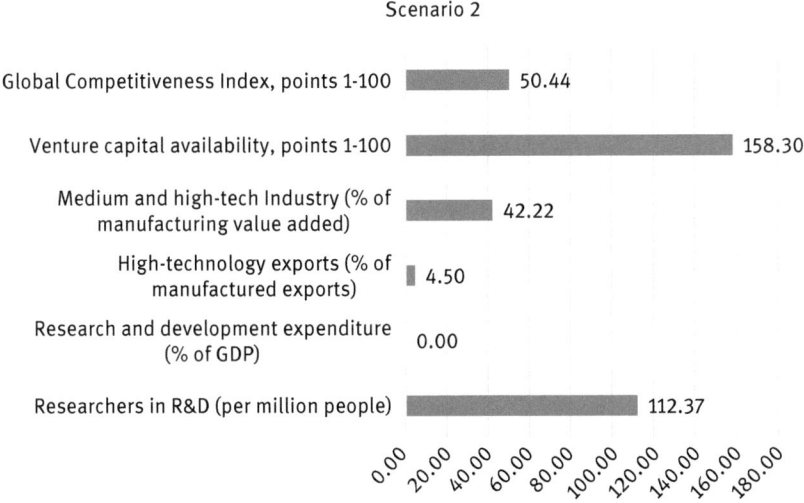

Figure 20.3: Scenario of internally oriented economic & legal management of innovative development in underdeveloped countries.
Source: developed and compiled by the authors.

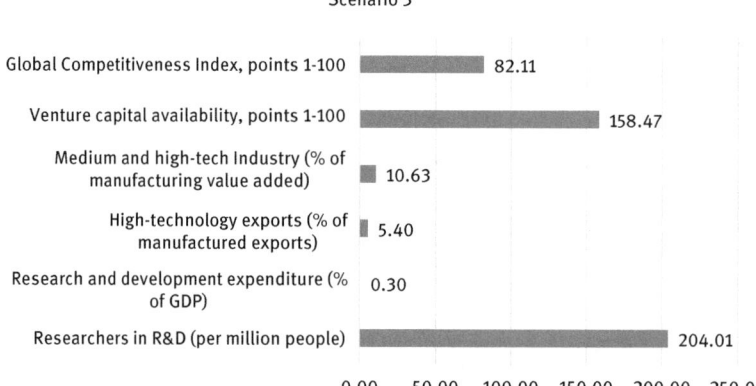

Figure 20.4: Scenario of economic & legal management of innovative development in underdeveloped countries that is oriented at competitiveness.
Source: developed and compiled by the authors.

As shown in Figure 20.2, externally oriented economic & legal management of innovative development in underdeveloped countries allows increasing their global competitiveness by 11%, up to 55 points, by means of increase of the share of hi-tech export by 4 times – up to 22.50% in the structure of industrial export. This requires increase of venture capital availability up to 90.52 points (by 168%), increase of R&D expenditures up to 0.39% of GDP (by 27%), and reduction of number of researchers in R&D to 105.23 by 1 million people (by 22%) – i.e., automatization of R&D.

As is shown in Figure 20.3, internally oriented economic & legal management of innovative development in underdeveloped countries allows increasing their global competitiveness by 1.5% (up to 50.44 points) by means of increase of the share of mid-tech and hi-tech productions by 4 times, up to 4.50%, in the structure of industrial production. This requires increase of venture capital availability up to 158.30 points (by 368%), full refusal from R&D expenditures (transfer to private investments), and reduction of number of researchers in R&D to 112.37 per 1 million people (by 17%) – i.e., authomatization of R&D.

As shown in Figure 20.4, economic & legal management innovative development in underdeveloped countries that is oriented at competitiveness allows increasing their global competitiveness by 65%, up to 82.11 points (average level of top 10 developed countries in 2020) by means of increase of the share of hi-tech export by 20%, up to 5.40%, in the structure of industrial export and by means of increase of the share of mid-tech and hi-tech productions by 26%, up to 10.63%, in the structure of industrial production. This requires increase of venture capital availability up to 158.47 points (by 369%), reduction of R&D expenditures to 0.30% of GDP (by 2%), and increase of the number of researchers in R&D up to 204.01 per 1 million people.

Conclusion

Thus, we have determined the future scenarios of innovative development of the global economic system depending on the economic & legal features of this process management in underdeveloped countries. The scenario of externally oriented and the scenario of internally oriented economic & legal management of innovative development in underdeveloped countries envisage total automatization of R&D, which is not accessible for underdeveloped countries at the current stage of digitization, and ensure moderate growth of competitiveness (by 11% and 1.5%, accordingly).

The most perspective scenario is the scenario of economic & legal management of innovative development in underdeveloped countries that is oriented at competitiveness – it allows increasing their global competitiveness by 65%, up to the current level of developed countries. Recommendations are offered, and quantitative landmarks for practical implementation of this scenario are outlined.

References

Andronova, I.V., Chernova, V.Y., Starostin, V.S., Degtereva (2019). Study of sector-specific innovation efforts: The case from Russian economy. Entrepreneurship and Sustainability Issues, Vsl Entrepreneurship and Sustainability Center, 7(1), p. 540–552.

Atkinsonk, R.D., Ezell, S.J. (2012). *Innovation Economics: the Race for Global Advantage*, New Haven, CT: Yale University Press.

Bogoviz, A.V., Ragulina, Y.V. (2020). Industry competitiveness in the new economy. Lecture Notes in Networks and Systems, 115, p. v–vi.

Bogoviz, A.V., Sergi, B.S. (2018). Will the Circular Economy Be the Future of Russia's Growth Model? In Bruno S. Sergi (Ed.). Exploring the Future of Russia'sEconomy and Markets: Towards Sustainable Economic Development, Bingley, UK: Emerald Publishing, pp. 125–141.

García-Quevedo, J., Segarra-Blasco, A., Teruel, M. (2018). Financial constraints and the failure of innovation projects. Technological Forecasting and Social Change, 127, p. 127–140.

Gumba, H.M., Vlasenko, V.A. (2017). Strategy of development of innovative activity in industry and construction: The rationale of the regional dimension. Izvestiya Vysshikh Uchebnykh Zavedenii, Seriya Teknologiya Tekstil'noi Promyshlennosti, 2017-January(2), p. 14–18.

Haabazoka, L. (2019). A Study of the Effects of Technological Innovations on the Performance of Commercial Banks in Developing Countries – A Case of the Zambian Banking Industry. In: Popkova E. (eds) The Future of the Global Financial System: Downfall or Harmony. ISC 2018. Lecture Notes in Networks and Systems, vol 57. Springer, Cham, Online ISBN 978-3-030-00102-5, https://doi.org/10.1007/978-3-030-00102-5_132

Harfst, J., Pichler, P., Fischer, W. (2017). Regional Ambassadors-An Innovative Element for the Development of Rural Areas? European Countryside, 9(2), p. 359–374.

Institute of Scientific Communications (2020). Data set "Big data of the modern world economy: digital platform for intelligent analytics – 2020". URL: https://www.archilab.online/en/data/sounting-data-set (data accessed: 09.04.2020).

Kuznetsova, O., Kuznetsova, S., Yumaev, E., Kuznetsov, V., Galtseva, O. (2017). Formation and Development of the Training System for Innovative Development of Regional Industry. E3S Web of Conferences, 15,04019.

Li, X., Subrahmanyam, A., Yang, X. (2018). Can financial innovation succeed by catering to behavioral preferences? Evidence from a callable options market. Journal of Financial Economics, 2(1), p. 34–42.

Petrenko, E.S., Shevyakova, A.L. (2019). Features and perspectives of digitization in Kazakhstan. Studies in Computational Intelligence, 826, p. 889–899.

Popkova, E.G. (2019). Preconditions of formation and development of industry 4.0 in the conditions of knowledge economy. Studies in Systems, Decision and Control, 169(1), 65–72.

Popkova, E.G., Sergi, B.S. (2020). Human Capital and AI in Industry 4.0. Convergence and Divergence in Social Entrepreneurship in Russia. Journal of Intellectual Capital, In press, 2020.

Popkova, E.G., Egorova, E.N., Popova, E., Pozdnyakova, U.A. (2019). The model of state management of economy on the basis of the internet of things. Studies in Computational Intelligence, 826, pp. 1137–1144.

Popkova, E.G., Gulzat, K. (2020). Technological Revolution in the 21st Century: Digital Society vs. Artificial Intelligence. Lecture Notes in Networks and Systems, 91, p. 339–345.

Popkova, E.G., Parakhina, V.N. (2019). Managing the global financial system on the basis of artificial intelligence: possibilities and limitations. Lecture Notes in Networks and Systems, 57, pp. 939–946.

Popkova, E.G., Poluyufta, L., Beshanova, Y., Popova, L.V., Kolesnikova, E. (2017). Innovations as a basis for marketing strategies of Russian oil companies in the conditions of oil prices reduction. Contributions to Economics, (9783319606958), p. 449–455.

Popkova, E.G., Zmiyak, K.V. (2019). Priorities of training of digital personnel for industry 4.0: social competencies vs technical competencies. On the Horizon, 27(3–4), p. 138–144.

Popkova, E.G., Sergi, B.S. (2018). Will Industry 4.0 and Other Innovations Impact Russia's Development? In Bruno S. Sergi (Ed.) Exploring the Future of Russia's Economy and Markets: Towards Sustainable Economic Development (pp. 51–68). Bingley, UK: Emerald Publishing Limited.

Popkova, E.G., Sergi, B.S. (Eds.) (2019). Digital Economy: Complexity and Variety vs. Rationality. Berlin: Springer International Publishing.

Ragulina, Y.V. (2019). Priorities of development of industry 4.0 in modern economic systems with different progress in formation of knowledge economy. Studies in Systems, Decision and Control, 169, p. 167–174.

Ragulina, Y.V., Alekseev, A.N., Strizhkina, I.V., Tumanov, A.I. (2019). Methodology of criterial evaluation of consequences of the industrial revolution of the 21st century. Studies in Systems, Decision and Control, 169, p. 235–244.

Ramanathan, R., Ramanathan, U., Bentley, Y. (2018). The debate on flexibility of environmental regulations, innovation capabilities and financial performance – A novel use of DEA. Omega (United Kingdom), 75, p. 131–138.

Sergi, B.S. (2003). Economic Dynamics in Transitional Economies: The Four-P Governments, the EU Enlargement, and the Bruxelles Consensus. New York: Routledge.

Sergi, B.S. (Ed.) (2019). Tech, Smart Cities, and Regional Development in Contemporary Russia. Bingley, UK: Emerald Publishing Limited.

Sergi, B.S., Popkova, E.G. Bogoviz, A.V., Litvinova, T.N. (2019). Understanding Industry 4.0: AI, the Internet of Things, and the Future of Work. Bingley, UK: Emerald Publishing Limited.

Shulus, A.A., Akopova, E.S., Przhedetskaya, N.V., Borzenko, K.V. (2020). Intellectual Production and Consumption: A New Reality of the 21st Century. Lecture Notes in Networks and Systems, 92, pp. 353–359.

Stolyarov, N.O., Petrenko, E.S., Serova, O.A., Umuralieva, A.S. (2020). The Digital Reality of the Modern Economy: New Actors and New Decision-Making Logic. Lecture Notes in Networks and Systems, 87, p. 882–888.

World Bank (2020). Indicators. URL: https://data.worldbank.org/indicator (data accessed: 09.04.2020).

World Economic Forum (2020). The Global Competitiveness Report. URL: http://reports.weforum. org/global-competitiveness-report-2019/competitiveness-rankings/#series=EOSQ089 (data accessed: 09.04.2020).

Yao, M., Di, H., Zheng, X., Xu, X. (2018). Impact of payment technology innovations on the traditional financial industry: A focus on China. Technological Forecasting and Social Change, 2(1), p. 22–29.

Zavyalova, E.B. Studenikin, N.V. Starikova, E.A. (2018). Business participation in implementation of socially oriented Sustainable Development Goals in countries of Central Asia and the Caucasus region. Central Asia and the Caucasus, 19(2), p. 56–63.

Lee Jae Sung and Elena Zavyalova

21 Public-Private Prartnerships as an Efficient Boost for the Economic Development. The Case of the Republic of Korea

Introduction

The need to introduce a public-private partnership mechanism was increasingly felt in the Republic of Korea in the early 1990s, which was generally attributed to two main reasons. On the one hand, after several decades of rapid economic growth, the country began to experience a serious shortage of infrastructure facilities such as roads, railways, seaports and airports. On the other hand, the country's government realised that it would not be able to provide financing for all infrastructure facilities construction independently, and decided to foster private sector participation in investments. The solution was found in the development of the pablic-private partnership mechanisms.

Research

Korean researchers chronologically distinguish four main stages in the development of this mechanism (Kim J. H., Kim J. W., Shin S. H., Lee S. Y., 2011).

The first stage (from December 1968 to August 1994) was characterized by the implementation of individual projects using public-private partnerships based on separate legislative acts regulating the construction of roads and port facilities.

The beginning of the second stage (from August 1994 to March 1999) is associated with such an important initial mark in the formation of public-private partnership in specific projects implementation in Korea as "The Act on Promotion of Private Capital Investment in Social Overhead Capital" adoption in August 1994, which was supplemented by a Presidential Decree "Enforcement Decree of The Act on Promotion of Private Capital Investment in Social Overhead Capital. "

Within the prescribed period, the government established clear criteria for the duration of agreements on a concession basis, the collection of fees for the services use, the providing of state support, and also specified the mechanisms for projects implementation. However, despite all these changes, designed to stimulate the interest of private capital, an investments inflow was not achieved.

Lee Jae Sung, Elena Zavyalova, Moscow State Institute of International Relations, Moscow, Russia

https://doi.org/10.1515/9783110643701-021

In order to trigger PPP, a substantial revision of the "The Act on Promotion of Private Capital Investment in Social Overhead Capital", which was in force at that time, and its adoption in December 1998 in the form of "The Act on Private Participation in Infrastructure" were undertaken.

The third stage (from the beginning of 1999 to 2004) was marked by a number of steps with the aim of partnership projects promotion through various mechanisms within the framework of government policy.

The forms of state support included the "minimum income guarantee (MRG) program" and the "compensation of base cost", in which the authorities share investment risks within government spending, as if the case touched on the implementation of a state project.

In addition, the government tried to solve a number of organizational problems that impeded the development of public-private partnership. In particular, the partnership support system was optimized by reducing unnecessary links, a more precise algorithm was developed for organizing the projects implementation by classifying them into state (solicited) and private (unsolicited) (i.e., depending on which of the two sides is the project initiator), the practice of analyzing technical feasibility and economic efficiency in the selection of projects was introduced, and also decisions that allowed the purchase of a controlling stake by a private investor came on-stream.

A PPP development center was established. This function was entrusted to the "Public and Private Infrastructure Investment Management Center" (PIMAC), which emerged from the reorganization of the previously existing "Private Infrastructure Investment Center of Korea". The activities of the "Korea Infrastructure Credit Guarantee Fund" developed, and an infrastructure fund also appeared.

The entry of the public-private partnership in the Republic of Korea into the fourth stage (from 2005 to the beginning of 2015) is tied to the adjustment of some provisions of "The Act on Private Participation in Infrastructure", as a result of which, since January 2005, it became possible to use such a type of partnership as "BTL (Build, Transfer, Lease)" while executing infrastructure projects, and the document itself was called "The Act on Public-Private Partnerships in Infrastructure" (사회기반시설에대한민간투자법). Besides that, the state expanded the categories of the projects themselves, adding social and residential facilities to the production facilities.

The adoption by the government of a whole range of measures aimed to activate PPPs in April 2015, including the introduction of "BTO-rs" and "BTO-a" as improved types of partnership, granting the private partner the right to initiate BTL projects, the types of objects expansion for BTL projects (buildings government agencies, child care facilities, fleets of public taxis, etc.), the decision to adjust the system of "minimum income guarantee" can be considered the beginning of the current, fifth, stage of PPP development in the Republic of Korea. (Kim J. H., Kim J. W., Shin S. H., Lee S. Y., 2011)

The PPP sector in Korea is regulated by the key legislative document, "The Act on Public-Private Partnerships in Infrastructure". Together with the Presidential Decree "On the Application of the Act on Public-Private Partnerships in Infrastructure", "PPP Basic Plan" and "PPP Implementation Guidelines" this law mainly forms the regulatory basis for activities within the framework of partnership.

"The Act on Public-Private Partnerships in Infrastructure" clearly defines the types of infrastructure facilities, the parameters of the "PPP Master Plan", the role of the state and the private partner as interacting parties, the powers and authority of state structures in decision-making, types of procurement and organizational aspects of the procurement process, methods for projects implementation, requirements imposed on the corporation for the project implementation, forms of government support, dispute resolution mechanism, etc. The decree largely specifies the provisions of the law.

The "Basic Plan" and the "Methodological Recommendations" set the direction of the PPP policy, and also details the procedures for the implementation of projects, the rules for their financing and refinancing, the risk sharing mechanism, and government support measures. They are adjusted every year in order to ensure the maximum possible traking of legislation and regulations amendments, the market situation affecting the work of PPPs, as well as tasks which the government faces. (2014/15 Knowledge Sharing Program with Tanzania)

The institutional structure of PPPs is the following.

The central role is played by the Ministry of Strategy and Finance, which is entitled to ensure the fulfilment of the provisions of "The Act on Public-Private Partnerships in Infrastructure", the Presidential Decree and the "Basic Plan". The preparation of a draft budget appropriation for PPPs, direct participation in resolving issues of financing, preparation and implementation of investment projects within the framework of a partnership fall within the competence of the body.

The Minister of Strategy and Finance, acting as chairmanship, heads the PPP Review Committee, which is composed of representatives of 11 central government departments, mainly ordering parties of PPP projects, and no more than 8 private experts with extensive experience in partnership issues. The committee consists of deputy heads of leading ministries. The Minister of Strategy and Finance involve private experts in the work on a paid basis for a period of two years subject to contracts extention for another period (Enforcement Decree of The Act on Public-Private Partnerships in Infrastructure. Article 3). The Committee is authorized to participate in decision-making on issues of attracting private investment, development of the "PPP Basic Plan", as well as on large-scale partnership projects initiated by the state (Act on Public-Private Partnerships in Infrastructure. Last amended by Act No. 12248, January 14, 2014. Article 5.). Such activities fall into two categories. The first includes projects with a total value of over 200 billion Korean won, and the second – with investments of 100 billion Korean won, the implementation mechanism of which provides for the facility transfer to the concessionaire for temporary rental for management and operation (Enforcement Decree of The Act on Public-Private Partnerships in Infrastructure. Article 6.)

The Center for Management of Public-Private Investment in Infrastructure, established at the Korea Development Institute, from where the Methodological Recommendations for the Implementation of PPPs are published is another important element of the government system(2014/15 Knowledge Sharing Program with Tanzania)/ The tasks assigned to the Center include supporting the Ministry of Strategy and Finance in the work on the "PPP Basic Plan" and assisting other ministries and relevant government organizations during the procurement process. The center contributes to the search for promising undertakings and, through consulting services, attracting foreign investment in PPP projects. In addition, it is engaged in the development and implementation of training programs for management of preparations on project implementation issues and conducts research activities, studying the situation in those sectors of the economy where PPP is applied (Enforcement Decree of The Act on Public-Private Partnerships in Infrastructure. Article 20).

Ensuring the implementation of projects is assigned to relevant government departments and local authorities. They are also engaged in writing a feasibility study with an assessment of the price-quality indicator (in particular, if the project value does not exceed 50 billion won and if more than 30 billion won of government subsidies are not required – according to The National Finance Act. Article 38), managing the public procurement process, competitive selection, technical plan coordination and project launch.

There is a state auditor in Korea called "the Board of Audit & Inspection". This organization monitors the actions of state bodies. In particular, the board exercises independent control and supervision over the implementation of public-private partnership projects, especially at the stage of public procurement.

In regards to organizational aspects of the implementation of specific PPP projects, a "public-private partnership project corporation" should also be mentioned. This is a legal entity that acquires the status of a concessionaire after receiving a contract. The founders are those who represent the private sector – developers, investors and operator companies intending to participate in the project (Kim J. H., Lee S. Y. 2012).

The attitudes of the leadership of the Republic of Korea to solving issues of stimulating PPPs is formulated in "The Act on Public-Private Partnerships in Infrastructure". Along with this, certain important aspects of preferences and benefits granting to private companies participating in PPPs are confirmed in several other laws: "Act on the Acquisition of and Compensation for Land, etc. for Public Works","Restriction of Special Taxation Act","Local Tax Act" and "Restriction of Special Local Taxation Act".

In general, the support measures, which are considered in the Republic of Korea as ways of public-private partnerships stimulating, can be described as land issues regulation by the concessionaire with the help of the state to implement the project, providing financial assistance to the private participant of the partnership, and sharing of the risks arising from project implementation between the government and the private investor.

Financial assistance is expressed in the subsidies allocation for construction and the provision of tax benefits to a private partner, and risk sharing is achieved through the use of the "compensation of base cost" mechanism and the "early termination payment", as well as in organizing the activities of the Korean Infrastructure Credit Guarantee Fund.

Solving land issues in the interests of PPP projects. In the interests of public-private partnerships the "Act on Public-Private Partnerships in Infrastructure" entitles the concessionaire to "expropriate" and use land, property, and rights to carry out a private investment project. Although this law primarily focuses on the need and desirability of land acquiring as a result of negotiations and consultations, it allows for the possibility of the land expropriation for public use in situations when a productive dialogue does not produce a positive result. In addition, it should be noted that during the implementation of many projects on the basis of public-private partnerships, the costs of acquiring land are fully or partially compensated by the competent authorities. The only exceptions are projects with very high returns.

Construction subsidies. "The Act on Public-Private Partnerships in Infrastructure" provides for the subsidizing of the concessionaire by the central government or local authorities in case an affordable level of tariffs for infrastructure use is required to be ensured. The time-frame for the transfer of subsidies is determined in the process of preparing a concession agreement and depends on the level of project implementation, as well as on the plan, schedule and proportions of the private partner's investments in the project shares. Moreover, payments under the subsidy are distributed by annual or quarterly periods. The amount of the subsidy is established in each case and is fixed in the concession agreement. When informing about the project, the state party announces an approximate part of the construction cost, which it is ready to subsidize. The exact ratio of subsidies to construction costs is determined through negotiations with the concessionaire and is fixed in the concession agreement.

The state has established the amount of subsidies for the construction of roads in the range from 20% to 30% of the total project cost, railways – up to 50%, ports – up to 20%, container terminals – up to 30%, terminals for handling unpacked goods (wheat, metals, oil products) – up to 40 %(Kim Jay Hyung, Kim Jung Wook, Shin Sung Hwan, Lee Seung Yeon6 2011). Of course, in terms of size, construction subsidies for national and local projects are significantly different, as the scale of the former is much bigger.

Tax concessions. In order to facilitate the financing of infrastructure, the country's authorities are empowered to provide tax incentives. As a basic legislative provision in this matter Art. 57 of "The Act on Public-Private Partnerships in Infrastructure" should be considered, which states that the central government and local administrations have the right to reduce taxes or exempt from them under the conditions defined by the "Act on the Limits of Special Taxation" and the "Act on the Limits of Application local special taxation" (Act on Public-Private Partnerships in Infrastructure).

Compensation of the base cost was introduced by the state in August 2009 instead of the "Minimum Revenue Guarantee", which was used for almost a decade. It provided for the project and the "redemption agreement" conclusion by partners and was a kind of supplement to the construction subsidies. The government funded operating income with the help of it.

In the framework of the new system, the authorities undertake a part of the investment risk within the costs that the government would bear if the project was implemented at public expense. At the same time, the private company is compensated for the project base cost, calculated as the sum of private investments (minus interest on a construction loan) and interest rates on government bonds.

The amount of support is equal to the difference between the actual operating revenue and the share of state investment risk.

Advance Settlement Payment

The possibility of a "settlement payment upon early termination of the private party obligations" is a critical factor for the concessionaire's risks mitigation. This system is provided for the cases of force majeure of a political or non-political nature, when the parties cannot fulfill their obligations for reasons beyond their control, bankruptcy of the concessionaire or default of the government. In fact, "settlement payment upon early termination" allows the concessionaire to finance debts at attractive rates.

When, for various reasons, the private partner is unable to continue work on the infrastructure object (construction, management or use), it may ask the authorities to terminate the concession agreement and make the payment, which the parties provide in advance in case of early termination of obligations. In the event of such situation, the government (whether central or local authorities) buys the project, acquiring all the rights to the object. The methodology for determining the amount of payment and the circumstances of the termination of the concession agreement are stipulated in the agreement itself.

As of 2011, there were only two cases of early termination of concession agreements. One of the projects was forced to be abandoned as a result of public opposition to plans for the construction of a toll road. Since the government was the responsible party for the early termination, it made a settlement payment in installments over the course of three years. The second project was backstopping, and its implementation was given up after the cancellation of the main project. Settlement issues there were arranged through negotiations between the private partner and the government.

Korea Infrastructure Credit Guarantee Fund

Having acquired its modern features as a result of legislative amendments of 2005 and acting on the basis of Art. 30 of "The Act on Public-Private Partnerships in Infrastructure", the Korea Infrastructure Credit Guarantee Fund provides financial guarantees to private sector contractors. Its activity was markedly developed in the period from 1999 to 2004.

As a rule, guarantees bear the form of an urgent loan used to pay senior debt, or take the form of guarantees of a loan yield. The fund is formed from the budgets of the central and local governments, company investments, income from payment of guarantees and fund management, loans from financial institutions and other funds.

Areas of Application and Practical Forms of Public-Private Partnership

After the latest additions made in May 2016, "The Act on Public-Private Partnerships in Infrastructure" identifies 53 types of infrastructure facilities, which can be generally divided into 15 categories: highways, railways, seaports, airports, communications, water resources, energy, environment, forestry, logistics, social services, civil housing, military personnel housing, education, culture (including tourism) (Act on Public-Private Partnerships in Infrastructure).

Without rejecting in principle the possibility of using other options, the basic law (Article 4) at the same time focuses on the use of the following four basic schemes for implementing infrastructure projects of public-private partnership(Act on Public-Private Partnerships in Infrastructure):

– objects are transferred to the ownership of the central or local government after the construct completion, and the concessionaire is entitled to manage and operate the facility for a certain period of time;
– the concessionaire also obtains the right to manage and operate the facility for a certain period of time, the difference is that this happens on the basis of leasing relationship on the part of the state, which thus uses the facilities and receives income from them (the second scheme is largely similar to the first one);
– upon completion of construction, the concessionaire takes ownership of infrastructure facilities for a certain period, on the expiry of which the ownership is transferred to the central or local government;
– the concessionaire comes into possession of the object on the basis of the right of ownership upon the construct completion.

With reference to Article 4 of the Law "The Main PPP Plan" identifies the following eight types of partnerships that can be applied in the implementation of projects within the framework of PPP taking into account the accepted international classification (Basic Plan for Public-Private Partnership Projects):

- BTO (Build-Transfer-Operate);
- BTL (Build-Transfer-Lease);
- BOT (Build-Operate-Transfer);
- BOO (Build-Own-Operate);
- BLT (Build-Lease-Transfer);
- ROT (Rehabilitate-Operate-Transfer);
- ROO (Rehabilitate-Own-Operate);
- RTL (Rehabilitate-Transfer-Lease).

Results of Public-Private Partnerships Use and Prospects for its Development

PPP Projects and Investments

Analysis of official Korean statistics for 1999–2016 generally indicates the significant expansion that public-private partnerships received in the Republic of Korea, which is primarily expressed in the consolidated figures for the number and cost of infrastructure projects based on PPPs (Table 21.1).

Table 21.1: Consolidated figures for PPP projects implementation in the Republic of Korea in the period of 1995–2016.

	Number	Share, %	Investments, trillion won	Share, %	Average project investment, billion won
Total PPP projects	699	100	105.9	100	151.5
from consolidated figures:					
Central government	188	26.9	63.1	59.6	335.6
Provincial administrations	182	26.0	27.4	25.9	150.7
Local government	329	47.1	15.4	14.5	46.7
from consolidated figures:					
BTO	222	31.8	73.3	69.3	330.3
BOT	4	0.6	0.7	0.6	164.5

Table 21.1 (continued)

	Number	Share, %	Investments, trillion won	Share, %	Average project investment, billion won
BOO	7	1.0	1.2	1.1	170.1
BTL	466	66.6	30.7	29.0	65.9
	from consolidated figures:				
Public partner initiative	570	81.5	60.6	57.2	106.3
Private partner initiative	129	18.5	45.3	42.8	350.9
	from consolidated figures:				
Project management completed	10	1.4	0.5	0.4	45.6
Projects at the stage of management and use	601	86.0	74.3	70.2	123.6
Projects at the stage of construction	73	10.4	25.4	24.0	347.5
Projects at the stage of preparation for construction	15	2.1	5.8	5.5	385.1

Source: compiled by the author on the basis of data presented in the Report of the Public-Private Infrastructure Investment Management Center at the Korea Development Institute for 2016.

In total, over a twenty-year period, there are only 699 PPP projects in Korea (projects at various stages under which contracts are concluded) for a total amount of slightly less than 106 trillion won, or about $91 billion (total investment, including construction subsidies, as well as borrowed and own capital) with an average investment of 151.5 billion won (a little over $130 million).

Most of the projects (329, or 47.1% of the total) are under the authority of the municipal administrations, while, in terms of total investment, the majority are projects supervised by the central authorities (63.1 trillion won, or 59.6%).

Demonstrating year on year a natural increase over the entire period, the consolidated figures of the number of projects and attracted investments are at the same time characterized by more and more moderate growth rates in recent years.

Moreover, based on the analysis of annual trends, which are shown in Figure 2, it should be noted that the partnership developed most dynamically and progressively from the mid-1990s. to 2007.

Types of PPP and Project Initiators

Among 699 projects, 466 projects (66.7% of the total) with a total value of 30.7 trillion won (nearly $26.4 billion) are associated with BTL. However, if the amount of invested funds is taken into account, the leaders are projects within the BTO. 73.3 trillion won (about $63.1 billion) were invested in 222 projects related to partnerships of this type, or 69.3% of the total amount spent in 1995–2016. BOT and BOO were selected for 11 projects with an investments of 1.9 trillion won (about $1.6 billion). They account for 1.6% of all projects and 1.7% of investments (Report of the Infrastructure Investment Management Center at the Korea Development Institute, 2016).

A state partner initiated 570 projects worth 60.6 trillion won (i.e. 81.5% of all projects with a share of all investments of 57.2%). Most of them (over 80% of the number of projects) were BTL projects. Based upon the available statistics, all of the Korean 466 BTL projects were conceived by the state. The remaining 104 projects, the initiatir of which was the public side, are BTO, BOT and BOO worth 29.9 trillion won. Accordingly, a private partner proposed 129 projects (all BTO, BOT and BOO), investments in which amounted to 45.3 trillion won. (Report of the Infrastructure Investment Management Center at the Korea Development Institute, 2016).

Authorities at Various Levels as Partners in PPP Projects

Among state partners, institutions related to the central government have the largest share in total investments (59.9%), while the municipal authorities account for 47.1% of the total number of projects.

Of the 188 projects worth 63.1 trillion won which are managed by the central authorities, 62 projects with the investments amount of 47.6 trillion won belong to BTO (shares 33.0% and 75.5% respectively), BTL -121 project and 14.3 trillion won investment (shares 64.4% and 22.7%), 4 projects and 824 billion won belong to BOT (2.1% and 1.3%), 1 project and 314 billion won to BOO (0.5% and 0.5%). (Report of the Infrastructure Investment Management Center at the Korea Development Institute, 2016).

The performance indicators of provincial administrations are the following: 182 projects totaling 27.4 trillion won, including 40 BTO projects with investments of 18.9 trillion won (shares 22.0% and 78%) and 142 BTL projects with investments of 8.5 trillion won (78% and 22%).

Among 329 projects with total investments of 15.4 trillion won, which are supervised by municipalities, BTL projects prevail: 203 of such projects attracted 7.8 trillion won (61.7% and 51.0%). The remaining indicators are 120 BTO projects with investments of 6.8 trillion won (36.5% and 44.4%), 3 BOT projects and 366 billion won of investments (0.9% and 2.4%), and 3 BOO projects worth 344 billion won

(0.9% and 2.4%). (Report of the Infrastructure Investment Management Center at the Korea Development Institute, 2016).

Classification of PPP Projects by Infrastructure

Most of the projects are related to education (33.2%) and nature conservation (26.5%), however, roads (42.5%) and railways (18.7%) (come to the fore in terms of investment). (Report of the Infrastructure Investment Management Center at the Korea Development Institute, 2016)

Investments in 232 projects related to the construction of such educational institutions as schools, colleges and universities amount to 10.1 trillion (9.5% of the total figure for all years), and 185 projects for environmental facilities creation required 14.3 trillion won (13.3%). 45 trillion won were invested in 90 road network development projects (12.9% of the total), while the amount of funds that went to the implementation of 15 railway sector projects exceeded 19.8 trillion won.

In addition, PPP was used for the construction of military facilities (11.2% of the total number of projects and 5.9% of all attracted investments), culture and tourism facilities (6% and 1.7%, respectively), port facilities (2.4% and 5.8%), social facilities (2.1% and 0.5%), aerodrome facilities (2.0% and 0.8%), logistics infrastructure (0.9% and 1.2%), telecommunications sector (0.6% and 0.1%), civil housing (0.1% and 0.02%).

An analysis of the facilities in terms of using different types of partnership shows that roads (90 projects), port facilities (17 projects) and airport infrastructure (14 projects) were built exclusively on the BTO basis. Work on the premises for military personnel (78 projects), social facilities (15 projects) and civilian housing (1 project) used only BTL. Out of 185 environmental projects, BTO was used in 86 cases, and BTL in 99. The same is observed in the railway sector (10 BTO projects and 5 BTL projects), telecommunications (1 BTO project and 3 BTL) and the construction of educational institutions (1 BTO project and 231 BTL projects). When implementing 42 objects in the field of culture and tourism, four types of partnership were used with a significant share of BTL (3 BTO projects, 3 BOT projects, 2 BOO projects and 34 BTL projects). Logistic facilities were built using BOT (1 project) and BOO (5 projects). (Report of Investment Management Center at the Korea Development Institute, 2016).

The 10 projects considered to be completed were distributed between airports (4 projects and 354 billion won of investments), environment protection (3 projects and 87 billion won) and road sector (3 projects and 14 billion won). A significant part of 601 projects with investments of 74.3 trillion won in the process of implementation is accounted for by educational sphere (224 projects with 9.6 trillion won of investments), environment protection (157 projects and 11.2 trillion won), defense sector (68 projects and 5.5 trillion won), roads (60 projects 26.8 trillion won), culture and tourism (39 projects and 1.6 trillion won), port infrastructure (16 projects and 5.5 trillion won), railways (9 projects and 12.3 trillion won). The rest are social institutions (10 projects and 234 billion won), airports (10 projects and 461 billion won), logistics (4 projects and 943 billion won) and telecommunications (4 projects and 94 billion won). Among 73 projects under construction with investments of 25.4 trillion won environmental structures (22 projects and 2.3 trillion won of investments), roadway network (21 projects and 15.5 trillion won) prevail, along with which construction works under the PPP are related to the defense sector (8 projects and 530 billion investments), railways (4 projects and 5.2 trillion won), education (6 projects and 4013 billion won), ports (1 project and 645 billion won), social services (5 projects and 274 billion won), etc. As of December 2016, preparation for construction is being carried out on 15 projects for a total cost of 5.8 trillion won, including 6 highway projects (2.8 trillion won), 2 railway projects (2.3 trillion won), 3 environmental projects (394 billion won), 2 housing projects for military personnel (253 billion won) and 2 projects of educational institutions (76 billion won). (Report of Investment Management Center at the Korea Development Institute, 2016).

Share of PPP Projects in Government Investments in Public Infrastructure

In 1995, when the introduction of PPPs began, investments in such projects (using the BTO mechanism) accounted for only 0.5% of government investments in public infrastructure projects. Meanwhile, from 1995 to 2010, PPP projects (national BTO projects and BTL railway projects) raised 26.5 trillion won, that is, on average more than 10% of public investment in infrastructure projects annually (Kim Jay Hyung, Lee Seung Yeon.2012). In 2011–2016 PPP in investments in social infrastructure accounted for 15.6%.

Examples of PPP Projects Implementation based on BTO and BTL

BTO

The most striking instances of the implementation of WTO projects in Korea include the Seoul-Incheon Airport Expressway (length: 40.2 km), Daegu Busan (length: 82 km), Chonan-Nonsan, the northern section of the express ring road around Seoul (length: 36.3 km), the first and second phases of a new port construction in Mokpo, the 6-lane Incheon bridge (length: 12 km), line No. 9 of the Seoul metro (length: 25.5 km), a biogas power plant at a solid domestic waste landfill in the metropolitan area and the railway for commuter trains (length: 58 km) connecting Seoul with the airports "Incheon" (international lines) and "Gimpo" (domestic service).

BTL

Some of the best-known BTL-based projects include a housing complex for 200 military families in Chongzhu, the National Institute of Science and Technology in Ulsan, and the Anhwa High School building in Hwason (Yoo S. K. Korea's, 2010).

Prospects for PPP in the Republic of Korea

The prospects for PPP in the Republic of Korea should be considered in the context of the general approach of the South Korean administration to the economy development, as well as tasks in this area that arise from the current situation.

The concept of a "creative economy", proclaimed after the previous president Park Geun-hye came to power in 2013, as a whole remains relevant under the head of the current administration, Moon Jae In, with an increased emphasis on the "fourth industrial revolution". Such an approach implies a significant and dedicated strengthening of efforts, initiated by the previous governments, solving such a global problem as ensuring the country's transition to an economy driven not by export-oriented manufacturing and export of the finished-products, but by innovations based on the development of science and technology, more widespread adoption of cutting-edge information and telecommunication solutions.

Limiting large industrial and financial groups influence over the economy and promoting competition should be accompanied by appropriate "creativity" encouragement, formation of a favorable "ecosystem" for startups fostering, expansion of the role of venture businesses, small and medium enterprises in the economy, including their potency to go abroad, and creation of new industries and markets for new products. These ideas formed the basis of the "Three-Year Plan for Economic Innovation", adopted in 2014 and providing for structural reforms in the public sector, education, and employment (3-Year Plan for Economic Innovation.).

At the same time, the government is forced, along with structural reforms, to pay great attention to work on the current tasks of reviving the economy, in the context of the remaining unfavorable external conditions for the South Korean economy, caused by the slowdown in the development of the main trade partners of the country and the lack of positive dynamics in their markets. In this regard, steps to stimulate domestic demand by increasing private consumption and investment are emphasized (Policies Focus on Maintaining Recovery Momentum and Strengthening Growth Potential).

The situation is complicated by the fact that the government has to use financial resources to stimulate the economy, with a tight reform aimed at increasing fiscal sustainability and reducing the debt of state organizations (2015–2019 Fiscal Management Policies).

Attaching great importance to PPP in carrying out the budget reform, in April 2015 the government formulated a number of fundamental directions for the development of partnership in the coming years. The main goal that the state has set for itself is to provide reliable opportunities for free capital investment in the market and stimulate economic growth through its effective use, and the essence of the measures is to accelerate the growth of PPPs and create conditions for increasing the interest of a private partner in participating in promising projects. This is planned to be achieved by improving the mechanism for sharing risks between PPP partners, increasing the income of private investors, simplifying the requirements for preparing documents related to projects, reducing the time for consideration and conclusion of contracts. The next seven main areas have been outlined for which work is planned.

Conclusions

The Republic of Korea has mainly used Build-Transfer-Operation, or WTO, so far, when a private investor takes the main risks, and Build-Transfer-Lease, or BTL, in which the government does it. As the "new" types of partnership, the state plans to introduce "BTO-rs" and "BTO-a". The addition of "rs" to "BTO" means "risk sharing", which implies equal participation (50:50) of the public and private parties in investments in the infrastructure project and operating expenses. "BTO-a", or "BTO-adjusted" will be applied to projects where the government is going to reduce business risks and fees for the use of facilities, undertaking a larger share of investments and operating expenses (for example, about 70% of construction costs). The goal is to attract about 7 trillion won into projects using the "new" types of PPP. The importance of the construction of underground highways and urban rail lines (normal and "light" metro), as well as the development of water treatment systems as investment areas, is noted. Moreover, the need to include water supply facilities, old roads and infrastructure in the area of PPP projects application to address the problem of urban renewal is emphasized.

The government is counting on overcoming the recent stagnation in the field of PPPs and the passivity of private business in terms of investments in public infrastructure by using the BTO-rs and BTO-a mechanisms while implementing new projects (primarily roads and railways), which should not only stimulate private partner to work together, but also encourage to initiate such projects more often. Another direction of efforts to step up PPPs is to involve municipal companies, representatives of small and medium-sized businesses in the active search and implementation of BTL projects related to the construction of office blocks, water supply, public services and amenities, etc. Although these projects are not large in scale, they are very important for municipal authorities and population, since they contribute to improving the quality of life, and participation in PPPs of not the largest companies allows to create a more competitive local business environment.[1] Considering the task of enhancing the well-being of the population, proclaimed by the current President of the Republic of Korea, Moon Jae In, after coming to power in May 2017, an increased attention to BTL projects, which are largely designed to create life amenities can be expected in the coming years.

References

2014/15 Knowledge Sharing Program with Tanzania: Consultation for System Improvement and Capacity Building for PPP Projects in Tanzania. Ministry of Strategy and Finance, Korea Development Institute, Center for Korean Prosperity, Hankuk University of Foreign Studies. p.36. / http://www.ksp.go.kr/publication/policy.jsp?idx=10820

2015–2019 Fiscal Management Policies. Press-Release. Republic of Korea: Ministry of Strategy and Finance, 13.05.2015. / [Online source]. Access: http://english.mosf.go.kr/popup/20_PolicyFocusBanner/popup.html

2015–2019 Fiscal Management Policies. Press-Release. Republic of Korea: Ministry of Strategy and Finance, 13.05.2015. [Online source] // URL: http://english.mosf.go.kr/popup/20_PolicyFocusBanner/popup.html. Access: (06.04.2016).

2016 Policies Focus on Maintaining Recovery Momentum and Strengthening Growth Potential. Press-Release. Republic of Korea: Ministry of Strategy and Finance, 18.12.2015. / [Online source]. Access: http://english.mosf.go.kr/

2016 년도 KDI 공공투자관리센터연차보고서 (The report of the Center for management of public-private investments in infrastructure under Korean Development Institute on the work in 2016). 04.2017. [Online source] // URL: http://pimac.kdi.re.kr/study/study_list.jsp#원본

3-Year Plan for Economic Innovation. R.O.K. Ministry of Strategy and Finance. Information material. / [Online source]. Access: http://english.mosf.go.kr/popup/14_PolicyFocusBanner_20140401/popup.html

Act on Public-Private Partnerships in Infrastructure. Last amended by Act No. 14242, May 29, 2016. Article 2. [Online source] // URL: http://elaw.klri.re.kr/kor_service/lawView.do?hseq=41990&lang=ENG

Act on Public-Private Partnerships in Infrastructure. Last amended by Act No. 12248, January 14, 2014. Article 5. C. 8-9. / [Online source]. Access: http://elaw.klri.re.kr/eng_service/lawView.do?hseq=41990&lang=ENG

---

1 2016~2020 년국가재정운용계획 (Plan of measures for financial and budget policy in 2016–2020). Republic of Korea: Ministry of Strategy and Finance, 02.09.2016. C. 207. / [E-source]. Access: http://www.mosf.go.kr/nw/nes/detailNesDtaView.do?menuNo=4010100&searchNttId1=MOSF_000000000005220&searchBbsId1=MOSFBBS_000000000028

Act on Public-Private Partnerships in Infrastructure. Last amended by Act No. 14242, May 29, 2016. Article 2. [Online source]. – Access:http://elaw.klri.re.kr/kor_service/lawView.do?hseq= 41990&lang=ENG

Baldwin, J.R./Dixon, J. (2008) Infrastructure Capital: What is it? Where is it? How much of it is there?: Canadian Productivity Review, No 16, Ottawa: Statistics Canada, 108 p.

Basic Plan for Public-Private Partnership Projects. Ministry of Strategy and Finance. March 29, 2011. Part II. Chapter 1. Article 3. Pp. 11–12. / [Online source]. Access: http://pimac.kdi.re.kr/ eng/mission/ppp_guide.jsp/

Enforcement Decree of The Act on Public-Private Partnerships in Infrastructure. Article 3. P. 3. / [Online source]. Access: http://elaw.klri.re.kr/eng_service/lawView.do?hseq=45822&lang=ENG

Evaluating the environment for public-private partnerships in Asia. The 2018 Infrascope // The Economist Intelligence Unit, 2018. P. 35,163.

Gerrard M. B. Public-Private Partnerships: What Are Public-Private Partnerships, and How Do They Differ from Privatizations? Finance & Development, 2001, 38(3).

Grimsey D., Lewis M. K. Public Private Partnerships: The Worldwide Revolution in Infrastructure Provision and Project Finance. Cheltenham, UK; Northampton, MA: Edward Elgar, 2004.

Is it time for an infrastructure push? The macroeconomics effects of public investment // World Economic Outlook (WEO). Legacies, clouds, uncertainties. 2014. 243 p.

Kim J. H., Lee S. Y. 2012 Modularization of Korea's Development Experience: Public–Private Partnerships: Lessons from Korea on Institutional Arrangements and Performance. Ministry of Strategy and Finance. Korea Development Institute. 2013. P. 32. [Online source]. Access: http://www.ksp.go.kr/publication/modul.jsp?syear=&sage=&skey=&stem=&stype=&pg= 9&idx=92

Kim Jay Hyung, Kim Jung Wook, Shin Sung Hwan, Lee Seung Yeon. Public-Private Infrastructure Projects: Case Studies from the Republic of Korea. Volume 1: Institutional Arrangements and Performance. Executive Summary. Mandaluyong City, Philippines: Asian Development Bank, 2011. P. 15–16. // URL: http://www.adb.org/publications/public-private-partnership- infrastructure-projects-case-studies-republic-korea/

National Finance Act/ Article 38. / [Online source]. Access: http://elaw.klri.re.kr/kor_service/ lawView.do?hseq=40922&lang=ENG

The Report of the Public-Private Infrastructure Investment Management Center at the Korea Development Institute for 2016.

Toolkit for Public-Private Partnerships in Roads & Highways. Country Case Study: Korea. Public- Private Infrastructure Advisory Facility, 2009. // URL:https://www.ppiaf.org/sites/ppiaf.org/ files/documents/toolkits/highwaystoolkit/6/pdf-version/korea.pdf, Accessed: (06.04.2016).

What is Public-Private Partnerships? // Deloitte. – [online] // URL: https://www2.deloitte.com/cn/ en/pages/real-estate/articles/what-is-public-private-partnerships.html

Yoo S. K. Korea's Case of Public-Private Partnerships for Infrastructure Development. Seoul, 2010. P. 8. / [Online source]. Access: http://www.unescap.org/sites/default/files/rok.pdf

Elena G. Popkova, Aleksei V. Bogoviz and Artem I. Krivtsov

Conclusions: Economic and Legal Management of Modern Economic Systems' Innovative Development: A View into the Future

The book presents two perspective scientific conclusions, which are important for the modern theory and practice and which open a wide field for future research. The first conclusion is that management of modern economic systems' innovative development should be conducted with symbiosis of economic and legal measures. Organizational schemes during R&D, implementation of innovations, and creation and dissemination of innovative products are based on the existing legal field. Economic management is not limited by commercialization of innovations, and legal management is not limited by protection of intellectual property: at each stage of the innovative process it is necessary to use a complex – economic & legal – approach to management.

The second conclusion is that the sphere of innovations vividly shows the problem of imbalance of the global economic system – however, it also contains the key to solving this problem. Imperfection of the practices of economic & legal management of modern economic systems' innovative development does not allow for full realization of the potential of this development, due to which developed countries' technological progress is slow, but developing countries' underrun from them is growing.

The book presents a revolutionary view at leveling of the global disproportions in managing the innovative development of modern economic systems – not from the positions of slowdown of developed countries' progress or their support for developing countries, but from the positions of use of own innovative potential by underdeveloped countries. The offered applied recommendations will allow underdeveloped countries to increase the rate of innovative development, which, in the mid-term (until 2025), will lead to visible reduction of the level of differentiation of economic systems and to balance of the global markets of innovations and hi-tech.

However, in the course of studying the new sphere of economic & legal management of modern economic systems' innovative development there arose new problems, which require scientific attention. These include formation of effective mechanisms of supra-national regulation of the global practice of innovative development. Successful implementation of the authors' recommendations require

Elena G. Popkova, MGIMO University, Moscow, Russian Federation
Aleksei V. Bogoviz, Independent Researcher, Moscow, Russia
Artem I. Krivtsov, Samara State University of Economics, Samara, Russian Federation

https://doi.org/10.1515/9783110643701-022

reconsideration of the role of international organizations, which have to change the course of support for developing and underdeveloped countries from diffusion of obsolete technologies to stimulation of venture investments and breakthrough R&D. This should be studied in the future works, based on the conclusions that are presented here.

List of Figures

https://doi.org/10.1515/9783110643701-023

List of Tables

https://doi.org/10.1515/9783110643701-024

Index

https://doi.org/10.1515/9783110643701-025